Traffic Management

SECOND EDITION

Laurence M. Olivo

2007
Emond Montgomery Publications Limited
Toronto, Canada

Copyright © 2007 Emond Montgomery Publications Limited. All rights reserved. No part of this publication may be reproduced, stored in a retrieval system, or transmitted, in any form or by any means, photocopying, electronic, mechanical, recording, or otherwise, without the prior written permission of the copyright holder.

Emond Montgomery Publications Limited
60 Shaftesbury Avenue
Toronto ON M4T 1A3
http://www.emp.ca

Printed in Canada.

We acknowledge the financial support of the Government of Canada through the Book Publishing Industry Development Program (BPIDP) for our publishing activities.

The events and characters depicted in this book are fictitious. Any similarity to actual persons, living or dead, is purely coincidental.

Acquisitions and developmental editor: Jennifer McPhee
Marketing director: Dave Stokaluk
Supervising editor: Jim Lyons, WordsWorth Communications
Copy editor: David Handelsman, WordsWorth Communications
Proofreader: Cindy Fujimoto, WordsWorth Communications
Typesetter: Tara Wells, WordsWorth Communications
Production editor: Nancy Ennis, WordsWorth Communications
Assistant production editor: Debbie Gervais, WordsWorth Communications
Indexer: Paula Pike, WordsWorth Communications
Cover designer: John Vegter

Figures 1.1 and 1.2 are reproduced from *The Ontario Highway Traffic Act, Cross Referenced to Selected Regulations, 2007* (St. Catherines, ON: MacBeth Publishing, 2007). Reprinted with permission.

Figures 3.1, 3.2, 3.3, and 3.4 © Queen's Printer for Ontario, 2006. Reproduced with permission.

Library and Archives Canada Cataloguing in Publication

Olivo, Laurence M., 1946-
    Traffic management / Laurence M. Olivo. — 2nd ed.

Previous ed. written by John Grime and Laurence M. Olivo.
Includes index.
ISBN 978-1-55239-155-6

    1. Traffic violations—Canada.   2. Traffic regulations—Canada.
3. Traffic accident investigation—Canada.   I. Grime, John.   Traffic management.   II. Title.

HV8079.5.O45 2007   363.2'3320971   C2007-900013-4

To Joyce, as always

CONTENTS

Figures ix
Preface xi

CHAPTER 1
Introduction 1
    Overview of the Law Governing Traffic Management 1
    Chapter Summary 14
    Notes 14
    Review Questions 14

CHAPTER 2
The Highway Traffic Act: Defining Terms 17
    Introduction 17
    Definition of Vehicle, Section 1 18
    Chapter Summary 28
    Key Terms 28
    Review Questions 28

CHAPTER 3
Licences and Permits 35
    Introduction 36
    Vehicle Permits 36
    Vehicle Classes 45
    Vehicle Class Description, O. Reg. 340/94, Section 2(1), Table 47
    Driver's Licences 50
    Compulsory Automobile Insurance Act 57
    Chapter Summary 60
    Key Terms 60
    Review Questions 60

CHAPTER 4
Rules of the Road 67
    Introduction 67
    Rules of the Road: Speed 68
    Rules of the Road 71
    Vehicle Equipment Requirements 97
    HTA Road Offence Penalties Victim Surcharge 100
    HTA Driving Offences: The Demerit Point System 101
    Chapter Summary 105
    Key Terms 105
    Notes 105
    Review Questions 106

CHAPTER 5
Highway Traffic Act Offences 123
    Introduction 123
    Motor Vehicle Stops 124
    Suspect Apprehension Pursuits 126
    HTA Offences 127
    Criminal Code Driving Offences 136
    Chapter Summary 136
    Key Terms 137
    Notes 137
    Review Questions 137

CHAPTER 6
Impaired Driving and Other Criminal Code and
Highway Traffic Act Offences 141
    Overview of Jurisdiction over Motor Vehicle Law 142
    Criminal Code Motor Vehicle Offences 144
    Vehicle Searches 163
    Chapter Summary 164
    Key Terms 164
    Notes 164
    Review Questions 165

CHAPTER 7
Collision Investigation 171
    Introduction 172
    Collision Investigation and Reconstruction 172
    Steps in a Collision Investigation 172
    Chapter Summary 187
    Key Terms 187
    Review Questions 188

APPENDIX A
Short-Form Wordings and Set Fines from the
Provincial Offences Act 195

APPENDIX B
Provincial Offence Ticket and Summons 225

APPENDIX C
Suspect Apprehension Pursuits Regulation 233

Glossary 237
Index 239

FIGURES

Figure 1.1	Finding Regulations in the Index	8
Figure 1.2	Parts of the Highway Traffic Act	9
Figure 2.1	Highways	22
Figure 2.2	Highway with Two Roadways	23
Figure 2.3	Intersections	25
Figure 2.4	Unmarked Crosswalks	26
Figure 2.5	Marked Crosswalks	27
Figure 3.1	10-Day Permits	38
Figure 3.2	In-Transit Permit	39
Figure 3.3	Dealer and Service Permits and Plates	41
Figure 3.4	Six-Day Temporary Use of Plates	43
Figure 3.5	Vehicle Class Categorized by Passenger Capacity and by Weight	47
Figure 3.6	What Class of Driver's Licence Is Required by the Driver of These Vehicles?	49
Figure 3.7	Non-Resident Plate and Licence Exemptions	58
Figure 4.1	Uncontrolled Intersection	73
Figure 4.2	Overtaking Stopped Vehicle at Crossover	75
Figure 4.3	Overtaking Moving Vehicle Near Crossover	76
Figure 4.4	Right-Hand Turn	77
Figure 4.5	Left-Hand Turn	78
Figure 4.6	Wide Turns	80
Figure 4.7	Hand Signals	81
Figure 4.8	Yielding to Bus	82
Figure 4.9	Traffic Signals	84
Figure 4.10	Left Turn at Intersection with a Median 15 Metres Wide or Wider	85
Figure 4.11	Right and Left Turns on Red Signals	87
Figure 4.12	Giving Way to Emergency Vehicle on One-Way Highway	91

Figure 5.1	Provincial Offence Ticket (Top Page)	128
Figure 5.1	Provincial Offence Ticket (Second Page)	129
Figure 5.1	Provincial Offence Ticket (Last Page)	130
Figure 5.2	Provincial Offence Summons	132
Figure 6.1	Procedural Routes for CC Offences	145
Figure 6.2	Measuring Reasonable Suspicion and Reasonable Grounds to Believe	151
Figure 6.3	Stages of Alcoholic Influence/Intoxication	152
Figure 6.4	Breath Demands	154
Figure 6.5	Drunk Driving Offence Procedure at a Glance	162
Figure 7.1	Dangerous-Goods Symbols	177
Figure 7.2	Barricades	181

Preface

The law is an ever-moving target, and the practice and procedure involved in the enforcement of highway traffic laws are no exception. Since the first edition was published in 2000, there has been enough change to warrant a new edition.

The first edition of any textbook is always something of an experiment. John Grime and I structured the original book on existing Traffic Management courses that had been student-tested in the early days of the mandated Police Foundations Program. With the passage of time, we have heard from students and professors about what worked and what didn't and what additional material they wanted to see in a new edition. This book reflects their input.

When it came time for the second edition, John Grime, having just retired from his position as professor in the Police Foundations Program at Mohawk College, was moving on to other things, and could not participate in the writing of the new edition. I was sorry not to have John working with me and I wish him well in his pursuits. The basic idea and much of the material for the first edition were his.

For the second edition, we were fortunate in having an advisory team made up of professors in Police Foundation programs who agreed to share their expertise, advice, insights, and teaching materials. Their input allowed me to fine-tune the contents to better meet students' needs. In particular, I want to thank Simon Bradford (Georgian College), Dave Bedard (Cambrian College), Wayne Thomas (Humber College), Tony Altomare (Centennial College), and Michael Chesson (Durham College).

The late Peter Parise was also helpful and generous with his suggestions and in letting us draw from his copious training materials. His untimely death interrupted the work he was doing on the preparation of this edition. Nonetheless, we think he would have been pleased with the results. And we dedicate this volume to the memory of Peter Parise, whose 35 years of service with the Toronto Police Service, most of them in the Traffic Division and at C.O. Bick College, have left an indelible mark on traffic management and the policing community in Ontario. Most importantly, we want our readers—both students and instructors—to benefit from the shared wisdom and understanding that have been incorporated into this learning resource.

Laurence Olivo
Toronto
March 2007

CHAPTER 1

Introduction

CHAPTER OBJECTIVES

After completing this chapter you should be able to:

- Appreciate the breadth and complexity of the law relating to traffic management and motor vehicle law.
- Understand the importance of the Ontario *Highway Traffic Act* (HTA) to motor vehicle law.
- Understand the relationship between the HTA and the regulations made under it.
- Locate relevant regulations made under the HTA.
- Know how to find topics in a consolidated version of the HTA using the table of contents, index, table of contents for the regulations, and the general regulation.

OVERVIEW OF THE LAW GOVERNING TRAFFIC MANAGEMENT

The law governing motor vehicles is both broad and complex. It is broad because it covers many aspects of and activities related to motor vehicles. And it is complex both because of the subject matter and because of the overlap between provincial and federal jurisdiction governing motor vehicle law.

The breadth of motor vehicle law can be appreciated simply by looking at what is included among the topics covered by the Ontario *Highway Traffic Act* (HTA):

- establishment and operation of government offices and departments to administer motor vehicle law,
- vehicle permits,

- parking permits,
- licensing of drivers and driving instructors,
- licensing and regulation of garages and storage facilities,
- vehicle and equipment requirements and standards,
- vehicle loads and dimensions,
- vehicle weight,
- vehicle rates of speed,
- rules of the road,
- regulation of toll highways,
- regulation of medical transportation services,
- offroad vehicles,
- civil liability issues involving motor vehicles,
- municipal bylaws regarding motor vehicles,
- traffic enforcement rules (including procedure, arrest, and penalties),
- accident records and reporting, and
- red light cameras.

In addition to these topics covered by the HTA, there are still other topics covered by other legislation. Under federal law, the *Criminal Code* of Canada (CC) deals with more serious operating offences such as dangerous operation of a vehicle and impaired driving. There are also federal laws governing vehicle safety requirements, some of which overlap or complement provincial rules.

Considering the breadth of the topics, it is not surprising that the law can be quite complex. For example, the many types of vehicles and the varied uses to which they may be put create a complex licensing and permit system both for vehicles and for those who operate them. As well, some of the equipment and safety requirements for vehicles often result in detailed rules that incorporate engineering terms and references not easily understood except by experts. And because there is occasional overlap of federal and provincial law covering an activity, sorting out a potential jurisdictional conflict and deciding which law is appropriate to a situation can be complex. For example, careless driving (HTA, s. 130) requires proof that the accused drove "without due care and attention or without reasonable consideration for other persons using the highway." Dangerous operation of a motor vehicle (CC, s. 249) requires proof that the accused operated "a motor vehicle in a manner that is dangerous to the public, having regard to all the circumstances, including the nature, condition and use of the place at which the motor vehicle is being operated and the amount of traffic that at the time is or might reasonably be expected to be at that place." The grounds for laying the charge are determined by the circumstances involved in the incident. Generally, the greater the departure from ordinary negligence in the direction of an intentionally dangerous act, the more likely that a CC charge will be laid.

Because this is an introductory text, we will not touch on all of these topics. Instead, our focus will be on matters that police officers commonly deal with or need to know about in day-to-day law enforcement: vehicle and operator permits, equipment requirements, rules of the road, HTA offences, HTA charging procedures and penalties, CC driving offences, and duties of drivers involved in a motor vehicle collision. We will begin by learning to find our way through and use the HTA. Once you have learned how to do this, you will find that the techniques used can be applied to finding your way through other legislation, such as the CC, that we examine later.

The Relationship Between a Statute and Its Regulations, or the Devil Is in the Details

A statute (that is, a law) like the HTA sets out general legal principles, but it does not usually deal with technical details. Instead, the technical details are dealt with in the HTA's regulations. The statute will contain a section or sections that allow the government to make regulations dealing with specific technical areas described in the section of the HTA that creates a regulation-making power. For example, s. 56 of the HTA authorizes the demerit point system, but the details of the demerit point system—how many demerit points are deducted for each offence—are located in Ontario regulation (O. reg.) 229/94. Another example of a regulation that supports the Act with technical details pertains to seat belts. If you look up ss. 106(3) and (4) of the Act, they stipulate that both the driver and passenger in a motor vehicle shall wear the complete seat belt assembly when driving on a highway. The technical details are contained in regulation 613, "Seat Belt Assemblies," which lists certain exemptions for police officers, prisoners in custody, ambulance attendants, firefighters, and others.

EXAMPLES OF A STATUTORY PROVISION AND THE AUTHORITY TO MAKE REGULATIONS UNDER THAT PROVISION AND THE REGULATION ENACTED

Section 78 of the HTA states:

>   (1) **Television in motor vehicle**—No person shall drive on a highway a motor vehicle that is equipped with a television receiving set,
>   (a) any part of which is located in the motor vehicle forward of the back of the driver's seat; or
>   (b) that is visible to the driver while he or she is operating the motor vehicle. ...
>   (3) **Exemption from regulation**—The Lieutenant Governor in Council may make regulations exempting any class of persons or vehicles or any use of equipment or type of equipment from this section.

In the index to the HTA (discussed in more detail below), the entry under "Television" reads: "restriction, exemption R-587 9." This code refers to s. 9 of reg. 587 of the Revised Regulations of Ontario 1990.

9. **Non-Application of Section 78 of the Act**—Section 78 of the Act does not apply to a television receiving set or to a television set where either is used only
   (a) as an aid for the safe and efficient operation of a motor vehicle; or
   (b) in carrying out a service or conducting a business where the use,
      (i) does not involve recreation or entertainment, and
      (ii) does not affect the safe operation of the motor vehicle.

Organization of Statutes and Regulations

In order to understand how to find sections of the HTA and regulations made under its authority, we need to know how they are organized. Periodically, the statutes and regulations of Ontario are revised. The most recent revision was in 1990. At that time, all parts of the statutes and regulations that had been repealed since the last revision in 1980 were cut out, and all the new acts, sections of acts, regulations, and sections of regulations made since the previous revision were added in their current form as of the date of the 1990 revision. The revised version then sets out the law as it is at the time of the revision. This cut-and-paste operation brings statutes and regulations up to date. After the date of revision, of course, the law continues to change. New statutes or amendments to old ones are identified by the date of the legislative session or year in which they were passed. The same holds for regulations.

For example, the revised version of the HTA is cited as RSO 1990, c. H.8, which is the short form for Revised Statutes of Ontario 1990, chapter H.8. An amendment to the HTA might be cited as SO 1994, c. 123. "SO 1994" means that the amending act was passed by in the 1994 session of the legislature, and "c. 123" means that it was the 123rd act passed in that session.

The regulations citation system is similar. The revised regulation for seat belt assemblies under the HTA is cited as RRO 1990, regulation 613, meaning that is the 613th regulation in the Revised Regulations of Ontario 1990. If the regulation was amended after 1990 by a later regulation, that amending regulation would be cited as O. reg. 195/05, meaning that it was the 195th Ontario regulation passed in 2005.

Now that we have an idea of how the statutes and regulations are organized, let us consider how we locate or find topics under the HTA and its regulations.

Locating Topics in the HTA and Its Regulations: The Use of a "Pocket Book" Consolidation on the Job

Because police officers need to be familiar with many parts of the HTA and frequently use the Act, there are a number of "pocket book" or consolidated versions of the Act that assemble the HTA and some or all of its regulations, complete with a table of contents and a subject index. Like the official revised statutes and regulations, the consolidated HTA brings the Act up to date to include the HTA as amended or revised to that year, and it does the same thing for regulations. This is done on an annual basis. Your instructor will specify which of the consolidated versions you should use. Without a consolidated version, you would need to have available to you the 1990 revision of the HTA (in the Revised Statutes of Ontario), all of the amendments to the HTA since 1990, the 1990 revised HTA regulations (in the Revised Regulations of Ontario), and all of the regulations made since 1990.[1] The publications containing all of this material would take up several feet of shelf space, weigh about 25 kg, and cost more than you would like to spend. A consolidated version of the HTA and its regulations is an attractive alternative to this. However, if you are using a consolidated version, note the date to which it is current. In some circumstances, it may be necessary to update the statute or the regulations to be sure there have been no changes since the publication of the consolidated version you are using.

HTA Table of Contents

A consolidated HTA begins with a table of contents (often simply titled "Contents") that defines its part-by-part organization. Each part is titled and lists the page on which each part begins. Following this is a table of contents for the HTA that lists the titles of the parts of the HTA, and the titles of the sections within each part and their section numbers. For instance, in the example below, "Powers and duties of Ministry" is found in s. 2 of part I of the HTA. Note that just the sections are listed, not the subsections, clauses, or subclauses. This means that the table of contents gives you a general overview of how the Act is organized, but it is only a partial aid in locating topics; it merely skims the surface.

> **Example: Table of Contents of the HTA**
>
> *Part I   Administration*
>
> | | |
> |---|---|
> | Powers and duties of Ministry | 2 |
> | Registrar of Motor Vehicles | 3 |
> | Deputy Registrar | 4 |
> | Regulations re fees | 5 |

HTA Index

A more specific aid is the index at the back of the Act. The index to the Act is a more detailed list of subjects by pointer words, which is arranged alphabetically by subject. For example, one set of pointer words is "Licence Plates." Listed alphabetically under this heading are subheadings that are more specific pointer words, along with the section and subsection where the more specific topics can be located. For example, under the entry "Licence Plates," you will find the subheading "General" and under it several subtopics. One of these is "obstruct S-13(3)," which deals with the obstruction of licence plates.

> **Example: HTA Index**
>
> Licence Plates
>   General ...
>   obstruct S-13(3) ...
>   visibility, dirty, confuse, obstruct S-13.

The consolidated index also identifies any relevant regulation that is associated with a section of the HTA. Finding relevant regulations is discussed in more detail below.

Abbreviated Forms for HTA Offences

The Ontario *Provincial Offences Act* makes writing HTA tickets easier for an officer, by permitting the offence to be described by section number and an appropriate abbreviated description. This is referred to as the "abbreviated form" or "short form" of the offence.

The abbreviated forms can also be used like an index or table of contents to quickly find an offence, together with its section number.

The abbreviated forms are authorized by the *Provincial Offences Act*, and are found in schedule 43 to RRO 1990, reg. 950, "Proceedings Commenced by Certificate of Offence." The abbreviated forms are listed in appendix A.

Examples of Abbreviated Forms in the HTA

Fail to notify change of name	9(2)
Red light—fail to stop	144(18)
Follow too closely	158(1)

Table of Contents for the HTA Regulations

The table of contents for the regulations to the HTA in a consolidated version of the HTA usually follows the main body of the Act. For example, in the 2007 consolidated version of the HTA published by MacBeth Publishing, the table of contents for the regulations is found on page 251. The table of contents for the regulations consists of the titles of all the regulations to the HTA. It is arranged alphabetically like an index, but is much shorter.

If a topic covered by the Act is very detailed, there may be a regulation that also discusses it. For example, if you were looking for information on motorcycle helmets that meet required legal specifications, you would find that it is dealt with under s. 104 of the Act. And by scanning the table of contents for the regulations, you would find that this topic is also dealt with under regulation 610.

Example: Table of Contents for the Regulations

Regulations under the Highway Traffic Act

...

Restricted Use of the King's Highway (Regulation 609)	262
Safety Helmets (Regulation 610)	281
Safety Inspections (Regulation 611)	283

In this example, regulation 610 of the Revised Regulations of Ontario 1990 is found on page 281 of the consolidated version of the HTA.

HTA General Regulation

If a topic of fine detail is not described in the table of contents for the regulations, it may be covered in the regulation entitled "General." The general regulation (RRO 1990, reg. 596, as amended by O. regs. 537/97 and 213/03) is a mix of miscellaneous topics and is located alphabetically under "g" in the table of contents for the regulations. For example, if you were searching for the regulation that covers the amount of damage to property that requires the police to complete a motor vehicle accident report, you would not find it described in the table of contents for the regulations. However, if you turned to the page on which the general regulation is found and scanned the headings, you would find the heading "Damage to Property Accident Report."[2]

Example of a Provision in the General Regulation

11. For the purpose of subsection 199(1) of the Act, the prescribed amount for damage to property is $1,000.

Finding Regulations in the Index

If you look up a more detailed topic in the index, you will find references to sections of the Act, but also to the details set out in a relevant regulation that deals with the topic covered by the section of the Act. For example, if you look up "Television" in the index, you are referred to s. 78 of the Act and to s. 9 of RRO 1990, reg. 587, which expands on the general statement of the law in s. 78 of the HTA. (See figure 1.1.)

HINT In your copy of the consolidated version of the HTA, you should stick a tab at the beginning of

1. the table of contents,
2. the index,
3. the table of contents for the regulations, and
4. the general regulation.

This will make it quicker and easier for you to look things up in the Act and the regulations.

Usual Method of Locating a Topic in a Consolidated HTA

1. If your topic is general, check the table of contents, which lists general topics covered by the Act.
2. If you cannot find your topic, check the headings in the index, which provides a more detailed list of topics.
3. If your topic is very detailed, also check the table of contents for the regulations.
4. If you cannot find your topic in the table of contents for the regulations, turn to the general regulation and look for it in the section headings.
5. If you cannot find your topic in the general regulation, check the headings and subheadings in the index for topics that refer you to specific sections of the regulations.

See appendix A, "Short-Form Wordings and Set Fines from the Provincial Offences Act," at the back of the book with respect to offences under the HTA.

FIGURE 1.1   Finding Regulations in the Index

Highway Traffic Act

    race S-172 199
garage licences sell or wreck vehicles,
    misconduct S-59(7) 98
licence plates
    misconduct, contravention by holder S-47 66
vehicle permit
    accident, fail to remain, assist etc S-200 225
    can include driver's licence suspension S-1(2) 16
    careless driving S-130 174
    deface/alter plates/permit S-12 36
    false statement S-90(1) 127
    load security, violate requirements S-111(4) 153
    operate contrary to CVOR requirements S-20 43
    operate contrary to CVOR requirements S-47(8) 68
    operate vehicle, permit suspended S-51 82
    person does not hold vehicle permit S-54 83
    second permit, obtain possess S-47(5) 67
    vehicle dimensions, violate requirements S-109(15) ... 147
    weight of vehicle, violate requirements S-121(4) 160
Symbols
    licence plate bearing disabled symbol S-29 48
    pedestrian control sign S-144(30) 185

T

Taxi, illegal S-39.1 56
Television
    restriction, exemption R-587 9 267
    restriction, exemption S-78 114
Territory without Municipal Organization
    gross weight on a bridge S-123 161
    load restrictions S-122(5) 160
    regulation, speed S-128(7) 170
    regulation, traffic control S-131 174
Three Lane Highway
    traffic S-154 191
Time
    offence deemed "subsequent" S-41(2) 58
    purchase or sale notice S-11(2) 35
Tinted Windows
    obstructing view S-73(2-3) 112
Tires
    altered, marking required S-71(2) 110
    chains S-69(2) 109
    chains, school purposes bus R-612 3(1)(b) 322
    clamps S-69(2) 109
    cutting to produce tread,
        marking required S- 71(2) 110
    defects R-625 2 379
    devices S-69(2) 109
    flanges S-69(2) 109
    mixtures, of types R-625 380
    permit operation of vehicle,

FIGURE 1.2   Parts of the Highway Traffic Act

The Ontario Highway Traffic Act

Cross Referenced to

Selected Regulations

2007

MacBeth Publishing Ltd.

FIGURE 1.2 (Continued)

Highway Traffic Act

Contents

	Page
Introduction	4
Sectional List	5
Part I — Administration	19
Part II — Permits	21
Part III — Parking Permits	47
Part IV — Driver, Driving Instructor	49
Part V — Garage and Storage Licences	98
Part VI — Equipment	101
Part VII — Loads and Dimensions	145
Part VIII — Weight	155
Part IX — Rate of Speed	169
Part X — Rules of the Road	175
Part X.1 — Toll Highways	210
Part X.2 — Medical Transportation Services	211
Part X.3 — Off-Road Vehicles	212
Part XI — Civil Proceedings	213
Part XII — Municipal By-Laws	215
Part XIII — Suspension for Failure to Pay Judgements	217
Part XIII.1 — Civil Remedy on Conviction of Certain Offences	221
Part XIV — Records and Reporting of Accidents and Convictions	222
Part XIV.1 — Photo-Radar System Evidence	228
Part XIV.2 — Red Light Camera System Evidence	232
Part XV — Procedures, Arrest and Penalties	236
Part XVI — Pilot Projects	250
Regulations	251
Index	491

FIGURE 1.2 (Continued)

Regulations
under the Highway Traffic Act

Commercial Motor Vehicle Inspections (Regulation 575)	253
Covering of Loads (Regulation 577)	257
Designation of Highways (Regulation 579)	258
Driving Instructor's Licence (Regulation 586)	259
Equipment (Regulation 587)	263
Garage Licences (Regulation 595)	268
General (Regulation 596)	269
Highway Closings (Regulation 599)	273
Over-Dimensional Farm Vehicles (Regulation 603)	275
Reciprocal Suspension of Licences (Regulation 607)	277
Restricted Use of Left Lane by Commercial Motor Vehicle (Regulation 608)	278
Restricted Use of the King's Highway (Regulation 609)	262
Safety Helmets (Regulation 610)	281
Safety Inspections (Regulation 611)	283
School Buses (Regulation 612)	319
Seat Belt Assemblies (Regulation 613)	325
Signs (Regulation 615)	329
Slow Moving Vehicle Sign (Regulation 616)	377
Tire Standards and Specifications (Regulation 625)	379
Vehicle Permits (Regulation 628)	383
Vehicles on Controlled Access Highways (Regulation 630)	328
Administrative Driver's Licence Suspension (Regulation 499/96)	462
Hours of Work (Regulation 4/93)	405
Used Vehicle Information Package (Regulation 601/93)	410
Demerit Point System (Regulation 339/94)	415
Driver's Licences (Regulation 340/94)	425
Provincially Approved Screening Devices (Regulation 343/94)	414
Suspension & Impoundment of Commercial Motor Vehicles for Critical Defects - Section 82.1 (Regulation 512/97)	451
Orders to Impound or Release Motor Vehicles Under Section 55.1 of the Act (631/98)	461
Pre-Empting Traffic Control Signal Devices (Regulation 34/06)	464
Classification of Vehicles as Irreparable, Salvage and Rebuilt (Regulation 376/02)	465
Testing, Repair and Compliance Requirements for Unsafe Vehicles under Section 82 of the Act (Regulation 381/02)	471
Definitions and requirements under section 142.1 of the act (yielding right of way to buses) (Regulation 393/02)	460
Operation of Off-Road Vehicle on Highways (Regulation 316/03)	475
Security of Loads (Regulation 363/04)	483
Designation of Bus By-Pass Shoulders on King's Highway (Regulation 618/05)	487
High Occupancy Vehicle Lanes (Regulation 620/05)	488

FIGURE 1.2 (Concluded)

Highway Traffic Act

Index

A

Abandoned vehicle
    abandoned or unplated S-170(7) 196
    abandoned or unplated S-221 247
    cars stored, parked S-60(4) 99
Accessories. *See* individual accessory, i.e. mirrors
Accident
    amount of damage to report 272
    amount of damage to report S-199 222
    amount of damage to report S-201 225
    bond S-194 214
    claims fund, mentioned S-198(2) 217
    damage claim, time limit S-206 236
    onus on driver or owner, negligence S-193 213
    provide assistance, information, remain S-200 225
    recovery from injuries, penalties no bar S-209 237
    report completion, police S-205 226
    reports by;
        blank forms S-205 226
        charitable institutions S-202(2) 226
        Crown Attorneys S-202 225
        driver, passengers, damage amount R-596-11 272
        driver, passengers S-201 225
        driver S-199 222
        hospital and other officials S-202 225
        Police S-199 to 202 222
Address
    driver's licence, change R-340/94-33 449
    notice of change, CVOR certificate S-18 43
    notice of change, owner, lessee S-9(2-4) 34
    provide at accident S-200 225
    provide to police S-218 245
    provide to Police S-33 53
Affidavits
    administration R-7(23) 25
    false statement, make in S-9(1) 34
Age
    drive motor assisted bicycle S-38 55
    driver's minimum for vehicle types S-37 55
    driver's minimum, out of province driver S-37(1) 53
    employ, permit, driver under 16 S-37 55
Air bags
    installing rebuilt, prohibited S-71.1 111
    rebuilding, prohibited S-71.1 111
    rebuilt prohibited S-71.1 111
Air Brake Endorsement. *See* Driver's Licence

491

Correctly Identifying or Citing Sections of Acts and Regulations

Once we have found a section of a statute or regulation, we have to know how to identify or cite the section. You will note in your consolidated HTA that every section has a numeric identifying system so that every rule can be identified by a series of numbers and letters.

Care should be used in recording the correct alphanumeric code, particularly for offences. If there is an error in recording the code for an offence against a defendant, so that it describes an offence that the defendant did not commit, the offence may not be processed by the court office, or may, if it reaches trial, be dismissed.

For example, if you stop a motorist whose car does not display licence plates, you would probably wish to charge the motorist with failing to display licence plates under s. 7(1)(b)(i). However, in issuing the ticket if you in error wrote in s. 7(1)(b)(ii), you will have charged the motorist with the offence of failing to have historic licence plates on his vehicle, which is not the offence he apparently committed, and the charge as recorded would be dismissed.

Some General Considerations About Interpreting and Applying the Acts and the Regulations

In interpreting motor vehicle statutes and regulations, or in fact any statutes or regulations that set out offences, there are some things you should keep in mind.

WHERE DID THE OFFENCE OCCUR AND WHO COMMITTED IT?

Some offences under the HTA can be committed anywhere, but others can only be committed on a highway. Offences can be committed in some cases by anyone, but others only by a driver, and still others only by an owner (and some may be committed by drivers or owners).

For example, s. 32(1) of the HTA states:

> No person shall drive a motor vehicle on a highway unless the motor vehicle is within a class of motor vehicles in respect of which the person holds a driver's licence issued to him or her under this Act.

It is clear that everyone who drives a motor vehicle on a public roadway must have a licence, but just as important we also know that he or she must be properly licensed when driving on a highway. So, "anyone" may commit this offence, but only when driving on a highway. This means that if you do not have a licence but wish to drive a car on private property, you may do so without violating the HTA.

CHAPTER SUMMARY

This chapter introduces you to the major components of the legislative framework governing traffic management. We begin by exploring the relationship between a statute and the regulations made under the authority of a statute. General rules and principles are set out in statutes, and the details are set out in its regulations. We describe how the *Highway Traffic Act* (HTA) and its regulations are organized and set up so that you can find information in them easily. You are introduced to "pocket book" consolidations of the HTA, which police officers use on the job. The chapter then discusses the steps for locating a topic in a consolidated HTA. The first step is to check the table of contents of the Act. If the topic is more detailed, you will need to check the table of contents for the regulations, and after that the table of contents for the general regulation. If you still cannot find the topic, check the headings and subheadings in the index for the regulations. The chapter closes with some suggestions to assist you in identifying and citing sections of statutes and regulations.

NOTES

1. For more information on how to use the standard sources for finding and updating statutes and regulations, see generally M. Kerr, J. Kurtz, and A. Blatt, *Legal Research: Step by Step*, 2nd ed. (Toronto: Emond Montgomery, 2006) and R. Carson, "Legal Research: An Introduction," in L. Olivo, ed., *Introduction to Law in Canada* (Toronto: Captus Press, 1999).

2. Dollar amounts are often described in the regulations rather than in the statute because regulations can be quickly changed to reflect the impact of inflation.

REVIEW QUESTIONS

True or False?

Place a "T" next to the statement if it is true, or an "F" if it is false.

_____ 1. Statutes are federal and regulations are provincial.

_____ 2. An "abbreviated form" or "short form" of an offence is the form used for writing a ticket.

_____ 3. The General Regulation to the *Highway Traffic Act* is a mix of miscellaneous topics.

_____ 4. If an officer is distracted by the defendant and mistakenly writes s. 7(1)(b)(ii) on a ticket instead of s. 7(1)(b)(i), the charge will be dismissed.

_____ 5. The *Highway Traffic Act* applies equally to private and public roads.

Short Answer

1. What are the places to search for a particular topic such as seat belts in a consolidated *Highway Traffic Act*?

2. Using the HTA index and table of contents, find all the statute sections and regulations dealing with the following:

    a. automobile trailers

    b. fines for speeding offences

    c. motorcycle helmets

    d. lighting on bicycles

Discussion

If a person is driving in a parking lot of a Wal-Mart store, and she drives through a stop sign located in the parking lot, could she be charged under s. 136(1) of the *Highway Traffic Act*? If yes, what charges may apply?

CHAPTER 2

The Highway Traffic Act: Defining Terms

CHAPTER OBJECTIVES

After completing this chapter, you should be able to:

- Distinguish between the various definitions of "vehicle" in the Ontario *Highway Traffic Act* (HTA) and understand the reasons for the variations in the definitions.
- Understand the definitions of "highway," "roadway," and related terms used in the HTA and the reasons for those definitions.
- Appreciate that although the definitions discussed in this chapter are key definitions, there are others in the HTA that you will need to look up from time to time.

INTRODUCTION

This chapter defines and discusses some key definitions in the Ontario *Highway Traffic Act* (HTA). These include definitions of conveyances of various kinds, such as

- vehicle, s. 1;
- motor vehicle, s. 1;
- commercial motor vehicle, s. 1;

- trailer, s. 1;
- bus, s. 1;
- school bus, s. 175(1) and reg. 612; and
- school purposes vehicle, reg. 612, s. 1(4).

Other definitions include geographical elements over which conveyances travel, such as

- highway, s. 1;
- roadway, s. 1;
- intersection, s. 1;
- crosswalks, s. 1; and
- pedestrian crossover, s. 1.

Finally, there are some definitions about stopping conveyances on highways, such as

- stopping, s. 1;
- standing, s. 1; and
- parking, s. 1.

DEFINITION OF VEHICLE, SECTION 1

vehicle
includes a motor vehicle, trailer, traction engine, farm tractor, road-building machine, bicycle, and any vehicle drawn, propelled, or driven by any kind of power, including muscular power, but does not include a motorized snow vehicle or a streetcar

The definition of **vehicle** includes motor vehicles, such as cars, trucks, trailers, farm tractors, and road-building machinery (including steam rollers and graders). The definition also includes vehicles that operate by any other form of power, including muscular power, such as bicycles and horse-drawn carriages. In a recent case, *R v. Yick* ([2004] OJ no. 4166 (Prov. Ct.)), the Ontario Provincial Court found that a person on the roadway using inline roller skates was operating a vehicle, as defined in the HTA, and could be convicted of failing to stop at a stop sign. The definition of "vehicle" is used in connection with the "rules of the road" and is very broad so that drivers of a wide variety of vehicles can be made subject to the rules of the road. Streetcars and motorized snow vehicles (snowmobiles) are explicitly excluded from the definition, primarily because they are covered by other legislation. For example, snowmobiles are regulated under the *Motorized Snow Vehicles Act* (RSO 1990, c. M.44).

motor vehicle
includes automobiles, motor-assisted bicycles (mopeds), and motorcycles (which includes motor scooters), unless otherwise indicated in the HTA, as well as other vehicles propelled by anything other than muscular power, but does not include snowmobiles, farm tractors, self-propelled implements of husbandry (such as reapers and combines), road-building machinery, streetcars, and traction engines

Definition of Motor Vehicle, Section 1

The definition of **motor vehicle** includes automobiles, motor-assisted bicycles (mopeds), and motorcycles (which includes motor scooters), unless otherwise indicated in the HTA. It also includes other vehicles propelled by anything other than muscular power. However, the following vehicles are not included in the definition:

- **snow**mobiles,
- **f**arm tractors,
- self-propelled **i**mplements of husbandry (such as reapers and combines),
- **r**oad-building machinery,
- **s**treetcars, and
- **t**raction engines.

You can remember which vehicles are excluded by using the mnemonic "snowfirst."

The definition of "motor vehicle," with the "snowfirst" exclusions, is generally used for rules regarding vehicle permits, driver's licences, and equipment requirements under the HTA. It is narrower and more restrictive than the definition of "vehicle." The "snowfirst" exclusions are regulated under other legislation, or are left unregulated.

Definition of Commercial Motor Vehicle, Section 1

A commercial motor vehicle is a vehicle that has a truck or delivery body attached to it. "Delivery body" is not defined by the HTA, but it can be assumed that it is a vehicle primarily for carrying cargo or objects rather than people. Other vehicles specifically included in the definition are

- ambulances,
- hearses,
- fire apparatus,
- buses, and
- tractors used for hauling on highways.

The definition of "commercial motor vehicle" is not based on the purpose or function of the vehicle, but on its structure and physical description. Therefore, if someone uses a hearse as a domestic family vehicle, it is still defined as a commercial vehicle because of its structure and physical description. This definition is used in the HTA to describe the type of motor vehicle that requires commercial motor vehicle licence plates. Commercial plates have a different colour (black, rather than blue, on a white background) and the number sequencing is different from that for passenger motor vehicles. With respect to vans, if there is a seating capacity of 4 or more, the van is considered a passenger motor vehicle; if there are fewer than 4 seats, the van is considered a commercial motor vehicle. If a van has more than 10 seats and is used for transporting people, it is considered a commercial vehicle, but will also be defined as a bus.

Definition of Trailer, Section 1

A trailer is any vehicle drawn on a highway by a motor vehicle, but excludes the following:

- a **m**otor vehicle being towed,
- a **m**obile home designed and used as a residence or working accommodation and exceeding 2.6 m in width *or* 11 m in length,
- an **i**mplement of husbandry (for example, a hay wagon),
- a **s**ide car on a motorcycle, and
- any device or apparatus not designed to **t**ransport persons or property and that is temporarily drawn on a highway (for example, a portable cement mixer).

You can remember which vehicles are excluded by using the mnemonic "mmist."

The definition of "trailer" describes vehicles that require trailer plates. Such vehicles must be pulled by a motor vehicle and pulled on a highway. If the vehicle does not fit the definition or is one of the exceptions, it does not require trailer plates.

Definition of Bus, Section 1

A bus is a motor vehicle designed and used for carrying 10 or more passengers. This definition is used for the purpose of determining who must have a bus driver's licence.

Definition of School Bus, Section 175(1) and Regulation 612

As in the definition of "bus," the definition of "school bus" has two parts: a definition by physical description, and a definition by use. A school bus is chrome yellow in colour. It has the words "SCHOOL BUS" marked on the front and rear and the words "DO NOT PASS WHEN SIGNALS FLASHING" on the rear. It also has red flashing lights at front and rear. A school bus is used for transporting children anywhere for any reason, or transporting developmentally handicapped adults to or from a training centre. Buses that fit this definition must meet the safety equipment requirements and the rules for operation of safety equipment for the loading or discharging of passengers, and drivers must meet licensing requirements specific to school buses.

Definition of School Purposes Vehicle, Regulation 612, Section 1(4)

The definition of "school purposes vehicle" covers buses of any colour that are operated by or under a contract to a school board for the transportation of children anywhere for any reason. It also includes chrome-yellow school buses. This definition is broad enough to cover any driver who will be in charge of transporting children.

Definition of Highway, Section 1

The term "highway" is described very broadly and includes a public street, avenue, parkway, driveway, square, place, bridge, viaduct, or trestle that is intended for or used by anyone to pass over in a vehicle. It includes not only the space over which the vehicle moves, but also the land on either side of the roadway between the lateral property lines. In many parts of the province, **road allowances** that constitute the highway are one **chain** (66 feet) wide (33 feet on either side of the centre of the roadway). In some cases, where the roadway is narrower than the road allowance, private property owners have encroached on the highway where it is not clearly delineated, by planting lawns or shrubs on what is technically the road allowance and part of the highway. For practical reasons, on city streets, the highway includes the sidewalks on either side or, if there is no sidewalk, the shoulder or verge of the road up to the property line of properties adjacent to the highway. The illustrations in figure 2.1 will help you see that the highway consists of more than just the roadway itself.

road allowance
a continuous strip of land dedicated for the location of a public highway, usually one chain (66 feet) wide; the actual roadway may be considerably narrower, but the whole width of the road allowance constitutes the highway, within the meaning of the HTA

chain
a surveyor's measure, consisting of a chain or line that is 66 feet long

Definition of King's Highway, Section 1

The term "King's Highway" describes a class of highway, consisting of secondary and tertiary provincial highways designated under the Ontario *Public Transportation and Highway Improvement Act*. These highways are commonly known as provincial highways and are identified by numbered route signs posted along the highway.

Definition of Roadway, Section 1

The roadway is the travelled portion of a highway ordinarily used for vehicular traffic, and does not include the shoulders, even if they are paved. What is considered the roadway depends on the physical attributes of the road. For example, the roadway is,

- on a city street, the paved portion between the curbs on either side;
- on a street where there is no curb, the paved portion between the edges of the pavement on either side of the travelled portion; and
- on a gravel or snow-covered road, the travelled portion (note that this kind of road can change width, depending on how much of the right of way is gravelled or cleared of snow).

To summarize, a roadway is the travelled part of a highway. Where there are median dividers and exit and entrance ramps, a highway, like Highway 401, can include more than one roadway, as figure 2.2 illustrates.

The definition of a driver in s. 1 is restricted to someone who drives a vehicle on a highway. Therefore, if the term "driver" is used in the description of an offence, the location of the offence is restricted to a highway, as defined in the HTA. This means that offences committed on private drives, driveways, or in private parking lots, including the parts used for traffic circulation, cannot be subject to charges under the HTA; a private parking area or drive is not a highway under the HTA (*R v. Mansour*, [1979] SCR 916).

FIGURE 2.1   Highways

City: Storefront to storefront

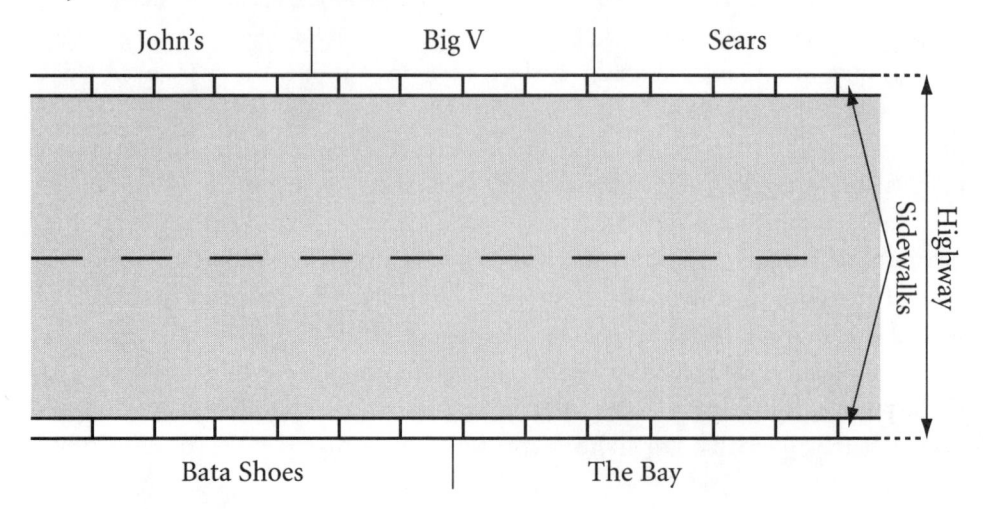

Suburb: Mid-lawn to mid-lawn

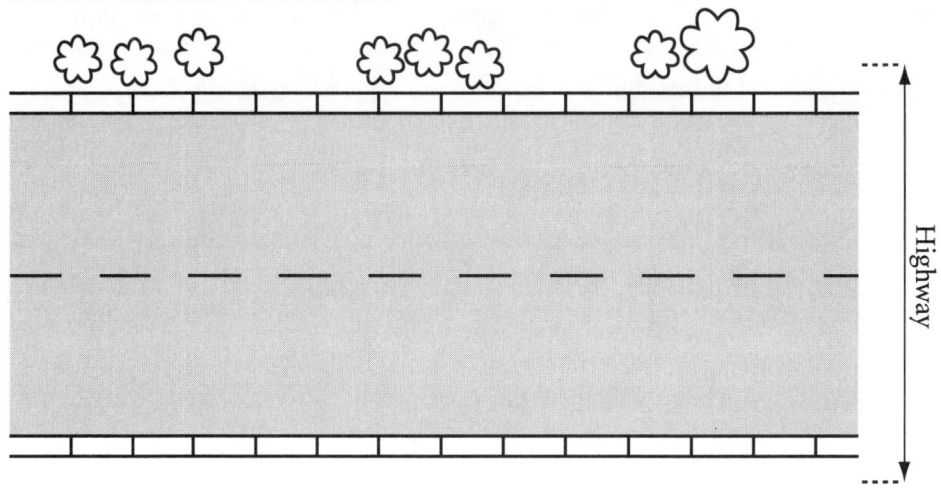

Country: Fence line to fence line

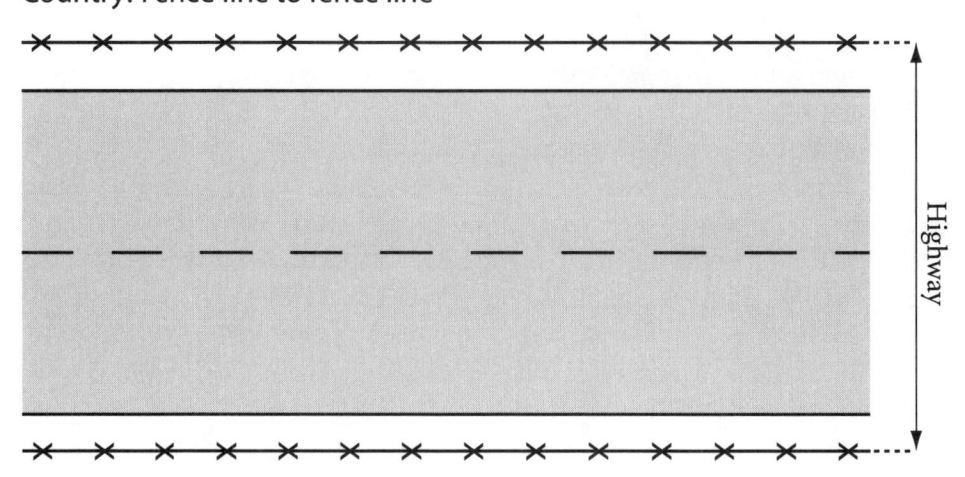

FIGURE 2.2 Highway with Two Roadways

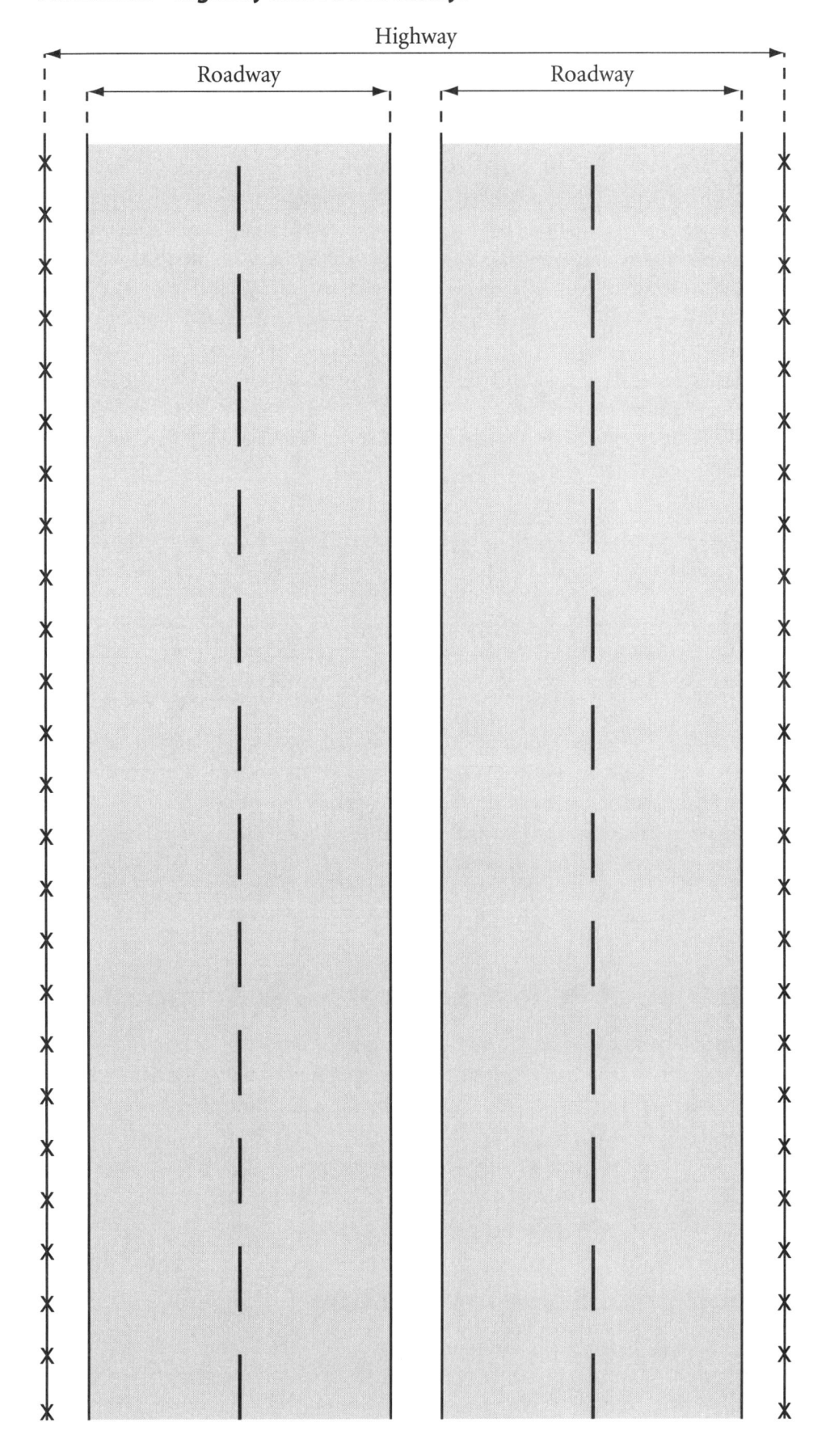

Definition of Intersection, Section 1

An intersection is the area of the highway that falls within the extension of the curb lines or, if there is no curb, it is the area that falls within the extension of the lateral boundary lines of two or more highways that join one another at an angle, whether or not the highways cross each other. Note that if there are curbs, the definition seems to describe a roadway, yet if there are no curbs, the reference to lateral boundary lines seems to suggest the more encompassing definition of a highway rather than the narrower one of a roadway. The angle of an intersection can be oblique or acute (as in the top portion of figure 2.3), although we usually think of intersections as two highways crossing each other at right angles (as in the bottom portion of figure 2.3).

The definition of "intersection" provides an important reference point for defining some driving offences. For example, the definition of "intersection" is invoked to describe the legal placement of a stop sign. A stop sign is probably only advisory if it is not placed where two highways intersect. For example, stop signs used in plaza or mall exits to highways are probably only advisory, and charges might not be laid successfully for failing to stop at such signs.

Definition of Crosswalks, Section 1

There are two kinds of crosswalks: marked crosswalks and unmarked crosswalks. Unmarked crosswalks are defined as that part of a roadway at an intersection that forms the area within the boundary created by the connection of the lateral lines of the sidewalks on opposite sides of the highway. More simply, an unmarked crosswalk exists only where there is an intersection with sidewalks on opposite sides. One of the sidewalks, if it were to continue, would cross the road to meet another sidewalk on the opposite side. See figure 2.4 for an example. This definition determines the place at an intersection where a pedestrian may safely cross the highway.

A marked crosswalk is any portion of a roadway, at an intersection or elsewhere, distinctly set out for pedestrian crossing by signs or markings on the roadway. Because a marked crosswalk can be posted at places other than intersections, the law requires that they be marked. See figure 2.5.

Definition of Pedestrian Crossover, Section 1

A pedestrian crossover is any portion of a roadway designated by a municipal by-law for pedestrian crossing by signs on the highway and by lines or other markings on the surface of the roadway, as prescribed by the regulations. This type of crossing is generally found in large cities, and there are prescribed stopping and passing requirements with respect to these crossovers that do not apply to ordinary crosswalks. Usually, crossovers have signs, lights, or both suspended over the roadway, although these are not required by law.

Definition of Stopping, Section 1

A "no stopping" area on a roadway indicates that a vehicle may not stop for any reason, except to avoid traffic or when required by the police, traffic signs, or traffic signals.

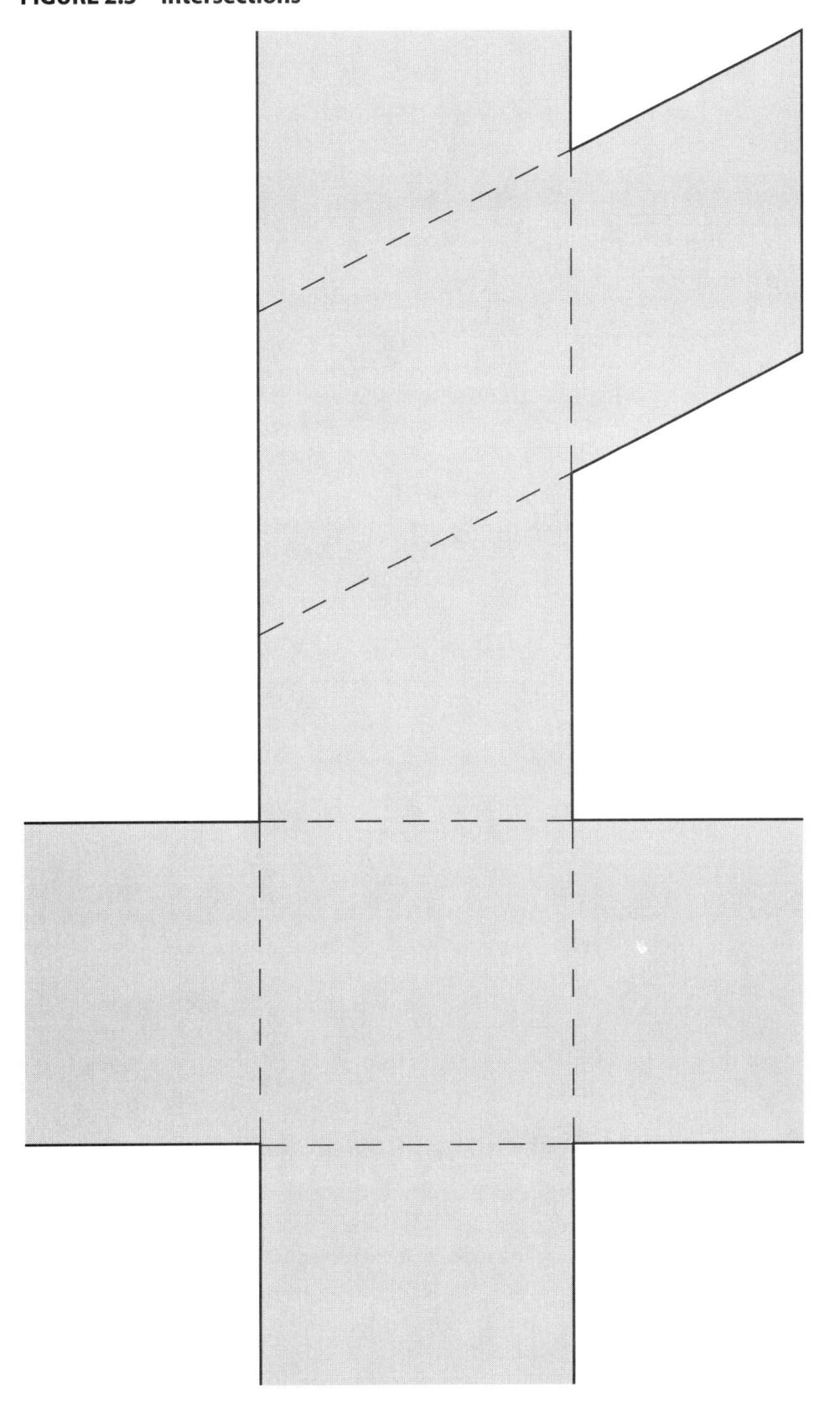

FIGURE 2.3 Intersections

FIGURE 2.4 Unmarked Crosswalks

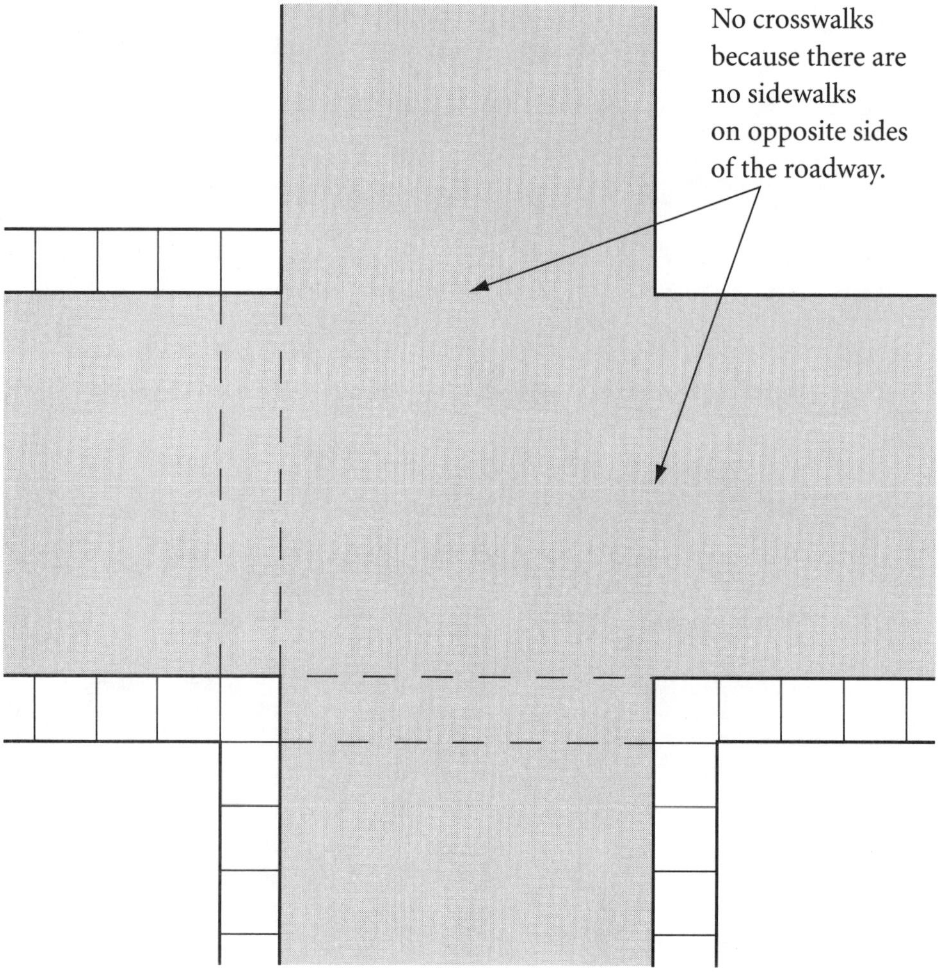

No crosswalks because there are no sidewalks on opposite sides of the roadway.

Three requirements:

1. at an intersection,
2. sidewalks on opposite sides, and
3. one of the sidewalks, if projected, must cross the road.

Definition of Standing, Section 1

A "no standing" sign means that a vehicle may not stop, except while engaged in picking up or dropping off passengers. Standing does not mean that a vehicle can stay to wait for passengers who are going to be picked up or dropped off.

Definition of Parking, Section 1

A "no parking" sign means that a vehicle may not be left standing, whether occupied or not, except when standing temporarily to pick up or drop off passengers or merchandise. A vehicle may not be left standing in a "no parking" area except while engaged in picking up or dropping off passengers or merchandise.

FIGURE 2.5 Marked Crosswalks

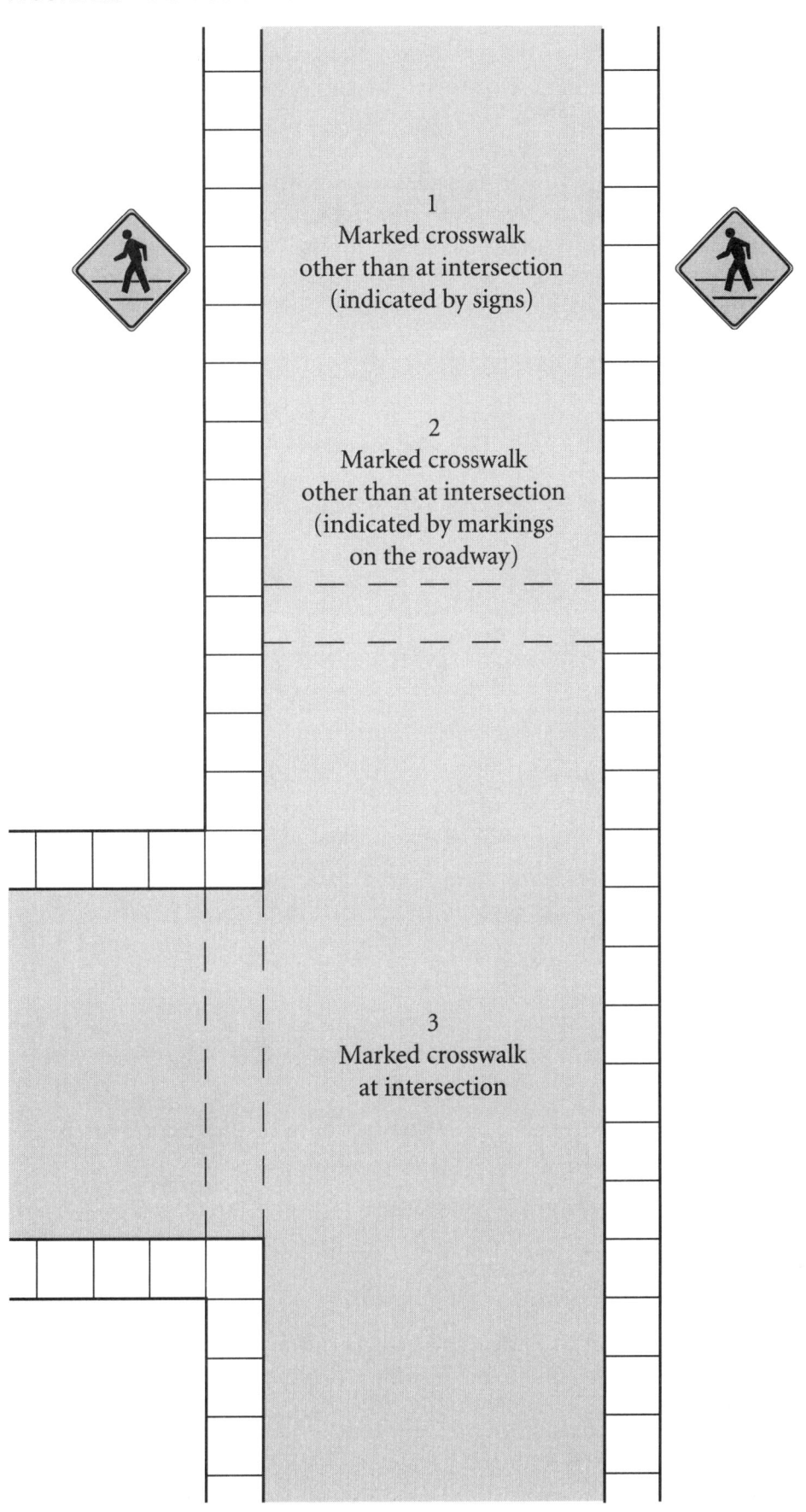

1 Marked crosswalk other than at intersection (indicated by signs)

2 Marked crosswalk other than at intersection (indicated by markings on the roadway)

3 Marked crosswalk at intersection

CHAPTER SUMMARY

This chapter introduces you to some of the basic terms and definitions in the HTA that you need to understand and apply to driving and permit offences. The general term "vehicle" is first defined, followed by its subcategories: motor vehicle, commercial motor vehicle, and various types of buses. The division of "vehicle" into subclasses is generally related to operator licensing requirements and, in the case of commercial vehicles and buses, to equipment requirements. The term "highway" is defined, along with its related component parts, including roadway, intersection, and crosswalk. These elements provide the necessary context for driving offences and collision investigation that concern police officers; they are discussed in more detail later in the book.

KEY TERMS

vehicle

motor vehicle

road allowance

chain

REVIEW QUESTIONS

True or False?

In the space provided next to each statement, place a "T" if the statement is true or an "F" if the statement is false.

__F__ 1. A roadway includes shoulders.

__T__ 2. A bicycle is a vehicle.

__F__ 3. A self-propelled farm harvester is a motor vehicle as defined in the HTA.

__T__ 4. A manure spreader, which is drawn along a highway by a truck, is a trailer.

__T__ 5. The only exception to prohibited parking is for picking up or dropping off passengers.

__T__ 6. A streetcar is a motor vehicle.

__T__ 7. A portable cement mixer, which is pulled by a dump truck, is a trailer.

__T__ 8. A road grader is not a motor vehicle.

__F__ 9. When a motor vehicle with a designed seating capacity of 14 people is carrying 7 people, the motor vehicle is considered a bus as defined in the HTA.

__T__ 10. In a residential area, the boulevard and sidewalk on either side of the roadway are considered part of the highway.

_F_ 11. A compressor, which is pulled by a half-ton truck, is a trailer.

____ 12. A highway is all the area between the lateral property lines of the road allowance.

____ 13. A motorcycle, a motor-assisted bicycle, a motor home, and a self-propelled cement truck are all motor vehicles as defined in the HTA.

____ 14. An exception to prohibited stopping is the temporary loading or unloading of cargo.

____ 15. A pedestrian crossover is only required to be designated by signs and a bylaw to be lawful.

____ 16. A chrome-yellow bus with the words "SCHOOL BUS" on the front and rear and "DO NOT PASS WHEN SIGNALS FLASHING" on the rear that is used for transporting a children's hockey team to a weekend tournament is a school bus.

Short Answer

Briefly answer the following questions in the space provided.

1. How does a marked crosswalk differ from an unmarked crosswalk, and how do both differ from a pedestrian crossover?

2. List four vehicles with motors that are excluded from the HTA definition of "motor vehicle."

3. Can you be charged for driving 80 km/h in the traffic circulation area of a private parking area in a plaza? Why or why not?

4. What is the difference between a highway and a roadway under the HTA?

5. If a half-ton truck is used only for personal use, can it be classed as a passenger motor vehicle rather than a truck?

6. How does a "school purposes vehicle" differ from a "school bus"?

7. What towed vehicles are excluded from the definition of "trailer" in the HTA?

8. Is a trailer that is pulled by a bicycle considered a trailer within the meaning of the HTA?

9. Can an unmarked crosswalk be located on a highway, 250 m from an intersection?

Discussion Questions

1. In *R v. Yick*, the accused was convicted of failing to stop at a stop sign while roller skating in the roadway. The court held that roller skates came within the definition of "vehicle" under the HTA. The brief oral decision on the case is set out below.

AUGUST J (orally):

[1] MS. PETERKIN: Good afternoon, Your Honour. For the record, the name is Peterkin, first initial K. Appearing on behalf of the City of Toronto. We can deal with number one-four, Winson-Wei Yick.

[2] MR. McKINNON: Yes. Good afternoon Your Honour. For the record, my name is McKinnon, first initials T.J., appearing as agent on behalf of the appellant who is not present before Your Honour's court, with your permission. Your Honour, this is a defence appeal for the conviction of disobey stop sign, fail to stop. The trial was held on January sixth, 2003, in C court. At that trial it was revealed that the defendant at that time, the appellant in this case, was roller-blading down the street. And the officer waved the appellant over and issued a Provincial Offences Notice to the appellant for the offence of disobey stop sign, fail to stop. Under that section, Your Honour, I would submit that the prosecution has the burden of proving that number one, the appellant was driving as it cites in s. 136(1).

[3] THE COURT: Is that in dispute?

[4] MR. McKINNON: Pardon me?

[5] THE COURT: Is that in dispute?

[6] MR. McKINNON: That he was driving the Roller Blades?

[7] THE COURT: Yes.

[8] MR. McKINNON: Yes, Your Honour. The crux of this appeal basically is that the Roller Blades, I would submit, are not classified as a vehicle, that you cannot drive Roller Blades, that they would be similar to skates or shoes or skis, something of that nature. I would submit that the intent of the law would be to prohibit vehicles, scooters, motorcycles, things of that nature. And that someone using Roller Blades would be the same as people in Nathan Phillips Square skating on the rink over there. I would submit that they are not driving or operating vehicles on the ice rink. I would say that Roller Blades would be very similar to shoes or boots and that you strap them on your feet, that they are part of your apparel. And I would submit that someone standing in Roller Blades would not be in a vehicle or operating a vehicle. That's the appeal.

[9] MS. PETERKIN: Your Honour, I would ... submit to the Court that I differ quite to the contrary, that notwithstanding first of all that it was never argued about the roller-blading not being a vehicle, I have provided some excerpts from the *Highway Traffic Act* as well as the *Oxford English Dictionary* and the *Black's Dictionary*. If I can pass up some information to Your Honour and as well as to Mr. McKinnon as well. I first highlighted the section itself, being 136(1)(a) from the *Highway Traffic Act*, which reads, "Every driver or streetcar operator approaching a stop sign at an intersection shall stop his or her vehicle or streetcar at a marked stop line, or if none, then immediately before entering the nearest crosswalk, or if none, then immediately before entering the intersection." I have further provided an excerpt for the *Black's Law Dictionary* with a definition of driving, which indicates, "To urge forward under guidance; compelled to go in a particular direction; urge onward and direct the course of." Further to that, the

definition of "driver" in the *Highway Traffic Act*, which is an essential element in the charge before us today, indicates—means, "a person who drives a vehicle on a highway." In the transcript before you on page—I believe it's line four, it clearly indicates. ...

[10] THE COURT: What page?

[11] MS. PETERKIN: Sorry. Page four, line 25. The officer indicates in his evidence that, "I observed a male roller-blading southbound on Beverly Street in the curb lane at a very fast pace. The male roller-blader went right through the intersection where there is a marked stop line for southbound traffic." I would submit there that the roller-blader was in fact on the highway, on the curb lane, which is a travel portion of the roadway by vehicles. I further went on to give a copy of the definition of "vehicle" from the *Highway Traffic Act*, which is different. There is a difference between a motor vehicle and a vehicle. And in the charge before us today it indicates, "vehicle," which includes a motor vehicle, trailer, traction engine, farm tractor, road-building machine, bicycle, and any vehicle drawn, propelled or driven by any kind of power including muscular power. And I'm submitting that roller-blading or in-line skating would fall in the definition of "vehicle," including "muscular power." It's quite obvious that the muscles being used amongst many, but certainly would be the leg muscles. And also further and lastly I have provided a definition of vehicle not only from the *Highway Traffic Act*, but also from the *Oxford English Dictionary*, that indicates, "A material, means, channel or instrument by which a substance or some property of matter is conveyed or transmitted from one point to another." And it also further goes on to mean, "A means of conveyance provided with wheels, or runners and used for the carriage of persons or goods." I'd respectfully submit that the defendant was roller-blading on [a] highway in the curb lane. He was on a means of conveyance. He was being transported by the Roller Blades, which in fact have wheels. And under those circumstances I would respectfully submit that roller-blading would fall in the definition of vehicle as I've provided today and that there was no error in law in the trial before the Court, and that the appeal should be dismissed.

[12] THE COURT: Thank you. Any reply?

[13] MR. McKINNON: Just briefly. I'm not sure if Your Honour's copy of the *Oxford English Dictionary* is highlighted as mine was, but after the highlighting for the first part, "A material, means, channel or instrument by which a substance or some property of matter, as sound or heat, is conveyed or transmitted from one point to another." And after that it says, "1615." Now I can't be sure what that "1615" means, but it sounds to me like a year, maybe when that definition was made. I would submit that they would have no comprehension of Roller Blades. I would submit that the muscular power is too broad in its wording and that my shoes are propelled forward by muscular power. By my friend's submission if I were to run through a stop sign my shoes would propel me through there by muscular power. I would submit that the Roller Blades should not be looked at as a vehicle, that they are part of someone's apparel, that they are basically footwear. Now they have wheels on the bottom but they are footwear, I would submit. And again, skates, I would submit if you're skating down the road that you would not contravene this section. I would submit that the reason why it includes muscular power is for things like bicycles, for scooters. Those things I would submit are vehicles and I concede that. However I would ask Your Honour to accept that Roller Blades are footwear and apparel and are not vehicles. And I'd ask Your Honour to allow the appeal and enter an acquittal.

[14] THE COURT: All right. Thank you. I choose to accept the submissions of the prosecution and I do not agree with the position taken by the appellant. And therefore the appeal is dismissed and the conviction and sentence are affirmed. ...

---

    a. Consider the opposing arguments made by counsel. Are there legitimate practical reasons for this decision, or is this a case of *de minimis non curat lex* (the law does not concern itself with trifling matters)?

    b. Would it have made any difference to the outcome of this case if Mr. Yick had been rollerblading on the sidewalk rather than in the roadway?

2. Babette has a four-wheel vehicle that seats one person and has a flat, horizontal deck behind the seat. It also has a mast and a sail; there is no motor. Using wind power, she is able to drive around the city. Does she require a vehicle permit under s. 7(1) of the HTA? If so, what kind?

3. Babette has added a larger deck and seating for 11 passengers to her wind-driven vehicle. She has accepted a contract for driving children to and from school. She drives this vehicle out of a shopping plaza parking lot and ignores the stop sign where the lot enters onto a highway. Discuss how this vehicle should be classified and whether or not, on the basis of these facts, Babette could be charged with failing to stop at a stop sign.

CHAPTER 3

Licences and Permits

CHAPTER OBJECTIVES

After completing this chapter, you should be able to:

- Know what restricted permits and their plates look like, and where to find them on a vehicle.

- Know the circumstances where a plate can be transferred from one vehicle to another.

- Know the procedure for transferring the ownership of a motor vehicle.

- Know the elements of the offences concerning unlawful use of plates and permits and validation tags.

- Identify the vehicle classes set out in the Ontario *Highway Traffic Act* (HTA).

- Assign a vehicle to an appropriate vehicle class by weight, purpose, passenger carrying capacity, use, or other factors.

- Know the levels and restrictions on graduated licences for G and M class licences.

- Determine which class of vehicle a licence holder of a certain class can drive.

- Know the elements of driver's licence offences.

- Understand the circumstances when reverse-onus rules apply to an offence.

- Know when you can arrest for an offence or ticket for an offence.

- Identify the circumstances where non-Ontario plates and licences can be used by a person driving on the highway.
- Know the requirements for vehicle insurance under the Ontario *Compulsory Automobile Insurance Act* (CAIA), and the related offences under this Act.

INTRODUCTION

In this chapter, we examine the requirements of the permit system for licensing different classes of vehicles and the requirements for different classes of operator's licences.

VEHICLE PERMITS

The permit is the document that licenses a vehicle to be used on the highways of the province and authorizes the attachment of metal number plates to that vehicle. There are two parts to a permit: the vehicle portion and the plate portion.

The statutory basis for the requirement of permits is s. 7 of the Ontario *Highway Traffic Act* (HTA). It reads as follows:

> 7(1) No person shall drive a motor vehicle on a highway unless,
> (a) there exists a currently validated permit for the vehicle;
> (b) there are displayed on the vehicle, in the prescribed manner,
> (i) number plates issued in accordance with the regulations showing the number of the permit issued for the vehicle, or
> (ii) number plates described in subsection (7.2) [re self-propelled implements of husbandry] if the vehicle is an historic vehicle and the Ministry has issued a currently validated permit for it; and
> (c) evidence of the current validation [**valtag**] of the permit is affixed, in the prescribed manner, to,
> (i) one of the number plates mentioned in subclause (b)(i) displayed on the vehicle, or
> (ii) to a mini-plate attached to the number plate exposed on the rear of the vehicle, if number plates described in subsection (7.2) are displayed on the vehicle. ...
> 7(5) ... [E]very driver of a motor vehicle on a highway shall carry,
> (a) the permit for it or a true copy thereof; and
> (b) where the motor vehicle is drawing a trailer, the permit for the trailer or a true copy thereof,
>
> and shall surrender the permits or copies for inspection upon the demand of a police officer.

valtag
short for "validation tag," which is attached to metal number plates to show that the plate is currently valid

Summary of Permit Requirements

HAVE: Any driver of a motor vehicle on a highway must have a permit for the motor vehicle that authorizes the number plates on that vehicle.

DISPLAY: Except in the case of temporary permits and motorcycles, there must be two number plates that are affixed to the front and rear of a motor vehicle operated on a highway, and the rear plate must be currently validated in the upper-right-hand corner of the plate. Motorcycle owners must affix only one number plate to the rear of their motorcycles.

SURRENDER: The driver of a motor vehicle on a highway must carry the permit or a true copy of it in the motor vehicle and surrender it to a police officer for inspection on demand.

Restricted Permits

There are three types of restricted permits for motor vehicles and trailers: 10-day permits, "in-transit" permits, and dealer and service permits and plates. All are authorized by s. 7(24) of the HTA and by reg. 628, ss. 11-13.

10-DAY PERMITS

These permits are temporary and are valid for a 10-day period (reg. 628, s. 11). They are used when it is necessary to move a vehicle on a highway, where the vehicle does not have permanent plates and where permanent plates are not being sought (for example, where the vehicle is being sold in the near future, but needs to be moved to another part of Ontario). These permits are sometimes referred to as "trip" permits, although this is misleading because the permits can be used for more than one trip within the 10-day period for which they are issued. Anyone may obtain these permits for any reason and for any use in Ontario.

A safety standards certificate is not required to obtain a 10-day permit because it is not issued for a change of ownership; however, the vehicle must be insured. The permit is a heavy paper sticker that takes the place of the ownership part of the permit and the metal number plates.

The permit must be placed in the inner top right section of the front windshield of the unplated vehicle for which it was issued or, in the case of a trailer, to the inner top right section of the windshield of the motor vehicle that is drawing the trailer. The expiry date and the vehicle identification number (VIN) are written on the face of the permit so that they are easily visible to an investigating officer from outside the vehicle. See figure 3.1.

If a motor vehicle or a trailer drawn by a plated motor vehicle is found on the highway with an expired 10-day permit, the violator is charged with driving a motor vehicle or drawing a trailer with no permit.

FIGURE 3.1 10-Day Permits

10-Day Permit for a Passenger Vehicle

Blue border and text

10 DAY TEMPORARY PERMIT
PERMIS PROVISOIRE DE DIX JOURS

A000000

ONTARIO

Expiry Date
*Date
d'expiration* ____ Y/A   M   D/J ____ V.I.N. / *N.I.V.* ____

White background with provincial symbol watermark

Black permit number

10-Day Permit for a Commercial Vehicle

Red border and text

10 DAY TEMPORARY PERMIT
PERMIS PROVISOIRE DE DIX JOURS

R000505

ONTARIO

Expiry Date
*Date
d'expiration* ____ Y/A   M   D/J ____ V.I.N. / *N.I.V.* ____

White background with provincial symbol watermark

Black permit number

IN-TRANSIT PERMITS

These permits are available only to a manufacturer or to a dealer in motor vehicles or trailers (reg. 628, s. 12). The permit shall be used only for the original trip that the vehicle takes from the manufacturer to the dealer.

The paper permit must be placed in a clearly visible place on the windshield of the motor vehicle or on the rear of the trailer for which it was issued. It is not a metal number plate. The permit takes the place of the paper ownership and the number plate normally required. The place of origin and the destination are written on the back of the permit and are visible from inside the motor vehicle. If these requirements are not met, the violator is charged with driving a motor vehicle or drawing a trailer with no permit. No safety standards certificate is required because these are used with new cars or trailers usually protected by warranty. See figure 3.2.

DEALER AND SERVICE PERMITS AND PLATES

Dealer and service permits (reg. 628, s. 13) and plates are issued to

- manufacturers of motor vehicles or trailers;
- dealers in motor vehicles or trailers;
- persons engaged in the business of repairing, customizing, or modifying motor vehicles or trailers; and
- persons engaged in the business of transporting motor vehicles or trailers.

Dealer and service permits and plates may be used only

- on a vehicle for sale that is owned by the permit holder;

FIGURE 3.2 In-Transit Permit

Orange border and text

White background

- to fix, test, or modify a vehicle by the person who owns the permit; or
- on a vehicle being transported by a person engaged in the business of transporting vehicles.

The permit and plates may not be used on a new vehicle that is being rented. Only one plate is issued, with red letters and numbers on a white background. The older plates with black letters and numbers on an orange background are being phased out. The plate must be attached in a conspicuous position on the rear of the rear-most vehicle being towed or driven on a highway. This suggests that the permit may apply to more than one vehicle, if they are linked together for transit. Dealer plates must be validated, and the valtag shall be affixed to the upper-right-hand corner of the plate. See figure 3.3.

Non-Restricted Permits

We can now look at the requirements for permits and number plates in the ordinary course of events, and we will do this for a number of common vehicle-transfer and vehicle-acquisition situations. There are two points that will help you make sense of the rules about permits. First, generally you cannot affix number plates to a motor vehicle until you have first obtained a permit from the Ontario Ministry of Transportation that authorizes the plates for that vehicle. As a general rule, you should get the permit before attaching the plates. Do not attach plates for which you have no authorizing permit. Second, number plates are issued to the person rather than the vehicle, which means that plates can be transferred by an owner from one vehicle he or she owned to another that he or she has bought. This means that if you buy a used or new car, you can transfer the plates to it from the car you previously owned, provided that you follow the rules prescribed in the legislation.

SELLER'S OBLIGATIONS, HTA, SECTION 11(1)

The seller, on selling a motor vehicle, is not obliged to notify the Ministry of Transportation, but is obliged

- to remove the number plates from the vehicle;
- to retain the plate portion of the permit;
- on delivery of the vehicle to the new owner,
  - to complete and sign the transfer application on the back of the vehicle portion of the permit, including the date of delivery, the date of the transfer, and the odometer reading; and
  - to give this portion of the permit to the new owner.

The seller or transferor may retain the plates that he or she has removed from the vehicle and affix them to another car that he or she owns under certain circumstances described in the HTA and its regulations (HTA, s. 11(3)). The newly acquired motor vehicle must be similar to the class of vehicle from which the plates have been removed—that is, you can transfer a plate from one passenger automobile to another passenger automobile, but not from a passenger automobile to a commercial vehicle. In addition, you must meet the following requirements set out in reg. 628, s. 10(1):

FIGURE 3.3 Dealer and Service Permits and Plates

Dealer Plate

Black text → ONTARIO ← Red plate number

D
E
A
L
E
R

SAM✠PLE

DEC 0 7

YOURS TO DISCOVER

White background

Service Plate

Black text and plate number

ONTARIO

435 ✠ DJD

YOURS TO DISCOVER

Yellow background

1. The number plate must be currently validated.
2. The driver must have in his or her possession the following documents:
   a. The vehicle portion of the permit issued for the vehicle that you are driving, with the transfer application completed on the back, signed by both seller and purchaser. If the motor vehicle is new and has not had a previous owner or lessee, a copy of the bill of sale or other ownership document or a leasing document may be substituted for the vehicle portion of the permit issued for the vehicle (reg. 628, s. 10(4)).

b. The plate portion of the permit corresponding to the plates you have transferred to the vehicle.

c. A valid safety standards certificate—that is, one issued within 36 days of the transfer. This is not required if the vehicle is new (reg. 628, s. 10(3)).

BUYER'S OBLIGATIONS, HTA, SECTION 11(2)

The buyer is obliged to apply for a new permit within six days of becoming the owner of a motor vehicle or trailer for which a permit was previously issued to someone else.

In general, if a person wants to take the number plates off one motor vehicle and transfer the plates to another motor vehicle, he or she should get a new registration permit authorizing the "old" plates to be used on the "new" motor vehicle before attaching the old plates to the new motor vehicle. However, the new owner may use plates issued for one vehicle on another temporarily without notifying the Ministry of Transporation for up to six days after becoming the owner. To do this, the buyer must comply with the requirements set out in reg. 628, s. 10(6), which states that the buyer must carry the documents or true copies (see reg. 628, s. 10(1)). Figure 3.4 sets out the requirements in a visual format.

The following scenarios illustrate some of the most common situations that might involve switching plates. Note that for some of the situations, switching plates is prohibited.

Transferring Plates from One Vehicle That You Own to Another Vehicle That You Own

Where you own two vehicles at the same time, you cannot use the six-day temporary use of plates provision because the plates are not from a vehicle that you no longer own, nor are they being transferred to a vehicle that you have purchased in the last six days. In this case, you must apply for a new permit authorizing the use of the plates on the vehicle before you can attach the plates to it and drive on the highway. Also, if you do this, you cannot transfer the plates back to the original vehicle by relying on the six-day temporary use rule.

Transferring Plates from One Vehicle That You Have Just Sold to Another Vehicle That You Have Owned for a Period of Time Prior to the Sale of the Other Vehicle

Where you owned two vehicles at the same time and sold one, you cannot use the six-day temporary use of plates provision if you did not obtain ownership of the vehicle to which you propose to transfer the plates within the last six days. Again, you can only resort to the six-day temporary use of plates provision if you bought the vehicle in the last six days and are using the plates within that six-day period. If stopped by the police, you will have to produce the old plate portion, the new vehicle portion, and a valid safety standards certificate. For example, Raj bought a Ford on January 3 and a Toyota on March 2. On April 3, he sold the Toyota. He removed the plates from the Toyota and would like to attach them to the Ford but cannot do this because he did not buy the Ford in the last six days before April 3.

FIGURE 3.4 Six-Day Temporary Use of Plates

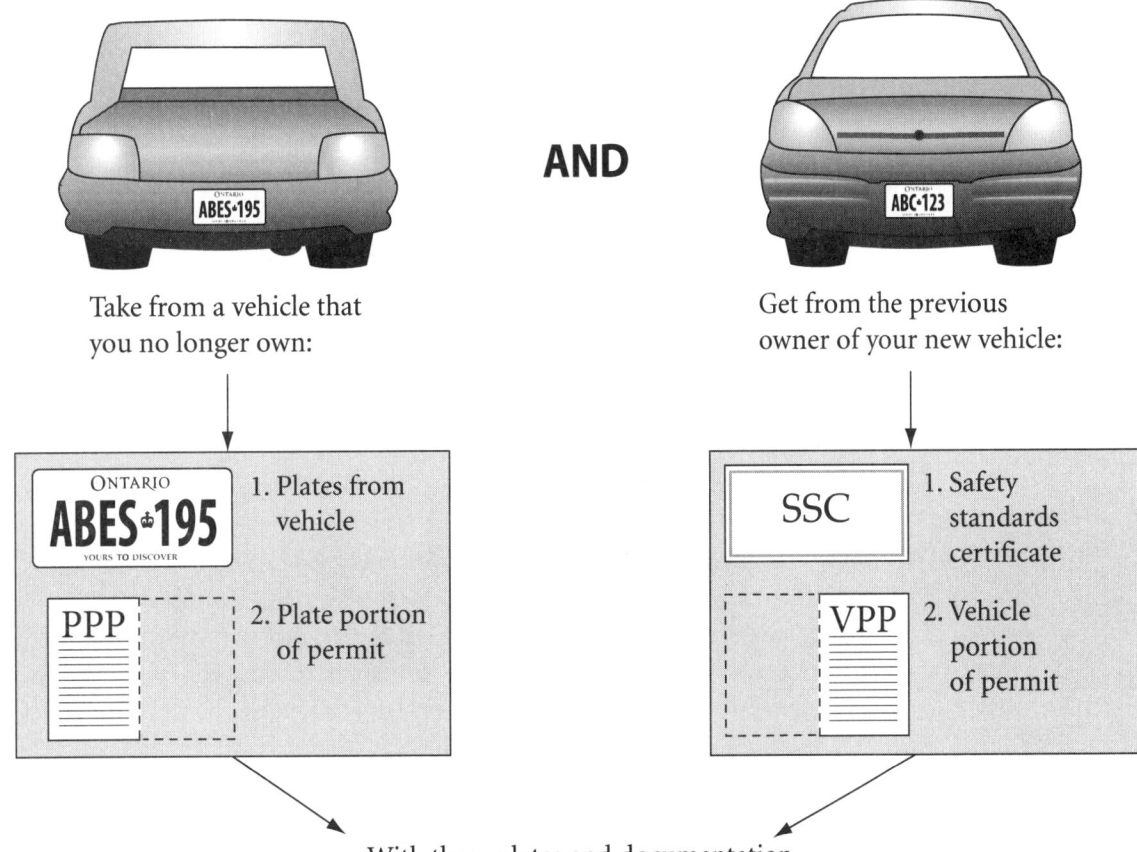

Take from a vehicle that you no longer own:
1. Plates from vehicle (ABES 195)
2. Plate portion of permit (PPP)

AND

Get from the previous owner of your new vehicle:
1. Safety standards certificate (SSC)
2. Vehicle portion of permit (VPP)

With these plates and documentation, your new vehicle may be driven for six days from the date of purchase.

Transferring Plates from a Vehicle You Previously Owned to a Used Vehicle That You Have Just Bought

Where you have sold one vehicle and then bought or leased a used vehicle, you *can* take advantage of the six-day temporary use of plates provision for six days from the date of purchase, at which time you must obtain a new permit from the Ministry of Transportation. During the six-day period, you are required to carry the plate portion of the old permit, the vehicle portion of the permit, and a valid safety standards certificate.

Transferring Plates by a Dealer Selling a "Demo" Model with Regular, Rather Than Dealer, Plates to Another Vehicle That the Dealer Bought in the Last Six Days

If you are a dealer, you cannot do this because dealers or other persons entitled to use "dealer" plates are not entitled to take advantage of the six-day temporary use of plates provision. In this case, the dealer would have to apply for a new permit authorizing the use of plates on the car before it can be operated on the highway.

Transferring Plates from a Vehicle You Previously Owned to a Brand-New Vehicle Where You Are the First Owner or Lessee

Where you have sold one vehicle and then bought or leased another brand-new vehicle from a dealer, you *can* take advantage of the six-day temporary use of plates provision for six days from the date of purchase, after which you must obtain a new permit from the Ministry of Transportation. In general, a dealer will do this as a courtesy for a new owner, although this ability to obtain a permit in the name of someone else is a cause for some concern because it makes it difficult to determine who actually owns a vehicle if a driver is stopped for a driving offence or if the vehicle is stolen and then recovered. During the six-day period, you are required to carry the plate portion of the old permit, a bill of sale, or a copy of the lease in lieu of the vehicle portion of the permit, since this car, because it is new, has never had a permit. No safety standards certificate is required because the car is new.

Plate and Permit Offences

Section 12(1) of the HTA sets out several offences involving the unlawful use of plates and permits. A person may be arrested for offences under s. 12 without a warrant. If a person is convicted of a s. 12 offence, he or she is liable to a fine of between $100 and $1,000, to imprisonment for not more than 30 days, or to both a fine and imprisonment. In addition, the convicted offender may have his or her licence suspended for up to six months.

DEFACING OR ALTERING PLATES OR PERMITS, HTA, SECTION 12(1)(a)

It is an offence to alter or deface any number plate, permit, or valtag.

USE OF DEFACED PLATES OR PERMITS, HTA, SECTION 12(1)(b)

In addition to altering or defacing, the use of an altered or defaced number plate, permit, or valtag is prohibited.

UNAUTHORIZED REMOVAL OF NUMBER PLATE, HTA, SECTION 12(1)(c)

It is an offence to remove a number plate from a vehicle or a trailer without the authorization of the permit holder. This offence is commonly related to the theft of a number plate.

USE OF UNAUTHORIZED NUMBER PLATE, HTA, SECTION 12(1)(d)

It is an offence to use or permit the use of a number plate on a vehicle other than the number plate authorized for use on that vehicle. Section 12(1)(d) can be invoked to charge someone who abuses the six-day temporary use rule.

UNAUTHORIZED USE OF VALTAG, HTA, SECTION 12(1)(e)

It is an offence to use or permit the use of a valtag on a number plate displayed on a motor vehicle that is not the valtag furnished by the Ministry of Transportation for that vehicle.

USE OF VALTAG OR PLATE CONTRARY TO THE HTA AND REGULATIONS, HTA, SECTION 12(1)(f)

Anyone who uses or permits the use of a number plate or valtag other than in accordance with the HTA and the regulations is guilty of an offence. This provision can be invoked for any future amendments to the legislation or for amended or new regulations.

SEIZURE OF EVIDENCE OF A SECTION 12 OFFENCE, HTA, SECTION 14(1)

This section authorizes the seizure of evidence of an offence under s. 12(1). It says that a police officer may seize the number plate, valtag, or permit, and retain it until the facts in issue have been determined if the officer has reason to believe that a number plate, valtag, or permit

- is not authorized for that vehicle,
- was obtained by false pretenses, or
- is defaced or altered.

This means that the items seized may be held until the trial has ended and the time for launching an appeal has elapsed. If an appeal is launched, the items may be held until the appeal is dismissed.

VEHICLE CLASSES

Motor vehicle classes for vehicles other than passenger automobiles are determined by passenger capacity, purpose, or weight, in the case of buses, and by weight, in all other types of commercial vehicles. These classifications are then used to determine the type of vehicle permit required and the class of licence that an operator must possess to operate a motor vehicle for each class.

Buses—Classed by Passengers

A motor vehicle is a bus if it has at least 10 permanent passenger seats. Buses with more than 24 passenger seats are a different class of motor vehicle than buses with 24 or fewer passenger seats. The two types of buses require different skills to operate and, therefore, require different driver's licences. The main reason for differentiating between "big" and "little" buses when the buses in question are school-purposes buses is simply to ensure that school-purposes bus drivers have been criminally screened.

Buses—Classed by Weight When They Do Not Have Passengers

A vehicle is not considered a bus for the purpose of driver's licence requirements unless the bus has at least one passenger. If there are no passengers on board, the weight of the bus is used to determine the class of driver's licence required by the driver. If, for example, a school bus carrying no passengers on a highway weighs only 9000 kg, the driver needs only a class G driver's licence to drive the bus lawfully on the highway. If a large bus carrying no passengers on a highway weighs 17 000 kg, the driver needs a class D driver's licence to drive the bus on the highway lawfully.

Weights and Vehicle Classes

towed weight
the weight of the trailer and its load

gross weight
the total weight of the motor vehicle, its trailer, and the load it is carrying; can be determined only by weigh scales

total weight
determined from either the gross weight of the motor vehicle, trailer, and load or the registered gross weight of the motor vehicle, whichever is more

registered gross weight
the weight of the vehicle and the load set out in the motor vehicle permit; the owner has prepaid the government to have the legal right to haul loads of that size in that vehicle on the highway

The **towed weight** is the weight of the trailer and its load. The **gross weight** is the weight of the motor vehicle, its trailer, and its load, and can be determined only by weigh scales of the type that you see on 400-class highways (highway 401, 407, etc.).

The **total weight** is determined from *either* the gross weight of the motor vehicle, trailer, and load *or* the **registered gross weight** of the motor vehicle, whichever is more. The registered gross weight is printed on the permit for commercial motor vehicles. This is the weight for which the owner has prepaid the government for hauling loads on the highway—a form of tax for highway carriers to defray the cost of repairing the damage caused to the roadway by heavy commercial vehicles. Generally, the registered gross weight is used to determine the class of the motor vehicle, even if it is empty and weighs far less than the registered gross weight. If, however, the truck is loaded, and the actual gross weight according to the weigh scales exceeds the registered gross weight, the larger weight is used to determine the motor vehicle class, and the driver or owner can be fined for exceeding the weight for which he or she has prepaid. The registered gross weight allows enforcement officers to determine the class of motor vehicle simply by checking the permit.

The registered gross weight always applies to a motor vehicle, not a trailer. The registered gross weight for a truck tractor (the tractor of a tractor-trailer combination) will always exceed 11 000 kg because of the size it needs to be to pull heavy loads. This means that even when the truck tractor is being operated independently without a trailer, the registered gross weight will exceed 11 000 kg, and the driver in this case would need a class D driver's licence. The moment that the driver hooks the trailer onto his vehicle, the total weight of the trailer and its load must be considered. The permit for the trailer has the empty vehicle weight printed on it. If the empty weight of the trailer is not more than 4600 kg, the driver still only needs a class D driver's licence. When the trailer is loaded so that the total weight of the trailer and its load exceeds 4600 kg, the driver needs a class A driver's licence. See figure 3.5.

FIGURE 3.5 Vehicle Class Categorized by Passenger Capacity and by Weight

Basis for classification	Class	Example
Passenger capacity		
If the vehicle is not actually carrying passengers, the basis for classification is weight.		
Up to 24 passengers	E	Board of education
	F	Ambulance
More than 24 passengers	B	Board of education
	C	Coaches and city buses
Weight		
Up to 4600 kg towed weight:		
—Up to 11 000 kg total weight	G	General vehicles
—More than 11 000 kg total weight	D	Dump trucks
More than 4600 kg towed weight	A	Moving vans

VEHICLE CLASS DESCRIPTION, O. REG. 340/94, SECTION 2(1), TABLE

Class A

A class A vehicle is any combination of a motor vehicle and towed vehicles, where the towed vehicles exceed a total gross weight of 4600 kg. This does not include a bus carrying passengers.

Class B

A class B vehicle is a school-purposes bus with a designed seating capacity of more than 24 passengers.

Class C

A class C vehicle is a bus with a designed seating capacity of more than 24, but not a school-purposes bus carrying passengers.

Class D

A class D vehicle is either (1) a motor vehicle that exceeds 11 000 kg total gross weight or registered gross weight or (2) any combination of a motor vehicle exceeding 11 000 kg total gross weight or registered gross weight and towed vehicles not exceeding a total gross weight of 4600 kg. This does not include a bus carrying passengers, even though it might otherwise meet the description of a class D vehicle.

Class E

A class E vehicle is a school-purposes bus with a designed seating capacity of 24 passengers or less.

Class F

A class F vehicle is any ambulance or any bus with a seating capacity of not more than 24 passengers that is not a school-purposes bus carrying passengers.

Class G

Class G vehicles include the following:

- Any motor vehicle, including a motor-assisted bicycle (but not a motorcycle), not exceeding 11 000 kg gross weight or registered gross weight.

- Any combination of a motor vehicle not exceeding a total gross weight or registered weight of 11 000 kg and a towed vehicle not exceeding a total gross weight of 4600 kg.

However, class G motor vehicles do not include a motorcycle, an ambulance when it is providing ambulance service under the Ontario *Ambulance Act*, or a bus when it is carrying passengers, even though these vehicles might otherwise fall within the weight limits that would make them class G vehicles.

A class D or G motor vehicle that is designed and used as a tow truck will not be deemed to become a class A motor vehicle if it is towing, on a highway, a disabled or unsafe motor vehicle or trailer that weighs more than 4600 kg (O. reg. 340/94, s. 2(2)).

A motor vehicle with a designed seating capacity of not more than 11 passengers would normally be a class F vehicle (small bus). However, if it is used for personal transportation without compensation, it is treated as a class G vehicle (O. reg. 340/94, s. 2(5)).

See figure 3.6 for examples of motor vehicles in different classes.

FIGURE 3.6 What Class of Driver's Licence Is Required by the Driver of These Vehicles?

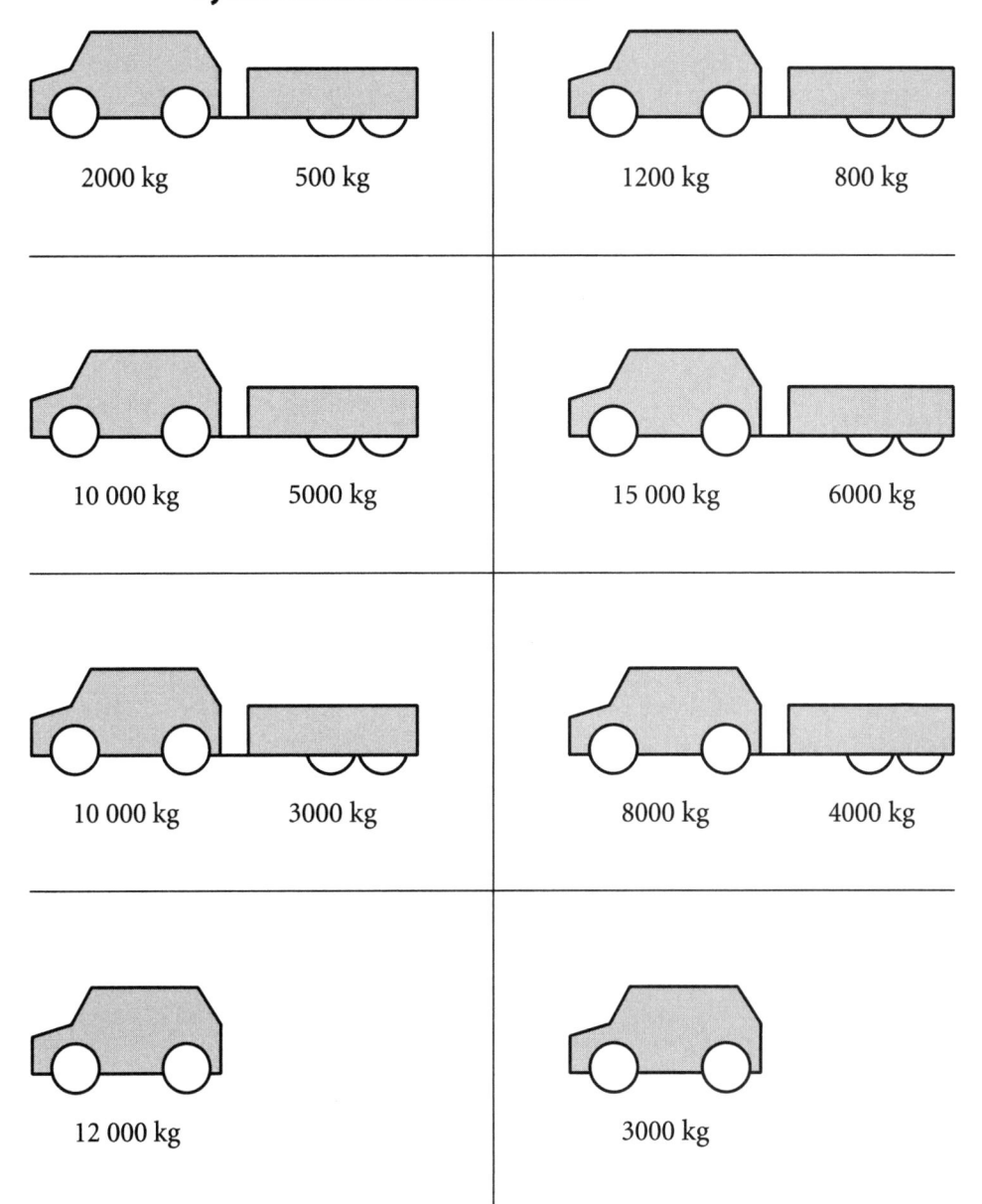

2000 kg 500 kg	1200 kg 800 kg
10 000 kg 5000 kg	15 000 kg 6000 kg
10 000 kg 3000 kg	8000 kg 4000 kg
12 000 kg	3000 kg

Remember:

1. If the towed weight is more than 4600 kg, a class A licence is required.
2. If the towed weight is not more than 4600 kg, the total weight is considered.
3. If the total weight is more than 11 000 kg, a class D licence is required.
4. If the total weight is not more than 11 000 kg, a class G licence is required.

DRIVER'S LICENCES

In this section, we discuss the requirements for various classes of driver's licences, and what motor vehicles can be driven by a person with a particular class of licence.

Graduated/Restricted Licences—G1, G2, G, and M1, M2, M

G1 DRIVER'S LICENCE

Ontario now has a graduated licensing system for obtaining a G licence. A person must first obtain a G1 licence, then a G2 licence, before graduating to the final class G licence. In order to obtain a G1 licence, the applicant must pass a written test. Once he or she obtains the G1, the person may drive a class G motor vehicle (passenger car, van, or light truck) when accompanied by a driver who has at least four years of driving experience and who is licensed to drive a class G vehicle. This accompanying driver must ride in the front passenger's seat beside the G1 driver. The back seat may hold as many passengers as there are seat belts for them.

A G1 driver must remain at that level for 12 months before he or she can graduate to the G2 level. However, if the G1 driver takes a recognized driver-education course, this period can be reduced by 4 months.

There are restrictions that apply to G1 drivers that do not apply to G drivers in general (O. reg. 340/94, s. 5). Drivers generally must have a blood alcohol level of less than 0.08 percent. However, a G1 driver must have a blood alcohol level of zero, and the accompanying driver must have a blood alcohol level that is less than 0.05 percent. G1 drivers also are prohibited from driving between midnight and 5 a.m. Also, they may not drive on any 400-series highway that has a posted speed of more than 80 km/h. In addition, a G1 driver may not drive on any urban expressways, including the Queen Elizabeth Way, the Don Valley Parkway, the Gardiner Expressway, the E.C. Row Expressway, and the Conestoga Expressway, unless accompanied by a licensed driving instructor.

In order to progress to the G2 class, the G1 driver must pass a road test. A driver who passes the G2 test enters that level and must remain there for a minimum of 12 months. Like G1 drivers, G2 drivers must also have a blood alcohol level of zero. The G2 driver, however, may drive alone and without an accompanying qualified class G driver. The G2 driver may have as many passengers as there are operable seat belts provided in the vehicle. After 12 months, the G2 driver may take a comprehensive road test and obtain the G licence. The G2 driver has five years from the time he or she obtained the G1 licence to take the comprehensive road test for the G licence. If the person does not apply to take the test within five years of obtaining the G1 licence, he or she must start over again and apply for a G1 licence.

The Graduated Licensing System for Obtaining a G Licence

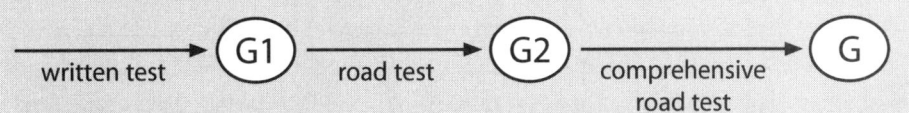

written test → G1 → road test → G2 → comprehensive road test → G

The only differences between a class G2 and a class G licence are that for the G2 licence,

- the driver's blood alcohol level must be zero, and
- the number of passengers must be limited to the number of operable seat belts.

Once the basic G class licence has been obtained, a class G driver can drive a class G motor vehicle, which includes

- any motor vehicle, including a motor-assisted bicycle (but not a motorcycle), that weighs less than 11 000 kg gross weight or registered gross weight; and
- any combination of a motor vehicle not exceeding a total gross weight or registered weight of 11 000 kg and a towed vehicle where the towed vehicles do not exceed a total gross weight of 4600 kg.

However, class G motor vehicles do not include motorcycles, ambulances when they are providing ambulance services under the *Ambulance Act*, or buses when they are carrying passengers, even though these vehicles might otherwise come within the weight limits that would make them class G vehicles (O. reg. 340/94, s. 2(1), table).

G2 drivers may drive any class G vehicle, except one equipped with air brakes, which requires training and a test.

G1 drivers may drive any class G vehicle, except heavy farm vehicles used by farmers for personal-use transportation and for shipping and moving their crops to market; these vehicles usually have "farm" number plates. Such heavy vehicles would usually be class D, but, if used for farm purposes, are deemed to be class G. However, these vehicles do not include large combines and harvesters that are driven on a highway, because these are considered self-propelled implements of husbandry and are not defined as motor vehicles. This means that, despite such a vehicle's size, a driver need not have a driver's licence of any kind to operate it on the highway (O. reg. 340/94, s. 2(3)).

Class F vehicles—such as paddy wagons operated by police officers and ambulances—are deemed to be class G vehicles when they are not carrying passengers and being used as paddy wagons or ambulances. But G1 drivers may *not* drive them when they are being used as paddy wagons or ambulances (O. reg. 340/94, ss. 2(3) and (4)).

Although a class G driver is limited in the vehicles he or she may drive, a class G driver can learn to drive any other class of vehicle as long as he or she is accompanied by a driver who is licensed to drive that particular class of vehicle.

M1 DRIVER'S LICENCE

Anyone who wishes to drive a motorcycle must obtain a class M licence. Like the class G licence, the class M licence is obtained through a graduated licensing system; the driver must obtain the M1 and then the M2 before obtaining the M licence. To obtain the M1 licence, the applicant must pass a written test that will permit the applicant to learn to drive a motorcycle. An M1 licence lasts for a minimum of 60 days and is valid for only 90 days. This means that the licence holder cannot take the road test for the M2 for at least 60 days from the date that the M1 was issued, even if the licence holder has taken a motorcycle safety course. However, the licence holder must take the test within 90 days; if he or she does not, the licence holder must apply for an M1 licence again.

There are specific operating conditions for M1 drivers (O. reg. 340/94, s. 7). The driver

- cannot carry any passengers on the motorcycle;
- must have a blood alcohol level of zero;
- must drive the motorcycle only during the daytime (one half hour before sunrise to one half hour after sunset);
- cannot drive on highways with speed limits in excess of 80 km/h, except highways 11, 17, 61, 71, 101, 102, 144, and 655; and
- must pass a road test to progress to the M2 licence.

M2 DRIVER'S LICENCE

Once the driver has passed the road test, he or she progresses to the M2 level, where he or she must remain for a minimum of 22 months. This period may be reduced to 18 months if the M2 licence holder completes an approved motorcycle safety course, which can be taken at any time while the driver is classed as an M1 or M2 licence holder.

The nighttime driving restriction is lifted for M2 drivers, but the M2 driver must have a blood alcohol level of zero. Once the driver has completed the minimum M2 licence period, he or she may take a comprehensive road test to qualify for a class M licence.

Holders of an M2 driver's licence can also drive a class G motor vehicle, but only under the conditions that apply to a class G1 driver's licence.

Once an M2 driver has passed the comprehensive road test and has become an M licence holder, he or she may lawfully drive any motorcycle and may also drive a class G vehicle, but only under the conditions that apply to a class G1 driver.

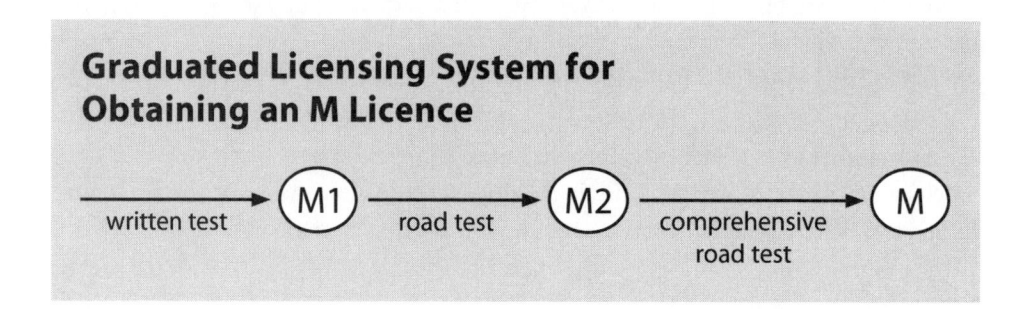

Graduated Licensing System for Obtaining an M Licence

written test → M1 → road test → M2 → comprehensive road test → M

Duration of Graduated Driver's Licences

G1 Lasts a minimum of 12 months (8 months, if lessons taken) and a maximum of 5 years.

G2 Lasts a minimum of 12 months and is valid for the remainder of the five-year period for which the G1 licence was valid.

M1 Lasts a minimum of 60 days and a maximum of 90 days.

M2 Lasts a minimum of 22 months (18 months, if safety course taken) and a maximum of 5 years.

Penalties for Violating Conditions of a Graduated M or G Licence

If a person is convicted of violating the conditions of a graduated licensing system, he or she will be notified that his or her driver's licence has been suspended. The suspension will last for 30 days from the date that the licence is surrendered or 2 years from the date that the licence is suspended if it is not surrendered.

The graduated system described here replaced the "learner" system that existed before 1994. It now takes much longer to obtain an unrestricted licence, and there are more restrictions on level 1 and 2 drivers than there were on learners under the previous system. Although there have been some problems with the graduated system—long waits for road tests, for example—there is evidence that jurisdictions using graduated licensing systems boast a reduction in collisions among young drivers. Furthermore, the reduction in collisions has been across the spectrum of drivers, regardless of age.

Non-Graduated Driver's Licences

Once a driver has obtained a G licence, he or she may go on to obtain other licences to drive other classes of vehicles. There is no graduated system for these licences; the only requirement is that a learner have an accompanying driver with a class of licence for driving that class of vehicle. For example, a person seeking a class A licence must have a person with a valid class A licence with him or her while driving a class A vehicle.

CLASS A LICENCE

A driver with this licence may drive either

- a class A vehicle, which is any combination of a motor vehicle and towed vehicles where the towed vehicles exceed a total gross weight of 4600 kg, but does not include a bus carrying passengers (which requires a B, C, E, or F driver's licence, depending on the size of or purpose of the bus); or
- a class D and G vehicle (O. reg. 340/94, s. 2(1), table).

CLASS B LICENCE

A driver with this licence may drive

- any school-purposes bus with a designed seating capacity of more than 24 passengers; and
- any class C, D, E, F, or G vehicle.

CLASS C LICENCE

A driver with this licence may drive

- any bus with a designed seating capacity of more than 24, except a school-purposes bus carrying passengers; and
- any class D, F, or G vehicle.

CLASS D LICENCE

A driver with this licence may drive

- a motor vehicle that exceeds 11 000 kg total gross weight or registered gross weight;
- any combination of a motor vehicle exceeding 11 000 kg total gross weight or registered gross weight and towed vehicles not exceeding a total gross weight of 4600 kg; and
- any class G vehicle.

However, a D licence holder may not drive a bus carrying passengers that otherwise might fit the class D definition. A bus that weighs over 11 000 kg cannot be classified as a class D vehicle once a passenger climbs aboard. Once a passenger is on board, the driver requires the appropriate bus licence.

CLASS E LICENCE

A driver with this licence may drive

- any school-purposes bus with a designed seating capacity of 24 passengers or less, and
- any class F or G vehicle.

CLASS F LICENCE

A driver with this licence may drive

- any ambulance;
- any bus with a seating capacity of not more than 24 passengers; and
- any class G vehicle.

However, an F licence holder may not drive a school-purposes bus carrying passengers.

AIR BRAKES

The Ministry of Transportation requires licence holders to have a Z endorsement on their licence in order to drive a vehicle equipped with air brakes. The Z endorsement on any class of driver's licence authorizes the holder of the licence to drive the class of vehicle he or she is otherwise permitted to drive if it is equipped with air brakes. The endorsement is not a separate class of licence; rather, it is in addition to the existing class of driver's licence. For example, the holder of a D licence who obtains an air-brake endorsement will receive a DZ licence, showing that he or she can drive a class D vehicle equipped with air brakes. To obtain a Z endorsement, the applicant must attend classroom instruction and pass an examination.

CALCULATING WHICH CLASSES OF MOTOR VEHICLE A DRIVER IS LICENSED TO DRIVE

There is an easy way to calculate all the classes of motor vehicles that a driver is legally licensed to drive on a highway in Ontario: the "Big Eddie" acronym, set out in the box at right.

The "Big Eddie" acronym is used to help remember the order of the right-hand column.

To calculate all the classes of motor vehicles that a driver is legally licensed to drive on a highway in Ontario, use the two columns with the system that follows:

1. Note the class letter of the driver's licence in the driver's possession.
2. Locate the letter in both of the columns.
3. Lay your pen so that it joins the same letter in both columns.
4. The driver can legally drive the class of motor vehicle for which he or she is licensed and any class of vehicle for which there is a letter in both columns below the pen.

The "Big Eddie" Acronym

A	B	(Big)
B	E	(Eddie)
C	C	(Can)
D	F	(Fool)
E	A	(All)
F	D	(Dumb)
G	G	(Guys/Girls)

Example of How to Use the "Big Eddie" Technique

A	B	(Big)
B	E	(Eddie)
C	C	(Can)
D	F	(Fool)
E	A	(All)
F	D	(Dumb)
G	G	(Guys/Girls)

The driver can legally operate class D vehicles and class G vehicles (G is the only letter that appears in both columns below the pen). Here's another example. If the driver has an E licence, he or she can legally operate class E, F, and G vehicles: F and G appear in both columns below the pen.

An exemption to these restrictions exists for police officers in the following situation. Any class of "Big Eddie" licence (B, E, C, F, A, D, or G) is authority for a police officer to drive any class of motor vehicle, including those equipped with air brakes, except for a motorcycle, on a highway in an emergency in the course of his or her duty. For example, a police officer is allowed to drive a large bus in an emergency with a class G licence. Similarly, a mechanic is also permitted this liberty while road testing a vehicle in the course of servicing it. Again, motorcycles are excluded.

Driver's Licence Offences, HTA, Section 32

Once a licence is issued, in addition to driving within the licence restrictions, the licence holder is required to have the licence in his or her possession when driving, and to surrender it for inspection by a police officer or other designated person.

Section 32(1) says that no person shall drive a motor vehicle on a highway unless the motor vehicle is within a class of motor vehicles for which the person holds a valid driver's licence. If a licence holder is convicted of driving a class of vehicle that he or she is not entitled to drive, he or she is subject to a fine of not less than $200 and not more than $1,000. If a streetcar is driven on a right of way that is on a highway, even though it is not a motor vehicle within the HTA definition, the operator must, nevertheless, have a driver's licence (HTA, s. 32(2)).

Section 33(1) requires every driver of a motor vehicle or streetcar to carry a driver's licence at all times while in charge of a motor vehicle, and to surrender it for reasonable inspection on the demand of a police officer or an officer appointed for carrying out the provisions of the HTA. If a person is unable or refuses to surrender his or her driver's licence in accordance with s. 33(1) or (2), the person shall give reasonable identification of himself or herself, and, for the purposes of s. 33(3), his or her correct name and address shall be deemed to be reasonable identification. Failure to comply with s. 33(3) can lead to an arrest.

If a citizen is driving a motor vehicle on a highway, the citizen is lawfully required to identify himself or herself if a police officer demands this information. This is one of the few instances when a citizen is lawfully required to identify himself or herself to a police officer. If an officer asks the person to identify himself or herself and the person tells the officer orally who he or she is, the officer cannot arbitrarily decide that the driver is not who he or she claims to be. The officer must have reasonable proof that the person is lying in order to arrest the person. This proof may require some investigation. Remember that the citizen has the right to remain silent and is not obliged to answer these investigative questions, and refusal to answer the questions is not proof that the person is lying. The refusal may lead to suspicion, but the officer needs more than suspicion for grounds to make an arrest.

If the driver is arrested for failing to identify himself or herself, he or she is released once the correct identification has been obtained. With the name and

> **Arrest Authority: Not Having or Surrendering a Licence or Not Identifying Yourself**
>
> - A person cannot be arrested for failing to have or failing to surrender a driver's licence, but a person can be charged.
> - A person can be arrested for failing to identify himself or herself after failing or refusing to surrender his or her driver's licence.
>
> The authority to arrest is for failing to identify, and is intended to secure the person until he or she can be identified.

address, the driver can be given a ticket for failing to surrender his or her driver's licence and for failing to identify himself or herself.

Authority for Use of Non-Ontario Plates and Licence

The issuance of Ontario plates and licences is tied to provincial residents. Only residents of the province may apply for vehicle permits and licences. Non-residents may, in general, drive vehicles on Ontario highways for limited periods of time. For these purposes, s. 15 (plates) and s. 34 (permits) of the HTA distinguish between residents of another province and residents of another country. The non-resident exemptions and conditions are set out in figure 3.7.

NON-RESIDENT EXEMPTIONS AND REVERSE-ONUS REQUIREMENTS

With the application of the *Canadian Charter of Rights and Freedoms* to criminal or quasi-criminal proceedings, the accused is no longer required to prove anything under a reverse-onus requirement in a statute, because reverse-onus rules have been held to be contrary to the Charter. An example of a reverse-onus clause in criminal law follows: in circumstances where the Crown proved that a person was inside premises unlawfully, the accused is presumed to have been there for the purpose of committing an indictable offence. It is then up to the accused to prove that he or she was not there for the purpose of committing an indictable offence. Under the Charter, however, the Crown must now prove every element of the offence, without the accused having to prove that he or she had not done something. This is described as the accused's right.

However, s. 47(3) of the *Provincial Offences Act* places the burden of proof on the accused to show that an exemption under ss. 15 and 34 of the HTA operates in his or her favour. Although this is clearly a reverse-onus clause, the courts in Ontario have accepted that driving is a privilege, rather than a right, so the reverse-onus provision is deemed lawful. This means that a driver in Ontario is presumed to require an Ontario driver's licence and Ontario number plates and that the onus is on the person to prove entitlement to the exemptions in ss. 15 and 34.

COMPULSORY AUTOMOBILE INSURANCE ACT

In addition to having the appropriate vehicle permits and licences, every owner of a motor vehicle registered in Ontario must maintain an insurance policy on the motor vehicle that conforms to the minimum insurance coverage requirements under the Ontario *Compulsory Automobile Insurance Act* (CAIA).

Failure to Have Insurance

Under s. 2(1) of the CAIA, no owner or lessee of a motor vehicle shall operate, or allow to be operated, a motor vehicle that is not insured. This section places the obligation to insure squarely on the owner or the lessee of the vehicle (unless the lessor

58 TRAFFIC MANAGEMENT

FIGURE 3.7 Non-Resident Plate and Licence Exemptions

Authority to drive in Ontario

	With out-of-province plates (section 15)		With out-of-province driver's licence (section 34)	
	Non-Ontario resident	New Ontario resident	Non-Ontario resident	New Ontario resident
From other province	One who resides in another province and who does not reside in or carry on a business in Ontario for more than six consecutive months in a calendar year.	One who no longer resides in another province and is a new resident of Ontario must obtain Ontario plates within 30 days. (Needs SSC.)*	One who resides in another province and who is at least 16 years old and has a valid driver's licence from that province can use his or her driver's licence so long as it is valid.	One who no longer resides in another province and is a new resident of Ontario must obtain an Ontario driver's licence within 60 days.
From other country	One who resides in another country and who does not reside in or carry on a business in Ontario for more than three months in a calendar year.	One who no longer resides in another country and is a new resident of Ontario must obtain Ontario plates within 30 days. (Needs SSC.)	One who resides in another country and who is at least 16 years old and has a valid driver's licence from that country can use his or her driver's licence in Ontario for no more than three months in a calendar year.	One who no longer resides in another country and is a new resident of Ontario must obtain an Ontario driver's licence within 60 days.

* Safety standards certificate

maintains the necessary insurance). Section 2(3) sets out stiff penalties for contravention of s. 2(1), and defines as a further offence the production of a false insurance card for inspection by the police that purports to show that the vehicle is insured when it is not. Fines of between $5,000 and $25,000 for a first offence, and between $10,000 and $50,000 for a subsequent offence, are steep enough that it is cheaper to maintain an insurance policy than to risk operating an uninsured vehicle. The offender, as defined in this section, is the owner or lessee of the vehicle. Charges would be laid under the penalty section, s. 2(3).

Failure to Surrender Insurance Card

Under s. 3(1), an operator of a motor vehicle shall have an insurance card for that motor vehicle in the vehicle, or an insurance card showing that he or she is insured on another contract of motor vehicle insurance other than the one for the car that is being driven. If the operator of the vehicle is not the owner, and he or she produces his or her own insurance card, rather than the one for the car he or she is driving, this does not relieve the owner of the vehicle that has been stopped of the responsibility for insuring the motor vehicle. The operator is obliged to surrender either his or her own card, or the owner's insurance card, for inspection by the police on request. A person who fails to produce either insurance card is guilty of an offence and may be fined up to $400 under s. 3(3). The offender, according to this section, is the operator of the vehicle. Charges would be laid under the penalty section, s. 3(3).

If the driver produces an insurance card for a motor vehicle other than the one he or she is driving, the police should check with the owner to see whether the vehicle is, in fact, insured. The police may ask the owner, even if the owner is at home, to surrender the insurance card. If the owner cannot or will not do this, the owner may be charged with permitting the operation of the vehicle without insurance, contrary to s. 2(1)(b) of the CAIA. Case law is clear that, even if the owner is in his or her own home, the owner must produce the card or be charged with the offence.

Failure to Disclose Particulars of Insurance

Under s. 4(1), an operator of a motor vehicle on a highway who is directly or indirectly involved in a collision shall, on request of any other person involved, disclose to that person the particulars of the contract of motor vehicle insurance that insures the motor vehicle. The particulars are identified in s. 4(2) as follows:

(a) the name and address of the insured,
(b) the make, model and serial number of the insured vehicle [identified by the vehicle identification number],
(c) the effective date and expiry date of the contract,
(d) the name of the insurer,
(e) the name of the insurer's agent, if any [some insurance is sold directly without an agent], and
(f) the policy number of the contract.

Failure to disclose particulars when requested can lead to a charge under s. 4(3) with a fine of up to $400 on conviction.

CHAPTER SUMMARY

This chapter deals with the law and procedures for issuing motor vehicle permits, plates, and driver's licences, and outlines related offences under the HTA. The classification of motor vehicles is explained in the context of both issuing vehicle permits and determining the restrictions on the type of vehicle that a licence holder can drive on the highway. Permits are either limited and restricted—in circumstances where a vehicle is being transferred to a new owner—or non-restricted and permanent. The class of permit required depends on the type of vehicle, and permit classes are categorized in terms of passenger capacity, purpose, or weight, in the case of buses, and weight, in the case of other commercial vehicles. The purpose of a commercial vehicle, however, sometimes alters the class into which a vehicle falls. After establishing the vehicle classes, we identify the classes of driver's licence available, noting which class of driver's licence is required for each class of vehicle. Special attention was paid to the requirements of the graduated licensing system for class G licences and vehicles. The chapter then sets out the "Big Eddie" technique for determining which vehicles a particular licence holder is permitted to drive, and discusses offences related to driver's licences. Lastly, the chapter sets out the requirements for vehicle insurance under the CAIA, describing the various offences involved in failing to produce insurance documents, and in failing to have a vehicle properly insured.

KEY TERMS

valtag

towed weight

gross weight

total weight

registered gross weight

REVIEW QUESTIONS

True or False?

Place a "T" in the space provided if the statement is true, and an "F" if the statement is false.

_____ 1. A 10-day permit is valid throughout the province of Ontario.

_____ 2. A mechanic, who has been issued a dealer and service plate, is permitted to use the plate on any motor vehicle that the mechanic is repairing.

_____ 3. Everyone who drives a motor vehicle on a highway in Ontario must have a permit for the motor vehicle and surrender the permit or a true copy at a police officer's request.

____ 4. The buyer of a motor vehicle must apply to the Ontario Ministry of Transportation for a new permit within six days of becoming the owner, even if the new owner does not plan to operate the motor vehicle on the highway.

____ 5. It is lawful to take the plates off a motor vehicle that you own and affix them to another motor vehicle of the same class that you have just purchased within six days and drive that motor vehicle on the highway as long as you carry the prescribed documents and surrender them at a police officer's request.

____ 6. An in-transit permit is only issued to motor vehicle dealers.

____ 7. If any of the requirements for the six-day temporary use of plates are violated, the plates are not lawfully authorized for use on the vehicle and the plates can be seized and the driver arrested.

____ 8. It is an arrestable offence to alter both a permit and a number plate.

____ 9. A dealer in motor vehicles, who wishes to transport a brand-new motor vehicle to any other location in Ontario, can lawfully use a dealer and service plate or an in-transit permit.

____ 10. A driver with a class B driver's licence can lawfully drive any bus on a highway.

____ 11. The holder of a class M2 driver's licence cannot drive at night or on any road with a speed limit above 80 km/h.

____ 12. A driver with a class F driver's licence can lawfully drive class D and G vehicles on a highway.

____ 13. A school bus with a weight of 10 000 kg when empty can be lawfully driven on a highway by a driver with a class G licence if the 20-seat bus has no passengers.

____ 14. A driver with a class B driver's licence could lawfully drive a tractor-trailer combination on a highway because a class B driver's licence is the "top" licence.

____ 15. Ambulances are considered to be class F vehicles.

____ 16. Class B and E vehicles are school-purposes buses and applicants for these classes of driver's licence are criminally screened.

____ 17. A person with any class of driver's licence that is determined by weight cannot lawfully drive any bus that is transporting passengers on a highway.

____ 18. To pull a trailer lawfully on a highway with a weight of 2000 kg, a driver of a 5000 kg motor vehicle would lawfully require at least a class D driver's licence.

____ 19. The holder of a class G1 driver's licence must be accompanied by a driver with at least four years of driving experience and at least a G driver's licence.

_____ 20. An M1 driver's licence is only valid for 90 days.

_____ 21. The holder of an M2 driver's licence can drive any motor vehicle on any highway.

_____ 22. The holder of a class M driver's licence can lawfully drive a class G vehicle under the conditions that apply to a class G1 driver's licence.

Short Answer

Briefly answer the following questions.

1. What are you required to do with the plates and permit of a vehicle that you are selling?

2. Where would you expect to find the valtag on a passenger vehicle? On a commercial vehicle?

3. If you are taking advantage of the six-day temporary use of plates provision, what documents must you have in your possession while driving the vehicle on the highway in the following circumstances?

    a. The car is a new car and you are the first owner.

b. The car is a used car.

4. What are the conditions precedent that must be met to acquire the following?

   a. A 10-day permit.

   b. An "in-transit" permit.

   c. A dealer and service plate.

5. Explain what class of driver's licence would be required in the following situations:

   a. A Greyhound bus (seating capacity is 48) that has been hired by a school board for a high school ski trip on a weekend.

   b. A motor vehicle pulling a trailer with a weight of 5000 kg, where the total weight of the motor vehicle and trailer is 15 000 kg.

6. Explain the circumstances in which vehicles in one class are treated as class G vehicles for the following situations. Explain the reasons for this reclassification.

   a. The classification of a class D farm truck as a class G vehicle.

b. The classification of a class D and G tow truck as a class G vehicle when towing a disabled vehicle.

c. The classification of a class F bus as a class G vehicle.

Discussion Questions

1. Orestes Smith has plates that were first issued in 1988. Each time he purchased a new car, he elected to transfer the plates from the old car he sold to the new car. It is now 2007. The plates were rusting, and most of the paint had worn off. Too cheap to buy new plates, Orestes bought a can of white paint, and a can of dark blue paint. He repainted both plates, with a white background and blue numbers and letters. The blue letters are very slightly different in tone from the original blue letters. The plates are more legible than they were prior to being repainted, although it is obvious on close inspection that they are old plates that have been repainted. A police officer sees the painted plates, and charges Orestes under s. 12(1)(a) of the HTA. Discuss the arguments in favour of, and against, conviction.

2. What were the reasons for the introduction of a graduated licensing system for G and M class drivers? Contrast the graduated system with the old system. How effective is the graduated system in dealing with the problems that gave rise to its creation? To answer this question, you may wish to examine collision statistics covering the period in which the graduated system and its predecessor operated, and do a microfilm search of a newspaper database from 1990 to the present. Or, try an Internet search—search for "collision statistics" on Google or at the Statistics Canada website (www.statcan.ca).

CHAPTER 4

Rules of the Road

CHAPTER OBJECTIVES

After completing this chapter, you should be able to:

- Determine what speed limits may apply to a highway, depending on location, type, or class of roadway, use of roadway, or other relevant factors.
- Determine the appropriate fine for a speeding offence under the Ontario *Highway Traffic Act* (HTA).
- Know the essential elements of speeding-related offences.
- Identify and understand the basic rules of the road.
- Identify exemptions, exclusions, and exceptions to the basic rules of the road.
- Understand the basis for the exemptions, exclusions, or exceptions to the basic rules of the road.
- Apply the rules of the road to given situations and determine whether any laws have been violated.
- Identify what equipment is mandatory on different classes of vehicles.

INTRODUCTION

This chapter covers the rules of the road as set out in part X of the Ontario *Highway Traffic Act* (HTA), ss. 133-191. We will also discuss the rules regulating speed that are set out in part IX, ss. 128-132, and key equipment requirements set out in part VI, ss. 61-107. Some of the statutory rules of the road also outline specific offences and their penalties.

RULES OF THE ROAD: SPEED

Speed

The standard speed on highways within a municipality or a built-up area is 50 km/h (s. 128(1)(a)). If the highway is in a municipality, but not in a built-up area, the speed limit is 80 km/h (s. 128(1)(b)). On a controlled access highway, whether it is within a municipality or built-up area, the speed limit is 80km/h (s. 128(1)(c)). However, the Minister of Transportation under s. 128(7)(b) may by regulation prescribe a speed limit that exceeds 80km/h, on any King's Highway, and that is the case for most of the "400 series" highways, such as Hwy. 401, which have speed limits of 100km/h. The ministry may also designate speeds for designated highway construction zones (s. 128(8)) and for provincial parks (s. 128(7)(a)). It may also, under s. 128(7)(c), set limits in areas that are not within municipalities. However, local municipalities[1] have been given broad powers under the HTA to pass bylaws to determine speeds in certain conditions and circumstances (s. 128(1)(d)):

1. On a highway that passes through the territorial jurisdiction of the municipality (HTA, s. 128(2)), the speed may be set by the municipality, at any speed up to 100 km/h and may prescribe different rates of speed for different times of day.

2. Where vehicles are driven in public parks or exhibition grounds within the municipality's jurisdiction, the speed may be set by the municipality, but shall not be below 20 km/h (HTA, s. 128(4)).

3. On highways within the municipality's jurisdiction that adjoin a school entrance, the speed may be reduced from the speed otherwise prescribed for 150 m on either side of the school entrance during the designated times (HTA, s. 128(5)).

4. On bridges within a municipality's jurisdiction, the speed may be set by the municipality (HTA, s. 128(6)).

In addition to prescribing maximum speeds on highways, the Ministry of Transportation may, by regulation, also prescribe speeds for different types of motor vehicles. When a municipality, under a bylaw, or the ministry, by regulation, has posted a speed for the highway, it is not valid and enforceable until the bylaw or regulation is posted and made public. Note that the validity of the speed limit does depend on the presence of, or the erection of, speed limit signs (HTA, s. 128(10)). If the bylaw or regulation is properly proclaimed and valid, the speed limit it prescribes takes precedence over the limits set out in s. 128(1)(a) of the HTA, and it is enforceable from that time provided speed limit signs have been erected.

Whatever the limit, the HTA exempts fire trucks, police vehicles, and ambulances from posted speed limits in the following circumstances (HTA, s. 128(13)):

- Fire trucks are only exempt when responding to a fire or emergency, not when returning from one.

- Police vehicles are only exempt when carrying out police duties.

- Ambulances are only exempt when responding to an emergency or transporting a patient in an emergency.

Remember that the exemption attaches to the use of the vehicle, and not merely to the vehicle itself.

Speeding Offences

Violations of s. 128, or regulations or bylaws made under its authority, may result in fines that increase progressively, depending on how much beyond the speed limit the person was driving (HTA, ss. 128(14)-(15)).

Speeding Fines

Less than 20 km/h over the limit	$3.00 for each km/h over the speed limit
Between 20 and 29 km/h over the limit	$4.50 for each km/h over the speed limit
Between 30 and 49 km/h over the limit	$7.00 for each km/h over the speed limit
50 km/h or more over the limit	$9.75 for each km/h over the speed limit and the court may also suspend the person's driver's licence for a period of up to 30 days

These fines are doubled if the offence occurs on a part of a highway designated as a "construction zone" by the province or by a municipality (where the highway is under municipal jurisdiction). The construction zone must be properly marked by signs as such (HTA, ss. 128(8), (8.1), (8.2), (10), and (10.1)).

These fines are also doubled if the offence occurs on a part of a highway designated as a "community safety zone" by the province or by a municipality (where the highway is under municipal jurisdiction). A community safety zone can be created under s. 214.1, where "public safety is of special concern on that part of the highway." For example, a stretch of highway where there have been frequent serious collisions due to excessive speed might attract this designation, as could a stretch of highway near a senior's residence, where risks to residents are high.

Breach of other provisions of the HTA, including most of the rules of the road in part X, will also attract doubled fines in a community safety zone (HTA, s. 214.1(1)).

Although the law is primarily concerned about excessive speed, the HTA also prohibits driving a motor vehicle at "such a slow rate of speed as to impede or block the normal and reasonable movement of traffic," except where a slow rate of speed is necessary for safe operation (for example, because of adverse weather conditions, or where the vehicle is involved in road maintenance). How slow is slow? There is no minimum limit set, and reference should be made to the maximum speed posted and the test set out in s. 132(1): Is the driver impeding or blocking normal and reasonable traffic flow?

In addition to speeding, another broadly described offence in part IX is careless driving, which is defined as driving on a highway "without due care and attention" or "without reasonable consideration for other persons using the highway" (see the boxes below). On conviction, the driver can be liable to a fine of between $200 and $1,000 or to imprisonment for a term of up to six months or to both a fine and imprisonment. In addition, the person's licence may be suspended for up to two years. Note that there are no specific acts that constitute this offence and that it is subjectively defined; in deciding whether a driver is guilty of careless driving, the court asks, What would a reasonable person consider an act of driving "without due care and attention" or driving "without reasonable consideration for other persons using the highway"? A person may be charged with careless driving when the commission of another HTA offence, such as speeding, results in a collision or in circumstances where a situation of great danger is created (HTA, s. 130).

Note that the intent required to support a careless driving charge under the HTA differs from the intent required to support a charge of criminal negligence in the operation of a motor vehicle and other *Criminal Code* (CC) offences. Generally, the intent under the HTA need be no more than negligence or carelessness. Under the CC, a greater intention to do harm is required. In the case of criminal negligence, for example, the required intent has been defined as a reckless or wanton disregard for the lives and safety of others—the driver has considered the risk, and demonstrated a positive acceptance of it without regard for the consequences. Although this does not amount to a positive intention to do harm, it is more than off-handed carelessness or mere indifference to consequences.

The grounds to lay a charge are determined by the circumstances involved in the incident. Also, definitions come into play; the definitions of "highway" and "motor vehicle" are interpreted differently in different acts and this affects which charge to lay. If a person were to commit a serious moving violation in a parking lot of a shopping mall, the charge of careless driving would not apply because this charge is restricted to careless driving on a highway.

Careless Driving

Case #1
Domingo Martinez was driving his car south on the 8th Line in the Township of Halton Hills. It was daylight and visibility was good. The road on which he was driving was straight and dry. He was driving at about 50 km/h on a road where the speed limit was 70 km/h. He was proceeding toward the 10th Sideroad, an east–west through highway. Traffic proceeding south on the 8th Line is required to stop at the 10th Sideroad. There was a clearly visible "stop ahead" warning sign on the 8th Line about 160 m north of the 10th Sideroad.

As Martinez drove south on the 8th Line, he entered the intersection without stopping. A van was proceeding through the intersection from the west. Martinez was more than halfway through the intersection before he applied his brakes. Martinez's car collided with the rear quarter panel of the van, causing the van to flip between five and seven times. The driver and sole occupant of the van died as a result of head injuries he sustained in the accident.

Martinez was originally charged with dangerous driving causing death contrary to s. 249(4) of the *Criminal Code*. At his preliminary hearing, he elected trial by a General Division (now Superior Court) judge sitting without a jury. After some evidence was heard, with the Crown's concurrence, he entered a plea of guilty to careless driving contrary to s. 130 of the HTA.

(*R v. Martinez*, 1996 CanLII 663 (Ont. CA), http://www.canlii.org/on/cas/onca/1996/1996onca10058.html)

Case #2
On November 13, 2002 at about 6:30 a.m., Michael Hutchings was driving his motor vehicle at about 65 km/h eastbound on Dixon Road between Kipling Avenue and Islington Avenue in Toronto. He struck and killed a pedestrian who was standing still in the centre of the left-turn lane in which Hutchings was travelling. The pedestrian had been looking away from the oncoming traffic. She was dressed in dark, non-reflective clothing with a hood over her head.

The traffic was light to moderate; the weather was cloudy, the road conditions were good, and the roads were dry. There was nothing obstructing Hutchings's view. Visibility was good, and the area was illuminated by the gradually rising sun, by streetlights, by lighting from the surrounding buildings in this densely populated area, and by the lights of other motor vehicles driving east and west along Dixon Road.

Careless Driving (concluded)

Hutchings was in good health; there was nothing wrong with his car, and his headlights were on. He had not consumed any alcohol or any non-prescription drugs. He had no physical or emotional problems that could have affected his driving, and he was familiar with the area. He did not see the victim at all prior to the accident, and therefore he did not apply his brakes until the impact. Hutchings was extremely remorseful.

At trial, Justice Kowarsky offered the following reasons for decision:

> On the totality of all the evidence before the Court, I am satisfied that the Crown has established a prima facie case of Careless Driving against the defendant. Mr. Hutchings has not provided a reasonable explanation as to why he did not see the victim prior to the collision so as to enable him to take action to avoid the collision. Consequently, the evidence does not raise a reasonable doubt that the defendant's manner of driving was careless in the circumstances. For these reasons I find that the Prosecution has proved its case beyond a reasonable doubt, and that the defendant's driving infringed Section 130 of the Highway Traffic Act in that he was driving without "due care and attention" as envisaged by the legislation. Accordingly, there will be a conviction registered against the defendant for Careless Driving.

(*R v. Hutchings*, 2004 ONCJ 155 (CanLII), http://www.canlii.org/on/cas/oncj/2004/2004oncj155.html)

Aggressive Driving and Road Rage

Aggressive driving and road rage are similar concepts and include tailgating, speeding, failing to yield the right of way, and cutting other drivers off, among other things. Often, the term "road rage" is used when a driver threatens violence or assaults another driver. Although aggressive driving and road rage are not specifically mentioned in the HTA, they can lead to charges under the Act, including careless driving.

The Canada Safety Council conducted a survey in 1999 in which it found that "[a]ggressive driving emerged second only to driver inattention as the perceived main cause of motor vehicle collisions—in fact, one in four respondents ranked aggressive driving ahead of impaired driving." A surprising finding was that "84 per cent of respondents admitted to at least one act of aggressive driving over the past year. With 20 million licensed drivers in Canada that means at least 16 million Canadians knowingly act aggressively behind the wheel." The respondents to the survey identified the most common acts of aggressive driving as tailgating, passing on the shoulder of the road, making rude gestures, pulling into a parking space someone else is waiting for, and changing lanes without signalling. (http://www.safety-council.org/info/traffic/aggress.html)

RULES OF THE ROAD

For each section of the HTA discussed in this chapter, you should refer to the short-form set wordings and fines in the *Provincial Offences Act* (POA) (see appendix A). The different wordings used in each section will help you understand the complexity of what is included in the section.

Direction of Traffic by Police Officer, HTA, Section 134

A police officer who is required to maintain orderly movement of traffic in order to prevent injury or damage to persons or property, or to deal with an emergency, may direct traffic and, in the event that his or her directions conflict with the rules of the road, the officer's exercise of discretion to direct traffic takes precedence over the rules of the road. As part of the power to direct traffic, an officer may also close a portion of a highway by posting signs or traffic signalling devices, in which case no one may drive on the closed roadway except emergency vehicles. Refer to the POA wordings to appreciate all the charges within this section.

Erection of and Effect of Signs, HTA, Section 182

Regulations may be made under the HTA to provide for or require road signs and markings on any highway in the province, and may prescribe the type of signs and markings to be used. Section 182(2) of the HTA makes obedience to the instructions given by signs or markings mandatory. This means that a sign may impose a duty in addition to that imposed by other rules of the road set out in the HTA. For example, s. 143 sets out a number of circumstances where U-turns are prohibited. In addition, U-turns would also be prohibited where a sign indicates that to be the case, even if it would otherwise be permitted under s. 143.

Right of Way: Uncontrolled Intersection, HTA, Section 135

Where two roads intersect and there is no traffic control sign or device, a driver approaching an intersection shall yield to a vehicle that has already entered the intersection from an adjacent highway. If both vehicles enter the intersection from adjacent highways at the same time, the vehicle on the right has the right of way over the vehicle on the left. Note that this section uses a broad definition of vehicle and explicitly includes streetcars. See figure 4.1.

Stop-Sign-Controlled Intersections, HTA, Section 136

When approaching a stop sign at an intersection, a driver is required to come to a full stop

- at the stop line or, if none,
- at a crosswalk or, if there is neither a stop line nor crosswalk, then
- immediately before entering the intersection.

If a driver stops on top of, rather than at, the stop line or crosswalk, he or she could be charged with "disobey stop sign—stop wrong place." If a driver proceeds all the way into the intersection (past the extension of the edges of the adjoining roadway), he or she should be charged with "disobey stop sign—fail to stop." The driver shall yield the right of way to traffic on the adjacent cross road that is in the intersection or so close to the intersection that to proceed would create an immediate hazard (for example, if the driver pulled out from the stop line, causing a vehicle with the right of way to brake sharply). Again, refer to the POA wordings to appreciate all the charges within this section.

FIGURE 4.1 Uncontrolled Intersection

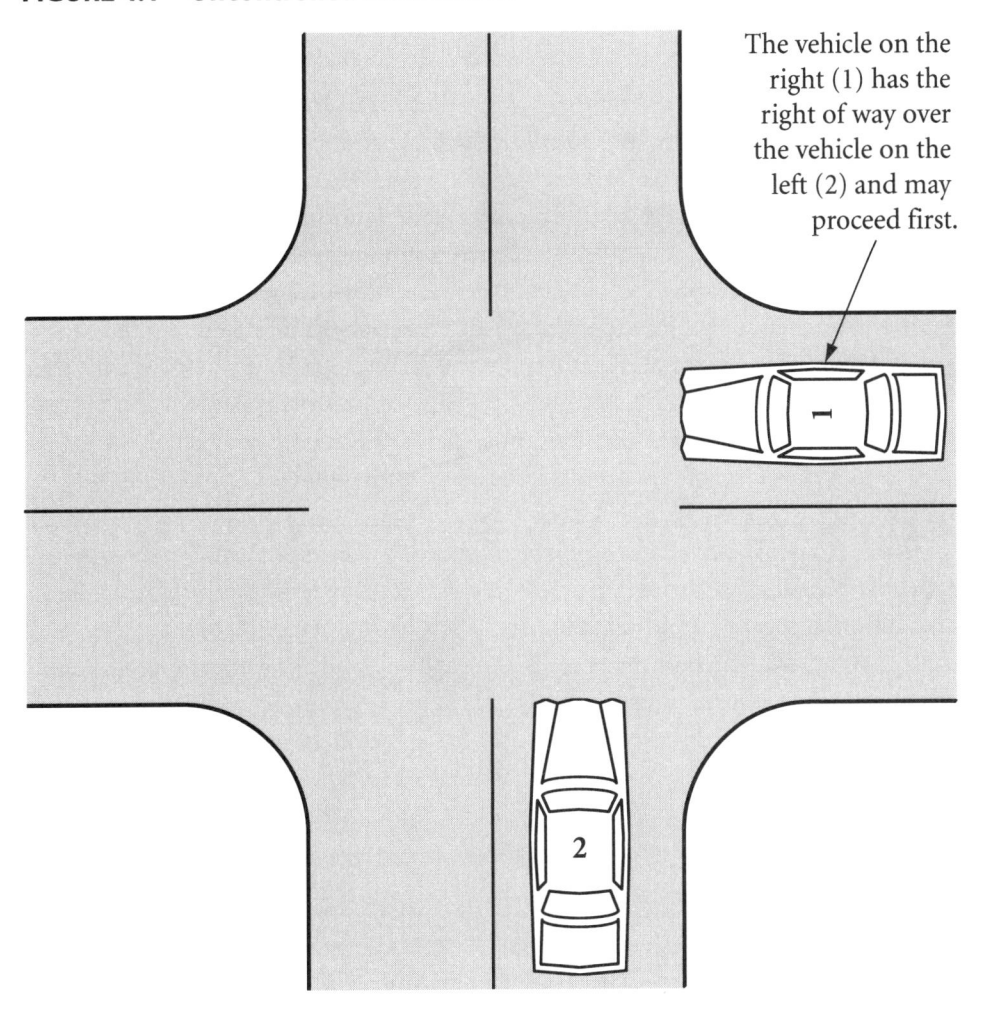

The vehicle on the right (1) has the right of way over the vehicle on the left (2) and may proceed first.

Yield-Sign-Controlled Intersections, HTA, Section 138

A driver approaching an intersection controlled by a yield right-of-way sign shall slow down or stop, if necessary, in order to yield the right of way to traffic already in the intersection or so close to the intersection that failure to yield would create an immediate hazard. When entering a highway from a private road, the driver is required to yield to highway traffic whether or not the private road is controlled by a yield sign (HTA, s. 139).

Pedestrian Crossovers, HTA, Section 140

A driver shall yield to a pedestrian or person in a wheelchair if the person is proceeding in the crossover on the part of the roadway that the driver is approaching or, if the person is proceeding on the other side of the roadway, the driver must still yield and wait until the pedestrian has safely crossed the roadway.

If one vehicle is overtaking another vehicle stopped at a crossover, the driver of the overtaking vehicle shall stop before entering the crossover and yield the right of way to any pedestrian who is in the crossover or who is approaching the part of the crossover that the vehicle is about to cross, unless proceeding would not endanger the pedestrian. See figure 4.2.

If a vehicle is overtaking another vehicle that is moving within 30 m of a crossover, the overtaking vehicle shall not allow the front of the vehicle to pass beyond the front of the vehicle that is being overtaken. Because the overtaking driver's view of a pedestrian to his or her right would be obstructed both while approaching the intersection or while stopped, this rule is intended to prevent the overtaking driver from hitting a pedestrian whom he or she cannot see until it is too late to stop. On the other hand, a pedestrian or person in a wheelchair is obliged not to enter an intersection where a vehicle is so close that it is impractical or impossible for the driver to yield the right of way. Also, cyclists who wish to use a crossover must become pedestrians by dismounting and walking their bikes across the highway. See figure 4.3.

Right-Hand Turns, HTA, Sections 141(2)-(4)

A driver intending to turn right onto an intersecting highway must, if there are marked lanes, use the right-hand lane or, if there are no marked lanes, must keep to the left of the right curb or the edge of the roadway, and shall make the right turn by entering the right-hand lane of the intersecting highway, or, if there is no right-hand lane, by keeping to the left of the right-hand curb or edge of the roadway being entered. If there is more than one lane designated as a right-hand turn lane, a driver shall approach the intersection in one of the lanes, and turn from that lane into the corresponding adjacent lane. See figure 4.4.

Left-Hand Turns, HTA, Sections 141(5)-(9)

A driver intending to turn left onto a roadway other than at an intersection—for example, to enter a private driveway—shall cross the path of vehicles approaching from the opposite direction only when it is safe to do so. It is safe as long as the driver does not cause an accident or an abrupt, panic reaction by drivers of approaching vehicles.

Where a driver intends to turn left at an intersection, he or she shall, where there are marked lanes, approach the intersection in the left-hand lane provided for use of traffic travelling in the direction in which his or her vehicle is proceeding, or, where there are no marked lanes, then by keeping immediately to the right of the centre line of the highway or its extension. He or she shall then leave the intersection by turning onto the intersecting highway, entering it in the left-hand lane for traffic moving in the direction he or she is proceeding. Where there is no marked left-hand lane in the intersecting highway, he or she shall make the turn entering the intersecting roadway to the right of the centre line.

If there is more than one left-turn lane, the driver shall approach the intersection in one of the lanes, leave the intersection in that lane, and enter the corresponding lane of the intersecting highway. See figure 4.5.

Exceptions to these rules can be made for long vehicles, such as tractor-trailers, that cannot make a right or left turn in the confines of the turn lanes provided. Such vehicles are deemed to be in compliance with s. 141 if they comply as closely as is practicable. In reality, a long vehicle may need to make a wide right turn, moving

Rules of the Road CHAPTER 4 75

FIGURE 4.2 Overtaking Stopped Vehicle at Crossover

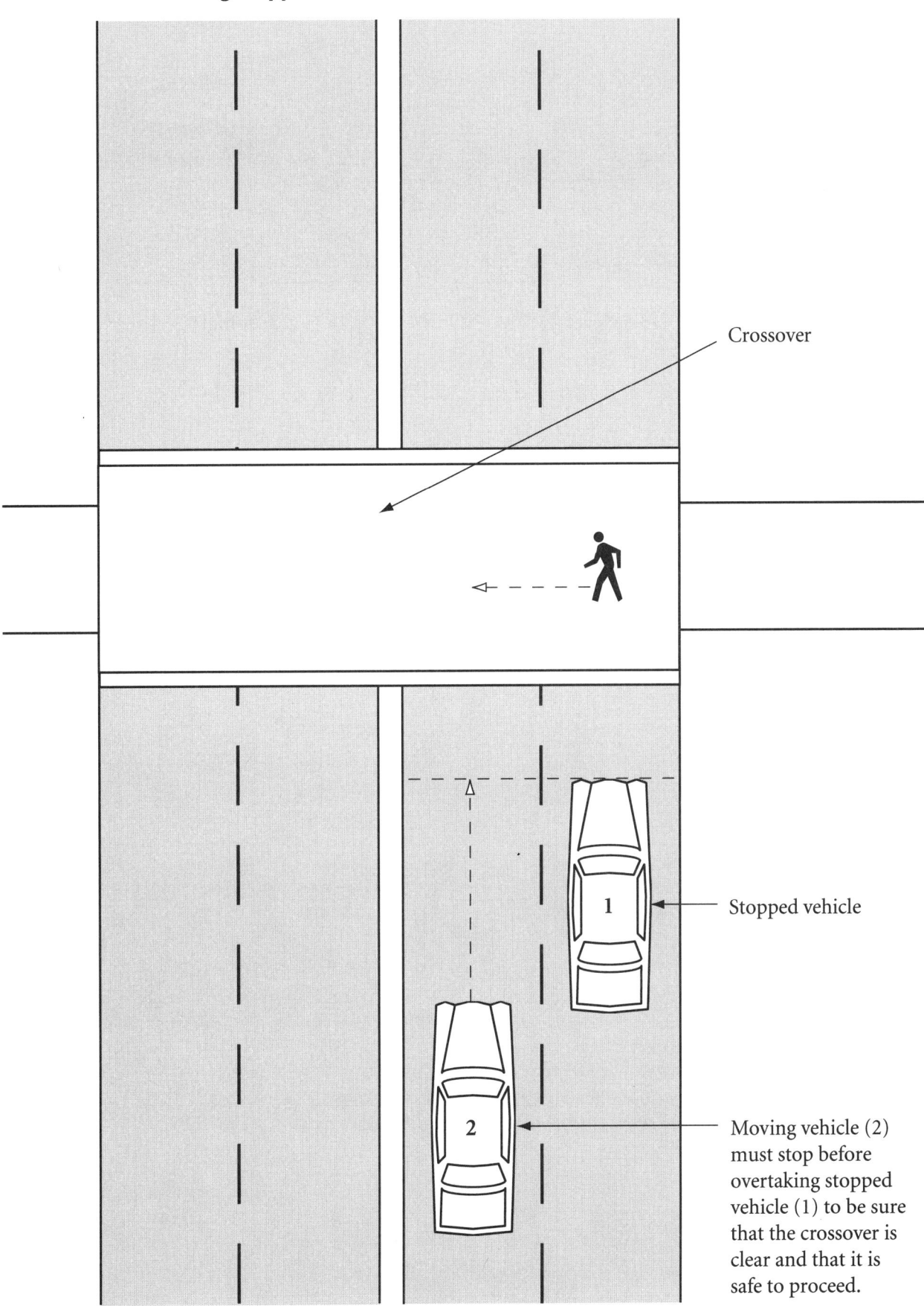

Crossover

Stopped vehicle

Moving vehicle (2) must stop before overtaking stopped vehicle (1) to be sure that the crossover is clear and that it is safe to proceed.

FIGURE 4.3   Overtaking Moving Vehicle Near Crossover

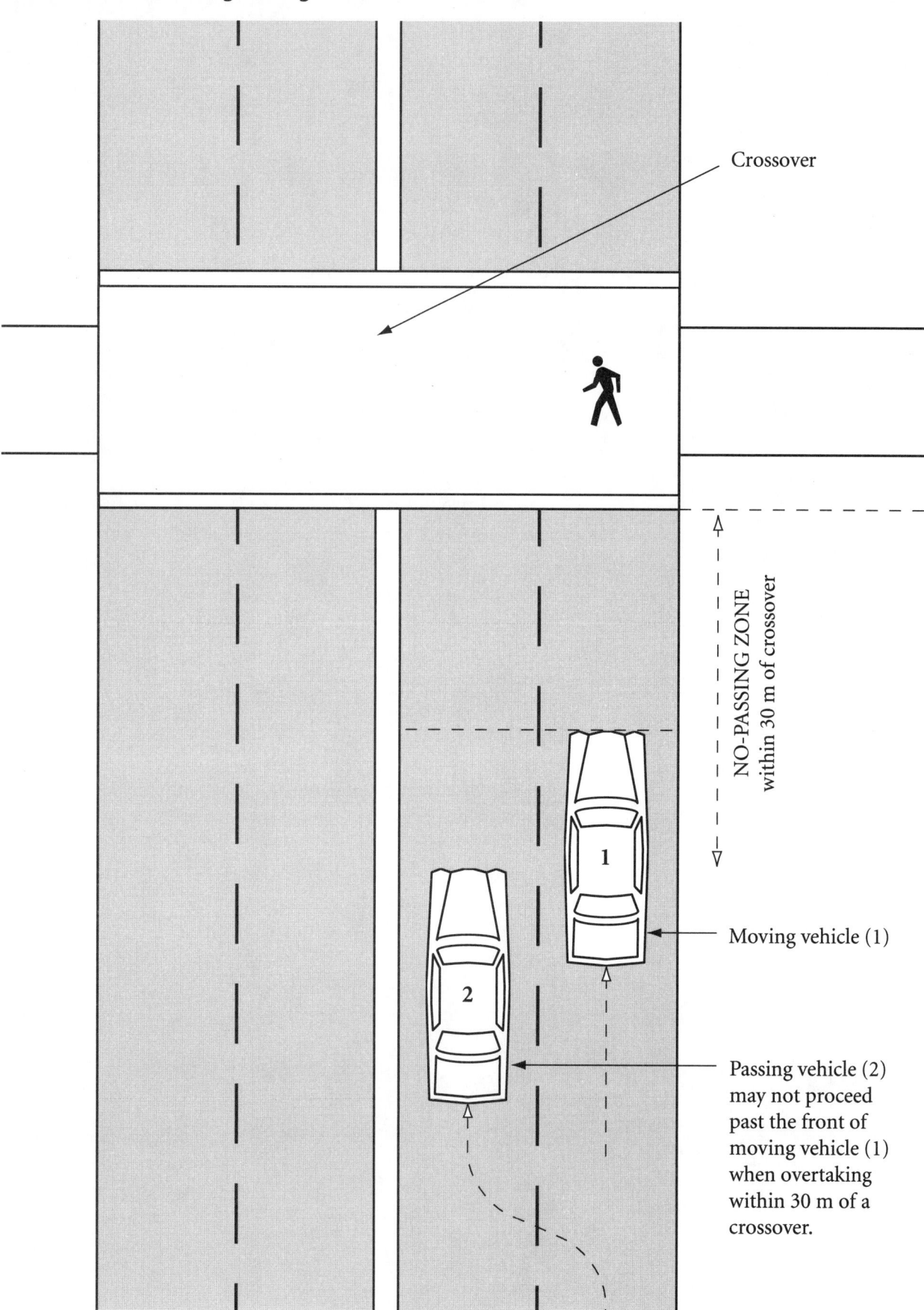

Crossover

NO-PASSING ZONE within 30 m of crossover

Moving vehicle (1)

Passing vehicle (2) may not proceed past the front of moving vehicle (1) when overtaking within 30 m of a crossover.

FIGURE 4.4 Right-Hand Turn

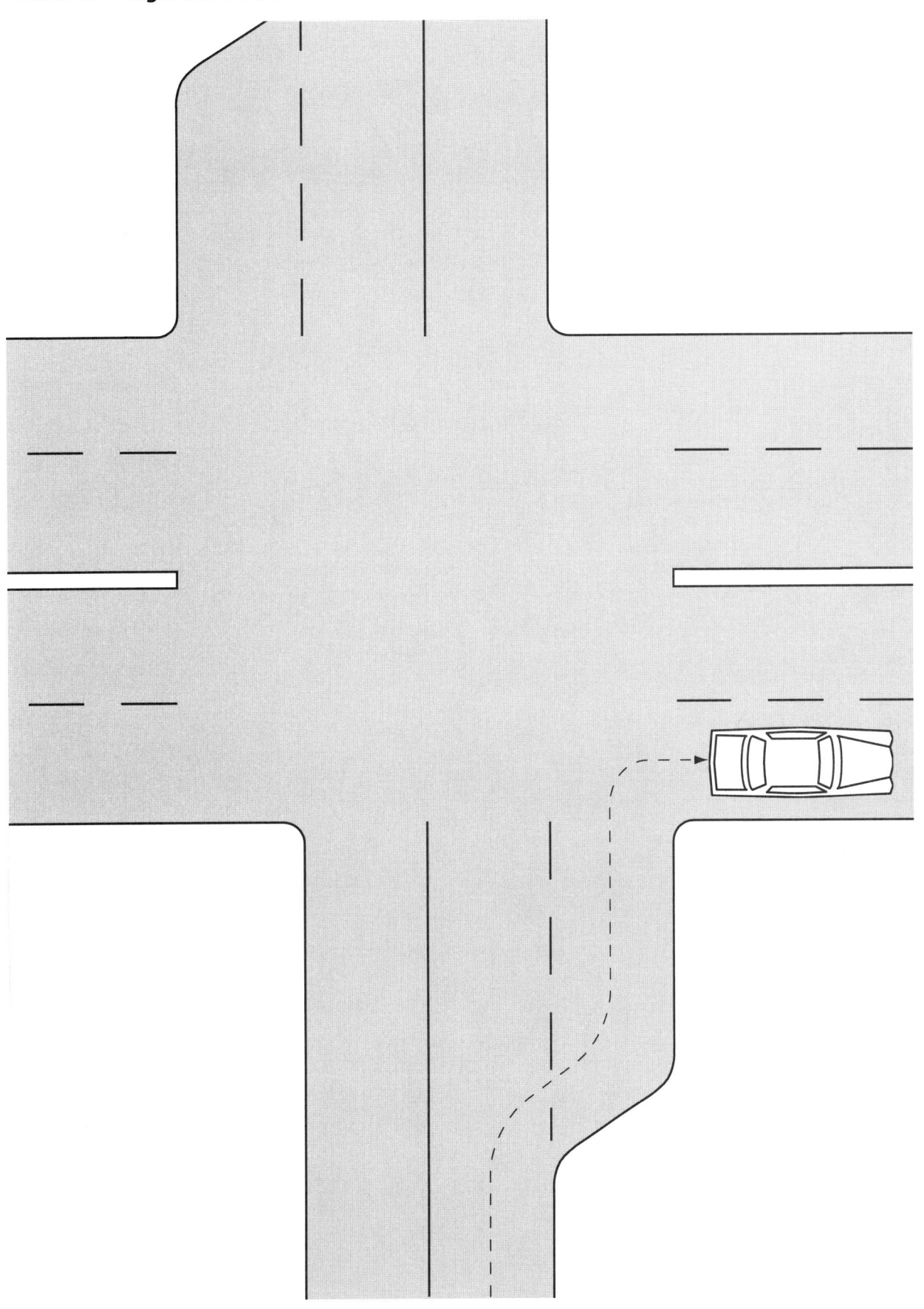

FIGURE 4.5　Left-Hand Turn

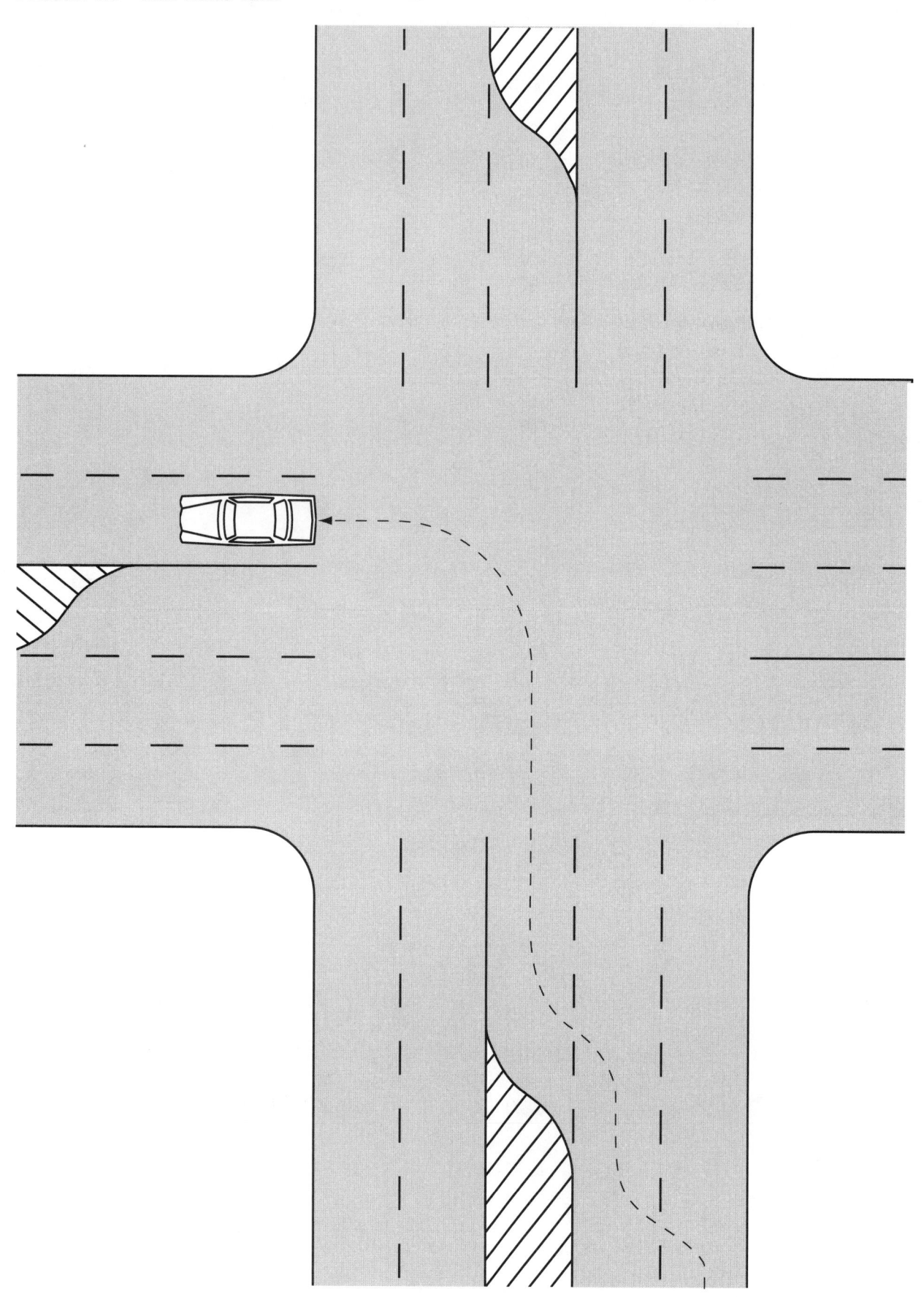

quite far out from the curb or the right-turn lane into an adjacent lane, or across the centre line, in order to complete the turn without running over the curb or the sidewalk. Similarly, a long vehicle may need to make a wide left turn in order to avoid side-swiping a centre-line road divider or traffic signal. See figure 4.6.

The turn rules are also relaxed for road-service vehicles (vehicles used for road maintenance by a municipality or other body with authority to conduct road maintenance), which may make right and left turns without complying with these rules if the turns can be made safely. A road-service vehicle may also proceed straight ahead through a left-turn lane, if it is safe to do so.

Signalling, HTA, Section 142

Drivers are obliged to signal right and left turns, lane changes, and exits from highways onto private roads or drives, if any other vehicle might be affected by the turn or manoeuvre. A turn can be made only after determining that it can be made safely. In other words, drivers are not required to signal if no vehicle is near them. Drivers are also required to signal when moving onto the roadway from a parked position. Signals may be given by mechanical/electrical means or by hand signals. The hand signals for each turn are as follows:

- Left turn: Extend the arm horizontally out the left side of the vehicle.
- Right turn: Extend the arm upward out the left side of the vehicle.

Drivers are also required to indicate stops. Usually, applying the brakes activates a red or amber light on the rear of the vehicle to indicate a stop. To signal a stop using hand signals, extend the arm downward out the left side of the vehicle. The cyclist's hand signals are the same as those for motor vehicle drivers, although a cyclist may also signal a right turn by extending the right arm horizontally on the right side of the bicycle. See figure 4.7.

Yielding to Buses in Bus Bays, HTA, Section 142.1 and O. Reg. 393/02

Drivers in a lane adjacent to a bus bay shall yield right of way to a bus leaving the bus bay and re-entering traffic when the driver of the bus has signalled his or her intention to do so. A bus driver shall not signal an intention to re-enter traffic until he or she is ready to do so, and the driver shall not re-enter the stream of traffic if a vehicle in the adjacent lane is so close that it is impractical for the driver of that vehicle to yield the right of way. O. reg. 393/02 defines a bus bay as a part of the roadway next to a bus stop from which passengers enter or exit the bus, and from which the bus exits and enters the adjacent stream of traffic. The bus bay may be inset, as indicated in figure 4.8, or it may be the lane nearest the curb where the bus stop is located. The regulation also requires buses to have a bus bay yield sign attached to the back of the bus .

FIGURE 4.6　Wide Turns

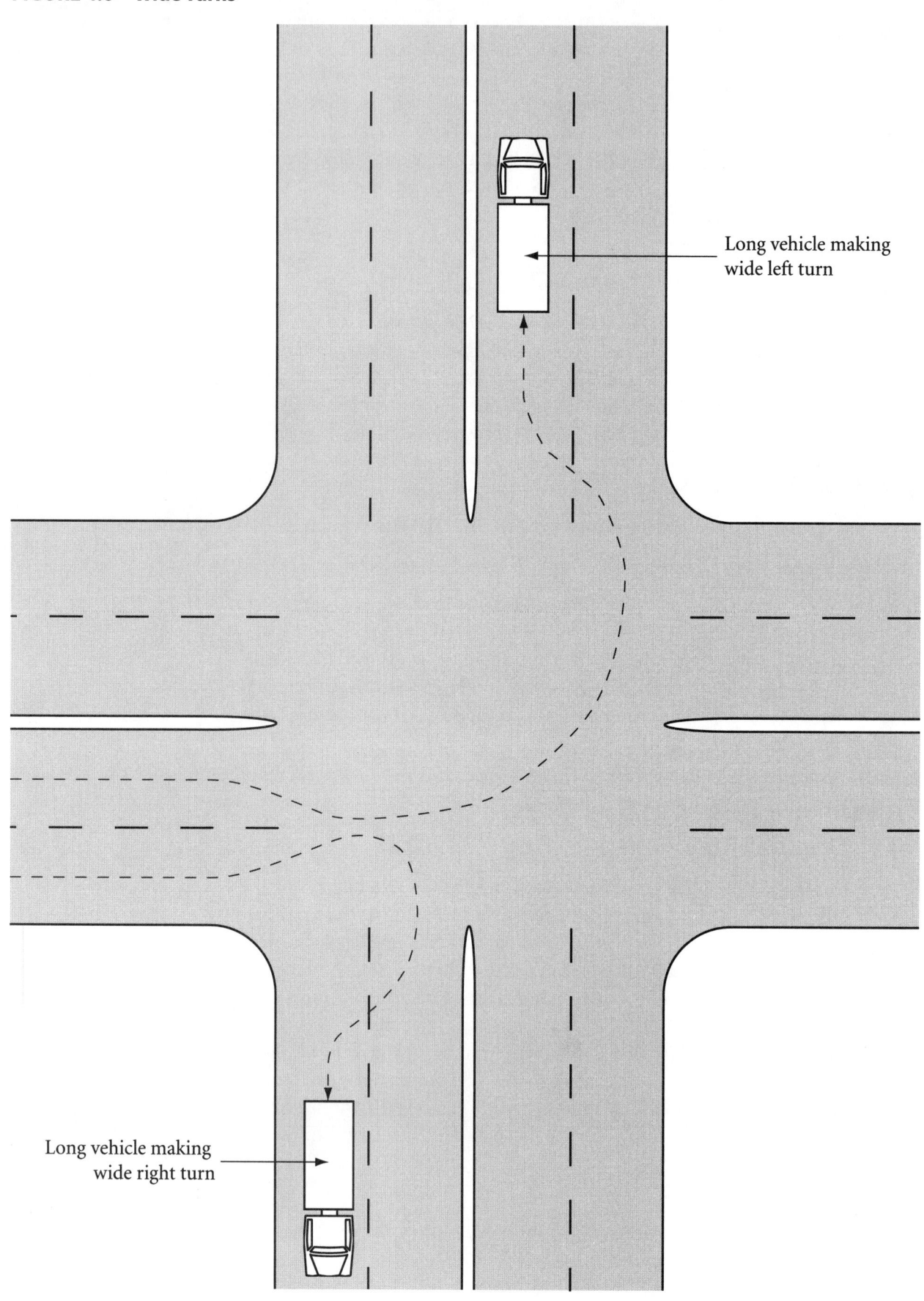

Rules of the Road **CHAPTER 4** 81

FIGURE 4.7 Hand Signals

Left-hand turn: Left arm straight

Stop: Left arm bent down

Right-hand turn: Left arm bent up

Right-hand turn on bicycle: Right arm straight

FIGURE 4.8　Yielding to Bus

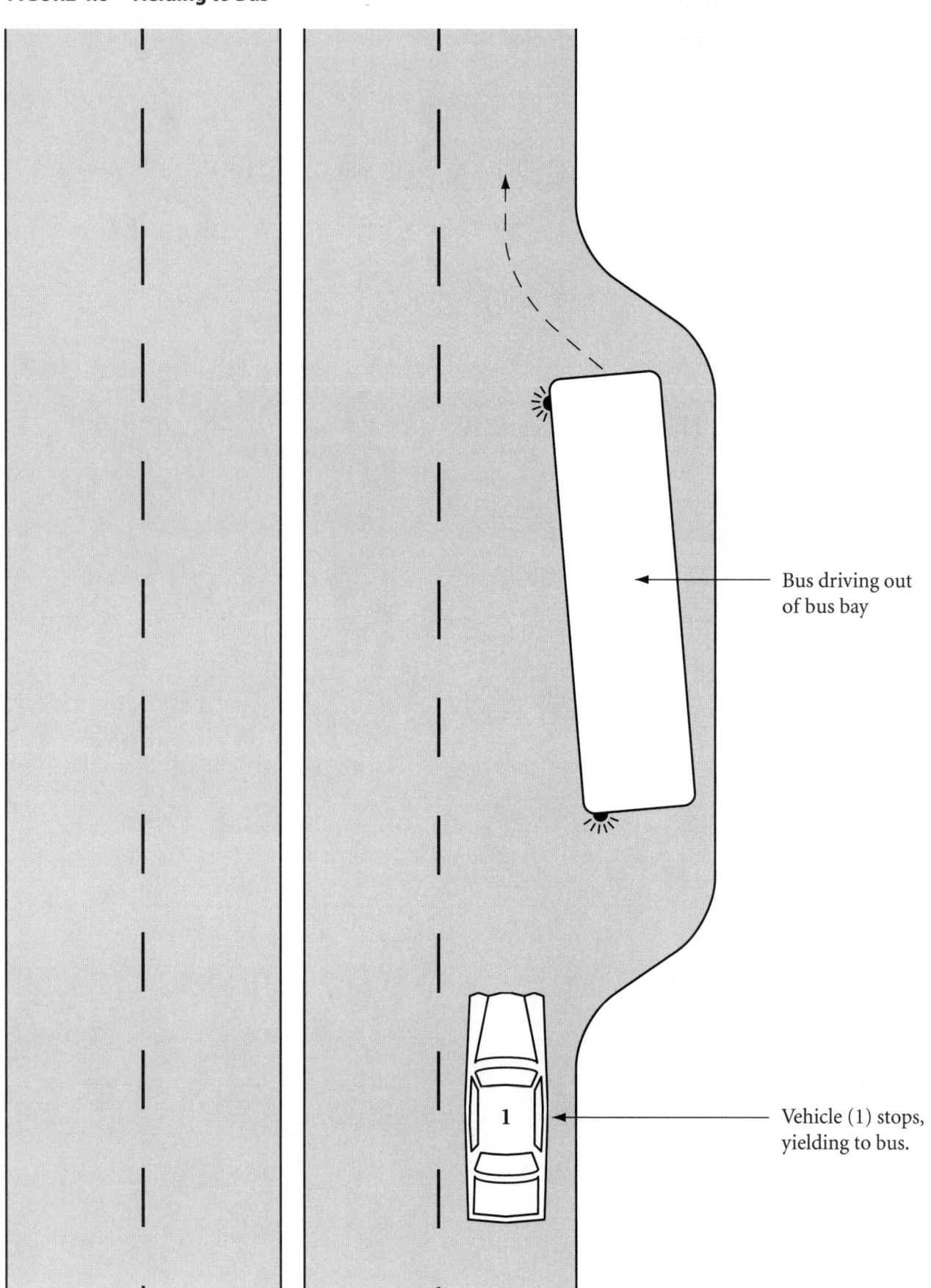

Bus driving out of bus bay

Vehicle (1) stops, yielding to bus.

U-Turns, HTA, Section 143

In general, drivers may make U-turns provided that it is safe to do so and that they signal their intention to do so. However, U-turns are prohibited in the following circumstances:

- on a curve, where traffic approaching from either direction cannot be seen by the driver making the U-turn within a distance of 150 m;

- on or within 30 m of a railroad crossing (absolute prohibition);

- on an approach or near the crest of a grade, where the turning vehicle cannot be seen by a driver of another vehicle approaching from either direction within 150 m; or

- within 150 m of a bridge, viaduct, or tunnel, where the driver's view is obstructed within that distance.

Traffic Signals, HTA, Section 144

Where there is a traffic signal at an intersection, a driver must stop at the stop line or, if there is no stop line, before entering a crosswalk or, if there is no sign or crosswalk, immediately before entering the intersection. If there is a traffic signal that is not at an intersection, the same rules apply, except that if there is neither a sign or crosswalk, the vehicle will stop at least 5 m back from the traffic signal. See figure 4.9.

Sections 144(2) and (3) provide that where a highway includes two roadways that are 15 m or more apart (whether or not the 15 m includes left-turn lanes), and it is crossed by an intersecting roadway, each crossing shall be considered a separate intersection. However, at the time of publication, these sections were not yet proclaimed in force. See figure 4.10.

When a driver is permitted to proceed, but there is a pedestrian lawfully in a crosswalk, the driver shall yield to the pedestrian in the crosswalk. For example, where the driver wishes to make a right turn on a green light and pass through a crosswalk, he or she must yield to any pedestrian lawfully walking through a crosswalk on a green signal. A driver who may turn right on a red signal must also yield to oncoming traffic in the lane he or she seeks to enter because the traffic facing a green signal has the right of way. This rule also applies to vehicles in private driveways and roadways controlled by a traffic signal where the driver faces a red signal and wishes to turn right.

Where there is a traffic signal system with different light or arrow signals for different lanes, the driver shall obey the signal for the lane he or she is in.

GREEN SIGNALS

A driver approaching a green circular signal may proceed or turn left or right, unless otherwise indicated. A driver approaching a flashing green light or a solid or flashing green arrow together with a circular solid green light may proceed forward or turn left or right. If a driver is approaching a green arrow, or arrows in combination with a red or amber circular signal, the driver may proceed only in the direction indicated by the green arrows.

84 TRAFFIC MANAGEMENT

FIGURE 4.9 Traffic Signals

Traffic signals at intersection: Where to stop

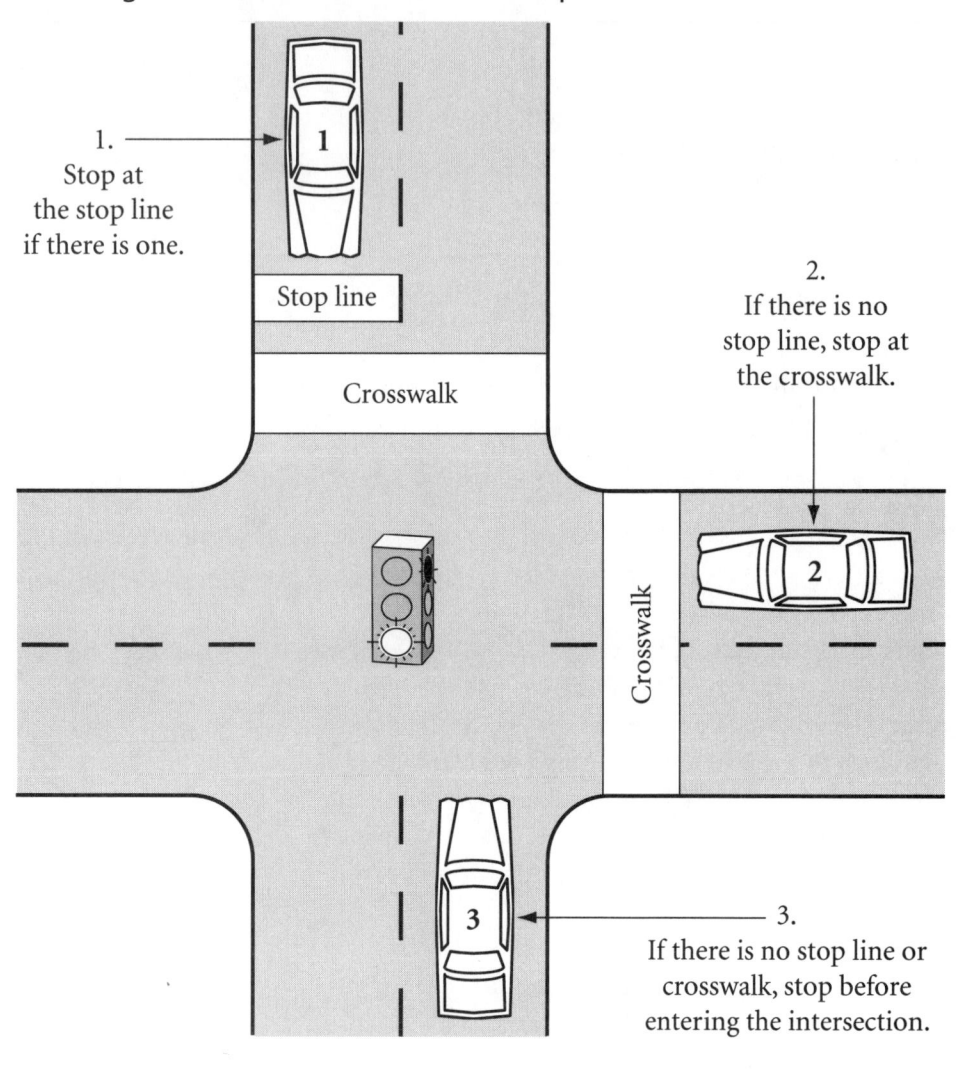

1. Stop at the stop line if there is one.

Stop line

Crosswalk

2. If there is no stop line, stop at the crosswalk.

Crosswalk

3. If there is no stop line or crosswalk, stop before entering the intersection.

Traffic signal where there is no intersection: Where to stop

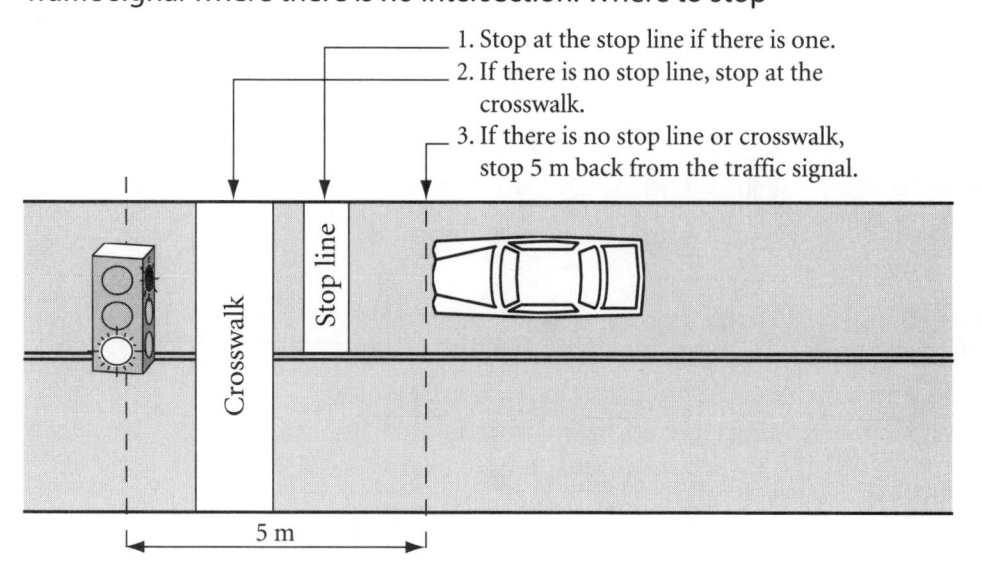

1. Stop at the stop line if there is one.
2. If there is no stop line, stop at the crosswalk.
3. If there is no stop line or crosswalk, stop 5 m back from the traffic signal.

Crosswalk

Stop line

5 m

Rules of the Road **CHAPTER 4** 85

FIGURE 4.10 Left Turn at Intersection with a Median 15 Metres Wide or Wider

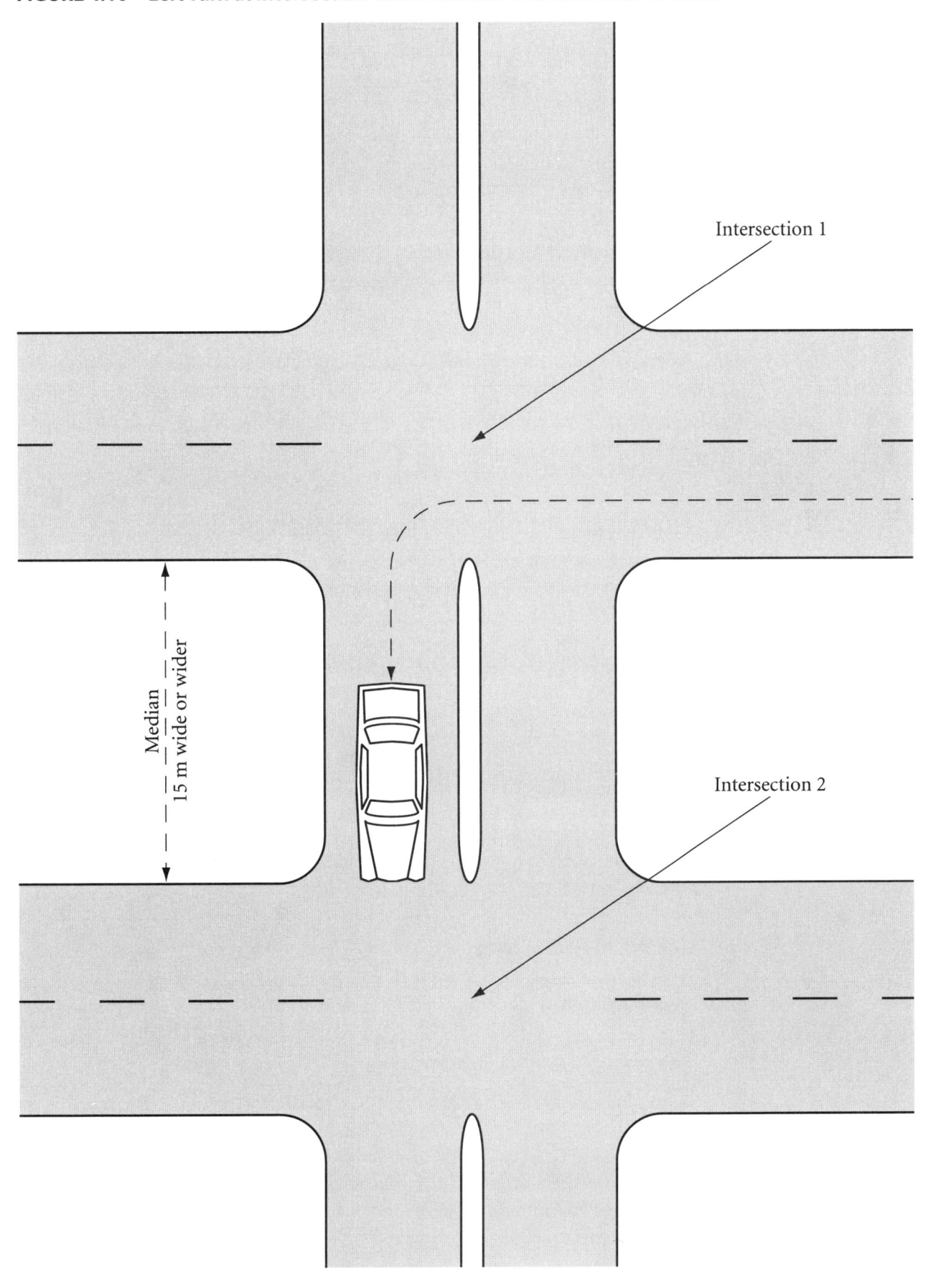

AMBER SIGNALS

A driver approaching an amber light shall stop his or her vehicle if he or she can safely do so; otherwise, he or she may proceed through the light with caution. Similarly, if a driver is approaching an amber arrow, he or she shall stop if it is safe to do so; otherwise, he or she may proceed with caution in the direction indicated by the amber arrow. A driver approaching a flashing amber light may proceed with caution; this light functions much like a yield sign.

RED SIGNALS

A driver approaching a red signal shall stop and not proceed until a green signal is shown. Anyone who violates the rule with respect to a red or amber signal is guilty of an offence under s. 144(31.2) and is liable to a fine not less than $150 and not more than $500. Sections 144(18.1)-(18.6) deal with a charge of running a red light where the evidence for the offence has been obtained by a red light camera. In this case, a charge is issued on the basis of the camera evidence and may be laid against the owner of the offending vehicle if the driver cannot be identified. The charge must be laid under s. 144(18.1) if it is against the owner, or under s. 144(18.2) if it is against the driver.

RIGHT AND LEFT TURNS ON RED SIGNALS

Despite the stop-on-red rule, a driver facing a red signal who stops and yields the right of way to approaching traffic may turn right on a red signal or turn left on a red signal from a one-way street into a one-way street. See figure 4.11.

RIGHT AND LEFT TURNS FOR TRANSIT AUTHORITY BUSES

A bus driver on a scheduled route approaching a traffic signal showing a white vertical bar may turn right or left with caution.

EMERGENCY VEHICLES

A driver of an emergency vehicle as defined in the HTA—that is, the vehicle is being used in an emergency—may, after stopping, proceed through a red signal if it is safe to do so.

FLASHING RED SIGNAL

A driver shall stop and proceed with caution, treating a flashing red signal in the same way as a stop sign.

TRAFFIC SIGNALS AND PEDESTRIANS

Pedestrians are not free to step out on the roadway at any time or place of their choosing, even though they generally have the right of way when lawfully crossing the roadway. First, where there is a crosswalk, a pedestrian must use the crosswalk and not simply cross the road at a location of his or her own choosing. A pedestrian facing a circular green signal, a green arrow pointed straight ahead, or a "walk" sign may cross the roadway in the direction indicated. However, a pedestrian facing

Rules of the Road **CHAPTER 4** 87

FIGURE 4.11 Right and Left Turns on Red Signals

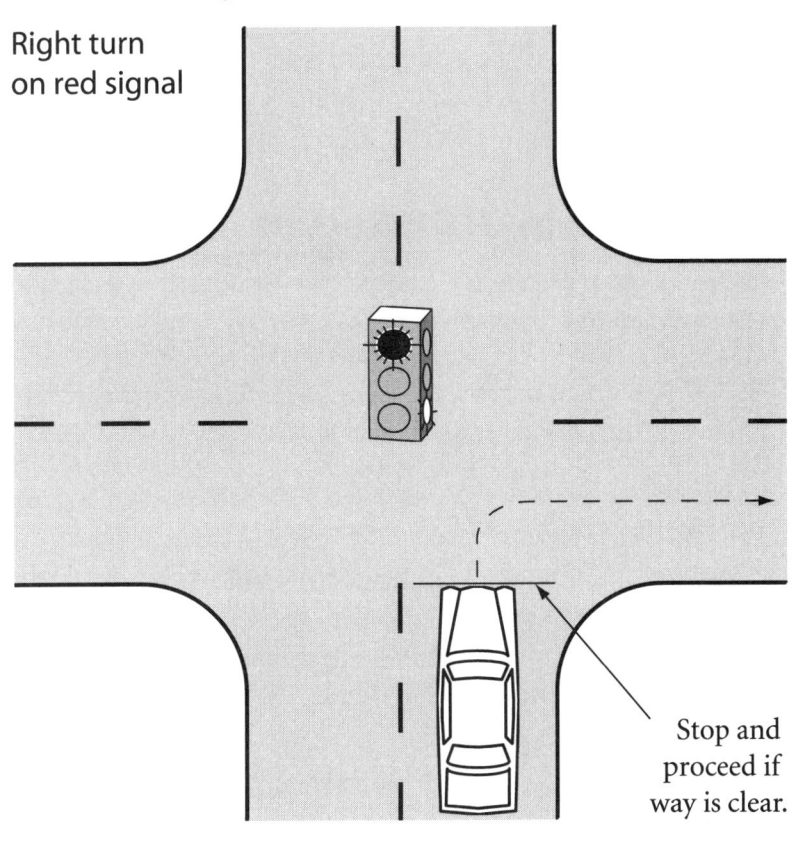

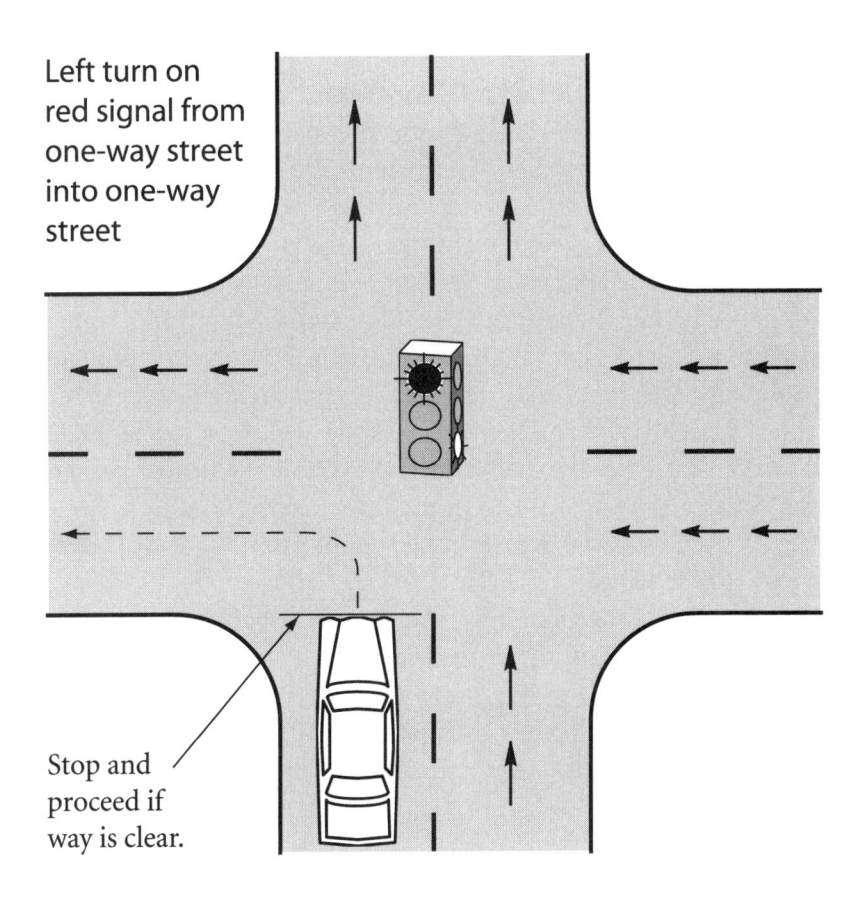

Right turn on red signal

Stop and proceed if way is clear.

Left turn on red signal from one-way street into one-way street

Stop and proceed if way is clear.

a flashing green signal or flashing green left-turn arrow in conjunction with a solid green signal shall not enter and cross the roadway. Nor shall a pedestrian, facing an amber or red signal or a "don't walk" signal, cross the roadway. Bicyclists are prohibited from riding in a crosswalk, and must dismount and walk if they intend to use a crosswalk.

Blocking Intersections, HTA, Section 145

Municipalities may pass bylaws prohibiting drivers from entering an intersection unless "traffic in front of him or her is moving in a manner that would reasonably lead him or her to believe he or she can clear the intersection before the signal … changes to … red." The bylaw does not apply to drivers entering an intersection to make a left or right turn if the driver has signalled an intention to do that.

Slow Vehicles, HTA, Section 147

A vehicle that is travelling at a slower speed than other traffic shall keep to the right-hand lane or, if there is only one lane, as close to the right curb as possible, except where a vehicle is slowing to make a left-hand turn or overtaking another vehicle. Road-service vehicles are exempt from this rule.

Passing (Overtaking), HTA, Section 148

The HTA considers two situations involving passing vehicles: vehicles meeting head on and vehicles travelling in the same direction. In the "head on" case, each driver is expected to turn to the right of the roadway to allow each other room to pass, assuming that the road does not have well-marked lanes of adequate width. Similarly, a motor vehicle meeting a bicycle is expected to give the cyclist sufficient room to pass. If one vehicle, because of weight or load, cannot turn to the right to make room for another to pass, the driver of the first vehicle shall stop and, if necessary, assist the other vehicle to pass. This scenario might arise with an oversized or long vehicle on a narrow highway with narrow lanes and/or no hard shoulder.

In the case of a vehicle or **equestrian** overtaking another vehicle or equestrian, the one being overtaken is required to pull to the right in order to permit the other driver to overtake him or her. Similarly, the overtaking vehicle is obliged to pull out to the left as far as necessary to avoid collision with the other vehicle or equestrian. The vehicle being overtaken is not expected to pull off the road, but is expected to leave one-half of the roadway free, if possible. Where a vehicle is passing a bicycle, the cyclist is expected to pull to the right to let the faster vehicle pass; at the same time, the driver or equestrian overtaking is expected to pull to the left to pass safely without running the cyclist off the road.

Whenever passing, it is the responsibility of the overtaking driver to ensure that the left lane is free of traffic to permit passing and that no one is overtaking him or her.

In general, no vehicle is to be driven or operated to the left of the centre of a highway designed for two-way traffic, when passing or otherwise, in the following cases (HTA, s. 149(1)):

equestrian
a person riding on a horse

- when approaching the crest of a hill, where the driver's view is obstructed;
- on a curve in a roadway, where the driver's view is obstructed;
- within 30 m of a bridge, viaduct, or tunnel, where the driver's view is obstructed so that an approaching vehicle cannot be seen within that distance; or
- within 30 m of a railway crossing, whether or not the view is obstructed.

There are some exceptions: highways divided into lanes, where there are more lanes in one direction than another, and one-way roads. Road-service vehicles also may be driven to the left of the centre line, provided that appropriate precautions are taken (HTA, s. 149(2)).

Passing on the Right and the Use of Shoulders, HTA, Section 150

Although passing on the right is usually prohibited, there are some circumstances where it is permitted:

- where the vehicle being overtaken is about to make a left turn and has signalled a left turn, and the pavement of the lane is wide enough to safely permit the manoeuvre (only if the shoulder is paved); and
- where a highway is designated for the use of one-way traffic.

However, no vehicle shall pull off the roadway to pass another vehicle. Remember that the roadway includes the travelled part of the pavement, but not the shoulder. There are exceptions to this rule—if the shoulder is paved, and the vehicle being overtaken has signalled and is making a left turn, passing on the right is permitted. Tow trucks responding to a police request for assistance, road-service vehicles, and emergency vehicles may also pass on the right. There is also a provision, which has not yet been proclaimed in force, which permits a person with authority, employed on a road-building machine or a road-service vehicle, to direct traffic to pass that vehicle on the right.[2]

The Ministry of Transportation may also designate, through a regulation and appropriate signs, any paved shoulder on a King's Highway for the use of traffic (HTA, ss. 151-152).

One-Way Traffic, HTA, Section 153

A one-way traffic lane is created by designation and by the posting of official one-way signs.

Multilane Highways, HTA, Section 154

A highway may be divided into several clearly marked lanes. A vehicle must be driven within a lane, and shall not change lanes until the driver determines that the lane change can be made safely. Where a highway is divided into three lanes, no vehicle shall be driven in the centre lane, unless the vehicle is overtaking, making a left turn, or the lane is designated and signed for the use of vehicles to travel in a particular direction. Before using the lane, a driver must be sure that the roadway is visible and clear of other traffic for a safe distance.

Any lane may be designated for a particular class of vehicles, for slowly moving traffic, or for traffic travelling in a particular direction where the lane has official signs posted (HTA, ss. 154-155).

Divided Highways, HTA, Sections 156-157

Traffic on a divided highway must stay on the roadway, and move in the direction indicated. Vehicles may not drive on the median, or cross the median to another roadway, unless a crossing has been provided. A road-service vehicle may operate off the roadway, but must stay on its side of the separation between roadways. Reversing is also prohibited on divided highways, on either the roadway or shoulder, where the maximum speed is more than 80 km/h. Emergency vehicles, road-service vehicles, and drivers reversing to render assistance to another driver are exempt from this rule.

Maintaining a Safe Distance, HTA, Sections 158-159

headway
the distance between one vehicle and another behind it

A driver of a vehicle following another vehicle is expected to maintain a safe **headway** between his or her vehicle and the vehicle in front. There is no specific rule setting out a distance in metres; rather, a driver shall have regard to speed, amount of traffic, and highway conditions. However, if the vehicle following is a commercial vehicle travelling more than 60 km/h, it must keep at least 60 m back from the vehicle in front. This rule should not be interpreted to mean that a following vehicle is prevented from drawing closer if it is overtaking and passing another vehicle.

When an emergency vehicle approaches a vehicle from any direction, with emergency signals on, the driver is obliged to pull to the right-hand curb and stop, provided that the vehicle does not stop in an intersection. Where there is more than one lane in the same direction, the vehicle may pull to the nearest curb or side of the road and stop; this means that traffic in the left lane of a one-way highway with two or more lanes in the same direction should pull to the left-hand curb. See figure 4.12.

If a driver is following a fire truck that is responding to an alarm (with its emergency signals flashing), the driver must keep back 150 m.

If an emergency vehicle is stopped on a highway with its flashers on, a driver on the same side of the highway must slow down and observe caution when passing (HTA, s. 159.1). If there are two or more lanes on the same side of the highway as the emergency vehicle, a driver shall move into another lane to leave an empty lane between the lane the driver is travelling in and the stopped emergency vehicle, if it is practical to do so. The fine for failing to slow down and use caution, or to leave a lane between the driver's vehicle and the emergency vehicle on a highway with more than one lane in the direction of travel, is between $400 and $2,000 for the first offence, with increased penalties for subsequent convictions.

Rules of the Road CHAPTER 4 91

FIGURE 4.12 Giving Way to Emergency Vehicle on One-Way Highway

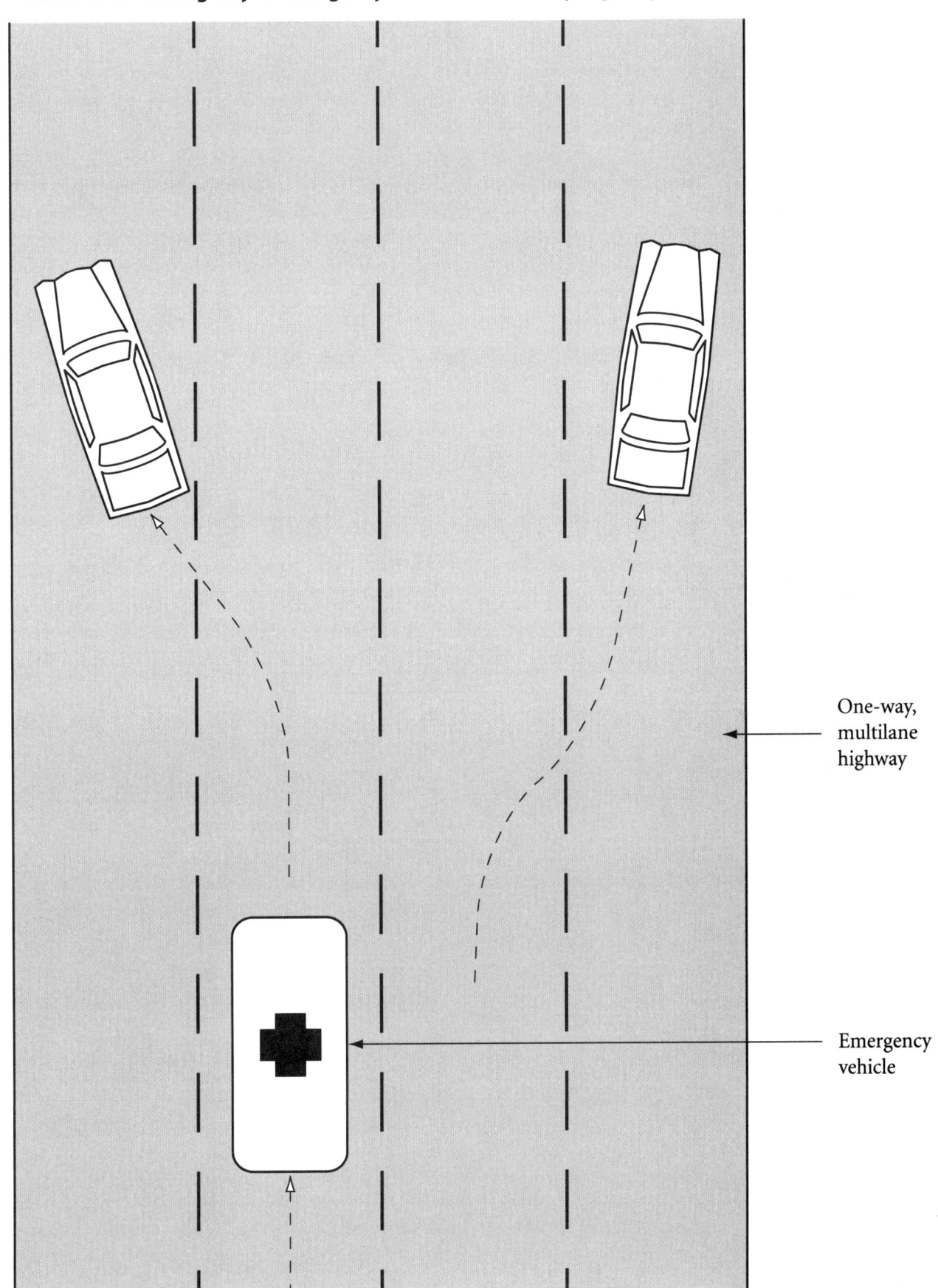

One-way, multilane highway

Emergency vehicle

Towing Other Vehicles, HTA, Sections 160-161 and 178

A vehicle may only tow one vehicle unless the towing vehicle is a commercial vehicle. This means that a sport utility vehicle, no matter how powerful, may not tow a camper trailer and a boat trailer at the same time. Nor shall any person ride as a passenger in any house or boat trailer in tow (HTA, s. 188). Towing a person on skates, a bicycle, skis, sled, toboggan, or toy vehicle is prohibited. Also, a person on a bicycle, skis, sled, toboggan, toy vehicle, or motor-assisted bicycle may not attach themselves to, or cling to, a motor vehicle on a highway (HTA, s. 178). A bicycle that is designed for one person shall not carry more than one person, and a motor-assisted bicycle, by definition, can carry only one person.

Crowding the Driver's Seat, HTA, Section 162

A driver shall not have persons or property in the front seat (if a bench seat) or driver's seat that impedes the management or control of the vehicle. Note that there is no precise or explicit list of prohibitions.

Stopping at Railway Crossings, HTA, Sections 163-164

A driver approaching a railway crossing when a flagperson or signal system is warning of an approaching train shall stop at least 5 m from the nearest rail and proceed only when it is safe to do so. If there is a crossing gate or other barrier, driving around or under it while it is closed or closing is prohibited. Remember that public buses and school buses are subject to special rules regarding precautions at railroad crossings. These are set out in s. 174 and discussed later in this chapter.

Opening Vehicle Doors on the Highway, HTA, Section 165

No one shall open a door on either side of a motor vehicle on the highway before ensuring that this will not interfere with the movement of any other person or vehicle. Similarly, no one shall open a door on the side of the vehicle available to moving traffic, or keep it open longer than necessary to pick up or drop off passengers. In urban areas, it is the violation of this section that often leads to cyclists getting the "door prize."

Approaching and Passing Streetcars, HTA, Section 166

No vehicle or equestrian shall overtake a streetcar standing in the roadway for the purpose of taking on or discharging passengers. All vehicles must stop at least 2 m back from the front or rear entrance of the streetcar on the side on which passengers are disembarking, and may not resume until all passengers have boarded the streetcar or are clear of it. Where a safety zone for loading and disembarking passengers has been created by municipal bylaw, other vehicles are not required to stop. As well, no vehicle shall pass on the left any streetcar that is operating in the centre of the roadway, whether it is standing or moving, except where the streetcar is operating on a one-way street.[3] Municipal fire trucks may pass a streetcar on the left in the course of responding to an emergency.

Approaching Horses Ridden or Driven on the Highway, HTA, Section 167

The driver of a motor vehicle or motor-assisted bicycle is obliged to approach with caution an equestrian, a vehicle being drawn by a horse or other animal, or a horse being led, so as not to frighten the animal or cause injury to persons riding on the animal or in a vehicle drawn by the animal. This section is of little significance in urban areas, but is of some importance where members of some Mennonite and other Anabaptist religious communities use horses and horse-drawn wagons and carriages on highways.

Use of Headlights, HTA, Sections 168-169

When vehicle lamps are required to be lit, the driver shall use the lower beam when approaching within 150 m of an oncoming vehicle and when following within 60 m of another vehicle, except when in the act of overtaking that vehicle. Emergency vehicles and public-utility vehicles may be equipped with high-beam lamps that produce alternate flashes of white light to be used when responding to an emergency.

Parking, Standing, or Stopping, HTA, Section 170

The general rule is that no vehicle shall park, stand, or stop on the roadway where it is possible to park off the roadway. If it is not possible to park off the roadway, there must be a clear view of the vehicle for 125 m in either direction. Exceptions to this rule are made for

- roadways in a city, town, village, township, county, or police village that has bylaws regulating parking, standing, and stopping;
- road-service vehicles, if they have parked safely; and
- vehicles that are so disabled that it is impossible to avoid temporarily contravening these provisions.

On many highways, parking is controlled by regulations or, in built-up areas, by municipal bylaws, so that the basic rule often does not apply. If there is a conflict between a municipal bylaw and a Ministry of Transportation regulation governing a stretch of roadway, the regulation will prevail. If a police officer or municipal bylaw enforcement officer with duties under the HTA finds a vehicle on the highway contravening these provisions, he or she may move the vehicle or have it towed.

A vehicle parked or standing on the highway must be secured to prevent the vehicle from being set in motion. This means that the parking brake or hand brake should be set and, if on a grade, the wheels should be blocked.

There are special safety rules for parking or standing commercial vehicles. If the highway permits a speed in excess of 60 km/h during a time when lights are required, the vehicle shall have a sufficient number of flares, lamps, or lanterns, approved by the ministry, that will display warning lights visible for 150 m for a period of eight hours. Alternatively, the vehicle may be equipped with ministry-approved reflectors. If the commercial vehicle becomes disabled and is parked on the roadway where the speed is in excess of 60 km/h at a time when lights are required, the driver is required to light the lamps or lanterns or set out flares and reflectors, which shall be placed 30 m in advance of the vehicle and 30 m behind the vehicle.

In no case shall a vehicle be parked to interfere with the movement of traffic or the clearing of snow. A violation may result in a fine of between $20 and $100. However, if there is a municipal bylaw that deals with impeding traffic or clearing snow, it shall prevail over the rule in the HTA. In either case, a police officer or by-law enforcement officer may remove the vehicle and store it in a suitable place, and the costs of doing this shall be a lien on the vehicle, enforceable like a civil debt. An unpaid lien may result in the vehicle being sold and the sale proceeds applied to pay off the debt.

Control of Tow Trucks, HTA, Section 171

Because tow-truck operators can monitor police and emergency communications, several may arrive at the scene of a collision, sometimes before police and ambulances. It is not hard to imagine a collision scene where several competing tow-truck operators are attempting to sell their services. In order to make it easier for emergency crews and police to do their jobs at a collision scene, the HTA sets out some rules governing what tow-truck operators may and may not do at a collision scene on a King's Highway:

- No tow-truck operator may make or convey an offer of towing services while the operator is within 200 m of the scene of a collision or a vehicle involved in a collision.

- No tow truck may park or stop within 200 m of a collision scene or a vehicle involved in a collision, if there are already enough tow trucks at the scene to tow vehicles damaged in the collision.

If the police, highway maintenance staff, a person involved in a collision, or other authorized person requests the services of a tow truck, the restrictions in s. 171 do not apply. Note that s. 171 applies to King's Highways (numbered provincial highways), but not to other provincial roads or county or municipal roads. However, counties, regional governments, and municipalities may regulate the activities of tow-truck operators through licensing and bylaws. Contravention of s. 171, where it does apply, may result in fines of between $200 and $1,000 for a first offence. A subsequent offence, within five years less a day of a previous conviction, may result in a fine of between $400 and $2,000.

Racing on Highways, HTA, Sections 172-173

Drag racing and other types of motor vehicle racing on a highway are prohibited, as is "driving ... on a bet or wager." With respect to betting on a driving activity, the language in the Act is broad, and includes betting on a race and other driving activities that might draw bets, such as driving headlong at another vehicle to see which driver will "chicken out" first. A conviction for this offence carries a fine of between $200 and $1,000, and/or imprisonment for up to six months. In addition, a person convicted of this offence may have his or her driver's licence suspended for up to two years. Note that racing bicycles or racing on in-line skates does not appear to be prohibited, because the more explicit term "motor vehicles" is used in defining the offence.

Racing animals on a highway by riding or driving a horse or other animal "furiously" is also explicitly prohibited. Because a horse or other animal may very well not exceed a posted speed limit, evidence of racing would consist of driving or riding the animal "furiously" at or near its apparent top speed.

Street Racing Under the Criminal Code

In June 2006, the federal minister of justice introduced amendments to the *Criminal Code* of Canada that would create a new and separate offence of street racing. Currently, someone involved in street racing can be charged under the HTA as noted in the preceding section. But, if the amendments are proclaimed, those engaged in street racing could be charged under the CC with offences that currently exist: dangerous driving (including dangerous driving causing bodily harm and dangerous driving causing death) and criminal negligence causing bodily harm or death. While dangerous driving by itself could be subject to summary conviction penalties, the other CC offences relevant to street racing carry maximum sentences of between 5 and 14 years, with criminal negligence causing death carrying a sentence of up to life imprisonment.

By its amendments to the CC, the government proposes to create a new substantive offence of street racing, which, for the purposes of imposing penalties, is tied to the existing dangerous driving and criminal negligence offences discussed above. However, under the proposed amendments, the penalties for those convicted of street racing where dangerous driving or criminal negligence is proved will be subject to greater penalties than currently exist for just dangerous driving or criminal negligence. In addition to longer maximum prison sentences, there will be mandatory driving prohibitions for first, second, and subsequent offences with up to lifetime driving bans.

Public Vehicles and School Buses at Railway Crossings, HTA, Section 174

A public vehicle is required to stop at a railway crossing that does not have gates or signal lights. The driver must look both ways, open the door to listen for a train, put the vehicle in gear, and cross the tracks without changing gears. A driver of a school bus must do the same at a railway crossing, even if the crossing is equipped with gates and signal lights.

Safe Operation of a School Bus, HTA, Section 175

A school bus driver who is about to stop to drop off or pick up children or developmentally delayed adults must switch on the overhead red signal lights on the bus, and, as soon as the bus is stopped, the driver must activate the school bus stop arm. These devices must remain on until all passengers who have to cross the highway to the other side or to a median strip have done so.

However, the signalling system is not to be used by the driver

- at an intersection controlled by traffic signals or within 60 m of it; or
- where there is a traffic signal, other than at an intersection, at a sign or roadway marking, indicating where a bus should stop, just before a crosswalk, within 5 m of a traffic signal, or within 60 m of the locations identified here.

Where there is a school bus loading zone, a driver must pull the bus as close to the right-hand curb of the loading zone as possible. The school bus driver need not use the stop signalling system if loading or unloading in a school bus loading zone.

Where a driver of a vehicle approaches a stopped school bus from either direction (other than at a highway separated by a median strip) with its stop signalling system on, the driver must stop before reaching the bus until the signal system is switched off or the bus moves. If a driver approaches the rear of a stopped school bus, he or she must stop at least 20 m behind the school bus. Failure to stop when required can result in a fine of between $400 and $2,000. For a subsequent offence committed within five years less a day of a previous conviction, a fine of between $1,000 and $4,000 may be levied.

School Crossing Guards, HTA, Section 176

A school crossing guard, about to direct children across a highway with a speed limit of not more than 40 km/h, shall display a school crossing stop sign. Where a driver of a vehicle approaches a crossing guard displaying this sign, the driver must stop before reaching the crossing.

Hitchhiking, HTA, Section 177

Hitchhiking is prohibited on all roadways, as is stopping or attempting to stop vehicles to sell the drivers or occupants goods or services. However, if a vehicle is stopped, offering goods and services to the driver or occupants does not appear to be prohibited under the HTA, although it may be prohibited under a municipal bylaw or other legislation.

Pedestrians Walk on the Left, HTA, Section 179

Where there is no sidewalk, a pedestrian walking on the highway shall walk on the left, keeping as close to the curb as possible. This does not apply to someone walking a bicycle, if crossing to the left side of the road is impracticable. Pedestrians may also be prohibited from walking on a highway, and a police officer may require a pedestrian in a prohibited area to accompany the officer to an intersection with the nearest highway where a pedestrian is permitted (HTA, s. 185(3)).

Littering or Depositing Snow or Ice on the Highway, HTA, Sections 180-181

Anyone who litters or deposits any kind of rubbish on the highway is guilty of littering; litter is broadly defined by the Act. Similarly, no one may deposit snow or ice on the roadway without the permission of the ministry or authority responsible for maintaining the road.

Logs to Be Kept by Drivers of Commercial Vehicles, HTA, Section 190

There is a blanket requirement that drivers of commercial vehicles maintain a daily log and carry it when in charge of a commercial vehicle. The log is used to record hours of work and other working-condition matters, as prescribed by the regulations. Similarly, the regulations may exempt various types of commercial vehicle drivers from keeping a log. A log must be surrendered to a police officer on request. Violation of s. 190 or the regulations made under it can lead to a fine of between $250 and $20,000 and/or to a term of imprisonment of up to six months.

VEHICLE EQUIPMENT REQUIREMENTS

Although many requirements with regard to the design and structure of a vehicle are the responsibility of manufacturers, there are some requirements that are the responsibility of the owner or driver of a vehicle. Often, when a police officer stops a motor vehicle, it is apparent that the vehicle does not meet equipment requirements or standards. In such cases, a police officer has some broad powers under s. 82 of the HTA to require the driver or owner of a motor vehicle, including a motor-assisted bicycle, to subject the vehicle to examination and tests as the officer sees fit (HTA, s. 82(2)). If the vehicle is found to be unsafe, it can be ordered off the highway until it is fixed. A written notice to that effect must be issued by the police officer, who also has the power to remove the plates from the vehicle (HTA, ss. 82(4)-(5)). There are similar provisions for commercial vehicles (HTA, s. 82.1). Some of the more frequently encountered equipment requirements are set out below.

Lighting Requirements, HTA, Section 62

The basic requirement is two white or amber lights in front, and one red lamp in back, to be switched on one half-hour before sunset to one half-hour after sunrise, or when fog or adverse weather reduces visibility. Lights must be visible at a distance of 150 m. In addition, front lights must be powerful enough for a driver to see a person clearly at a distance of 110 m. However, for those who would like to install banks of fog or flood lights on the front of a vehicle, the limit is four bright lights in total, including the headlights that are part of the vehicle. Again, the lights must be visible at a distance of 150 m and powerful enough for the driver to see a person clearly at a distance of 110 m. There are slightly different requirements for motorcycles, which must have two lamps: one white, in front, and one red, at the back. If the motorcycle has a side car, there must be two white lights in front on either side of the vehicle and one red light at the rear. The rear light on motorcycles and other motor vehicles must illuminate the number plate.

For long and wide vehicles, there are further requirements of marker lights on the side of the vehicle.

Bicycles are required to have a white or amber front light and a red tail light or reflector, visible for 150 m. The headlight does not have to cast as powerful a light as other motor vehicles do. Its primary purpose is to make the bicycle visible from the front to other road users, rather than to illuminate the roadway for the cyclist. As well, the front forks must have white reflector tape, and the rear must have red reflector tape.

Windshield Wipers and Mirrors, HTA, Sections 66 and 73

All motor vehicles, except motorcycles, are required to have windshield wipers. All motor vehicles must have mirrors that allow the driver to see vehicles behind him or her. Mirrors must allow a view through the rear of the vehicle, unless the driver can see behind his or her vehicle with side-view mirrors on either side of the vehicle. Windshields must be free of sight-line obstructions, such as stickers, and windshields and windows to the right or left of the driver may not be colour-coated in a manner that obstructs the view of the road or conceals a view of the interior of the vehicle.

Mufflers, HTA, Section 75

All motor vehicles, including motor-assisted bicycles with internal combustion engines, must have mufflers, and the use of "cut-outs" and hollywood mufflers is expressly prohibited. Excessive noise from horns or bells on a vehicle is also prohibited.

Radar Warning Devices, HTA, Section 79

Radar warning devices (called "speed measuring warning devices" in the HTA) are illegal and may be seized from a vehicle. No compensation is paid.

Commercial Vehicles—Wheels Becoming Detached, HTA, Section 84.1

In response to public concern about unsafe commercial vehicles on highways, it is now an offence if a wheel becomes detached from a commercial vehicle, or from a vehicle being towed by a commercial vehicle. This is a strict or absolute liability offence; an occurrence will result in a conviction, no matter how careful or diligent the operator and/or owner were in checking and maintaining the wheels.

Helmets, HTA, Section 104

Motorcyclists and their passengers must wear approved helmets while driving on a public highway. Bicyclists 17 years of age and younger must wear approved helmets while cycling on a public highway. Parents of children under 17 shall not knowingly permit or authorize a child to ride a bicycle without a helmet. Bicyclists 18 and over, however, are free to cycle without using an approved helmet, as apparently are those of all ages on in-line skates.

Bicycle helmets must meet prescribed standards, must be worn with a snug chin strap, and must be undamaged, as required by O. reg. 610.

Seat Belts

Motor vehicles in Canada are generally required to have seat belts for the driver and for each passenger seat in the vehicle. The technical requirements for motor vehicle seat belts are set out in the federal *Motor Vehicle Safety Act*, which makes seat belts mandatory equipment in vehicles manufactured after certain dates. In effect, nearly all motor vehicles on the road today have seat belts.

The requirements for child restraint systems and their use are discussed in the next section. For others, the use of seat belts is governed by s. 106 and reg. 613 of the HTA.

The general rule is that the driver and all passengers must use the seat belt provided for him or her, subject to some exemptions spelled out in the HTA and reg. 613. These exemptions are subject to change upon proclamation of amendments that were passed in 1996 but that have not yet been proclaimed. The general areas of exemption are as follows:

- those with medical certificates from a medical practitioner exempting them for seat belt use;
- those whose size or body build makes them unable to use a seat belt;
- those engaged in work where they must frequently enter and leave a vehicle; and
- those engaged in other kinds of work that makes the use of seat belts impractical or dangerous (guards transporting prisoners, ambulance attendants attending to patients and some other emergency workers, and taxi drivers).

A driver must ensure that passengers under the age of 16 are using seat belts as required (either child restraint systems or adult seat belts, depending on the age of the child). Other passengers are personally responsible for using seat belts and may be charged for not using them, unless they are exempt.

Under amendments introduced late in 2006, it is expected that the seat belt use requirement will change so that every passenger must use a seat belt. Currently, the HTA requires the use of a seat belt by a passenger if a seat belt is provided. This created a loophole that exempted passengers from seat belt use when a vehicle had more passengers than it was designed to carry so that there were not enough seat belts available for all.

Although there has been debate about requiring seat belts for passengers in school buses, there are no proposals to require this by legislation. The reason for this is that safety studies do not indicate that school bus passengers would be safer in a collision if seat belts were required.

Child Restraint Systems, O. Reg. 613

Sections 8-9 of O. reg. 613 govern child restraint systems. The regulation creates three categories of children under eight years of age based on size, with corresponding requirements for child restraint systems for each category:

- Infants: children weighing less than 9 kg.

- Toddlers: children weighing between 9 and 18 kg.

- Preschool to primary grade: children weighing between 18 and 36 kg who are less than 145 cm tall.

For each of these categories there is a specific type of restraint system as approved under the *Motor Vehicle Safety Act*. The restraint system must be installed and anchored as required by the manufacturer and by the regulations. It must also be used as required by the manufacturer—that is, all harnesses, belts, and other parts must be properly connected.

Preschool and primary-grade children shall not be secured in a seat for which there is an operating front airbag. This means that these children should not be sitting in the front seat of most vehicles because most vehicles on the road today have front airbags.

Short-term leased vehicles (60 days or less), taxicabs, and ambulances are exempt from these child restraint requirements. However, taxicabs and small buses under contract to transport children to and from school are not exempt. Passenger vehicles imported into or manufactured in Canada prior to January 1, 1974 are also exempt, because the restraint systems cannot be installed in them without substantial modification to the auto frame or body.

HTA ROAD OFFENCE PENALTIES VICTIM SURCHARGE

Any HTA fine, whether for speeding or any other HTA offence, will have added to it a victim surcharge. The victim surcharge is authorized under s. 60.1 of the *Provincial Offences Act*. The surcharge applies not only to fines under the HTA but also to any fine levied for any provincial offence. The surcharge was established as a mechanism to fund programs established to assist victims of crime.

The surcharge is calculated on a sliding scale, rising with the amount of the fine levied, as set out in the table below.

Fine range	Surcharge
$0-50	$10
$51-75	$15
$76-100	$20
$101-150	$25
$151-200	$35
$201-250	$50
$251-300	$60
$301-350	$75
$351-400	$85
$401-450	$95
$451-500	$110
$501-1,000	$125
Over $1,000	25 percent of the actual fine

HTA DRIVING OFFENCES: THE DEMERIT POINT SYSTEM

Under the HTA, the province does not tolerate without penalty those drivers who are constantly being charged with driving offences. Instead, it uses a demerit point system to track violations, assigning demerit points for each conviction of a driving offence or moving violation. The number of demerit points depends on the specific offence; some offences result in more points than others. Although demerit points are deleted from a driver's record after a period of time, once a driver has amassed a certain number of points, progressive corrective measures are taken, starting with a notice, followed by a mandatory interview by a Ministry of Transportation official, and ending with licence suspension. In theory, bad drivers who consistently commit driving offences, even minor ones, can eventually accumulate enough points to be taken off the road if they fail to correct their driving behaviour. Under the graduated licensing system, probationary and novice drivers are watched more carefully than those who are more experienced, and the threshold for intervention by the ministry is lower than it is for fully licensed drivers. For example, probationary drivers who accumulate demerit points during the probationary period may have their probationary period extended.

Set out in table 4.1 are the demerit points that may be given for specific HTA offences. Note that for speeding, just as fines are on a sliding scale, rising with the number of kilometres per hour over the speed limit, so are demerit points: the higher the speed is over the speed limit, the greater the number of points assigned.

TABLE 4.1 Demerit Point System Under O. Reg. 339/94

	Column 1	Column 2	Column 3
Item	Provisions for Offences	Number of Demerit Points	Short Description of Offences for Convenience of Reference Only
1	Section 200 of the *Highway Traffic Act*	7	Failing to remain at scene of accident
1.1	Section 216 of the *Highway Traffic Act*, except where a suspension order is made under subsection 216(3)	7	Driver failing to stop when signalled or requested to stop by a police officer
2	Section 130 of the *Highway Traffic Act*	6	Careless driving
3	Section 172 of the *Highway Traffic Act*	6	Racing
4	Section 128 of the *Highway Traffic Act*; subsection 13(3) of Regulation 829 of the Revised Regulations of Ontario, 1990; any provision of the National Capital Commission Traffic and Property Regulations CRC 1978, c. 1044 made under the *National Capital Act* (Canada) fixing maximum rates of speed and any municipal by-law fixing maximum rates of speed where the rate of speed is exceeded by,		
	(a) 50 km/h or more	6	Exceeding speed limit by 50 km/h or more
	(b) 30 km/h or more and less than 50 km/h	4	Exceeding speed limit by 30 to 49 km/h
	(c) more than 15 km/h and less than 30 km/h	3	Exceeding speed limit by 16 to 29 km/h
5	Subsections 174(1) and (2) of the *Highway Traffic Act*	5	Driver of public vehicle or school bus failing to stop at railway crossings
6	Section 164 of the *Highway Traffic Act*	3	Driving through, around or under railway crossing barrier
7	Subsections 135(2) and (3), clause 136(1)(b), subsection 136(2), subsection 138(1), subsection 139(1), subsection 141(5) and subsections 144(7), (8) and (21) of the *Highway Traffic Act*	3	Failing to yield right of way
8	Clause 136(1)(a), subsections 144(14), (15), (16), (17), (18) and (21), subsections 146(3) and (4) and section 163 of the *Highway Traffic Act*, any municipal by-law requiring a driver to stop for a stop sign or signal light, and the National Capital Commission Traffic and Property Regulations CRC 1978, c. 1044 made under the National Capital Act (Canada) requiring a driver to stop for a stop sign	3	Failing to obey a stop sign, signal light or railway crossing signal

(Continued on the next page.)

TABLE 4.1 (Continued)

	Column 1	Column 2	Column 3
Item	Provisions for Offences	Number of Demerit Points	Short Description of Offences for Convenience of Reference Only
9	Subsection 134(1) of the *Highway Traffic Act*	3	Failing to obey directions of police constable
10	Subsection 134(3) of the *Highway Traffic Act*	3	Driving or operating a vehicle on a closed highway
11	Subsections 199(1) and (1.1) of the *Highway Traffic Act*	3	Failing to report an accident
12	Subsection 148(8), sections 149, 150 and 166 of the *Highway Traffic Act*	3	Improper passing
13	Section 154 of the *Highway Traffic Act*	3	Improper driving where highway divided into lanes
14	Subsections 175(11) and (12) of the *Highway Traffic Act*	6	Failing to stop for school bus
15	Section 158 of the *Highway Traffic Act*	4	Following too closely
16	Section 162 of the *Highway Traffic Act*	3	Crowding driver's seat
17	Clause 156(1)(a) of the *Highway Traffic Act*	3	Drive wrong way—divided highway
18	Clause 156(1)(b) of the *Highway Traffic Act*	3	Cross divided highway—no proper crossing provided
19	Section 153 of the *Highway Traffic Act*	3	Wrong way in one way street or highway
20	Subsection 157(1) of the *Highway Traffic Act*	2	Backing on highway
21	Subsections 140(1), (2) and (3) of the *Highway Traffic Act*	3	Pedestrian crossover
22	Subsections 148(1), (2), (4), (5), (6) and (7) of the *Highway Traffic Act*	2	Failing to share road
23	Subsections 141(2) and (3) of the *Highway Traffic Act*	2	Improper right turn
24	Subsections 141(6) and (7) of the *Highway Traffic Act*	2	Improper left turn
25	Subsections 142(1), (2) and (8) of the *Highway Traffic Act*	2	Failing to signal
26	Section 132 of the *Highway Traffic Act*	2	Unnecessary slow driving
27	Section 168 of the *Highway Traffic Act*	2	Failing to lower headlamp beam
28	Section 165 of the *Highway Traffic Act*	2	Improper opening of vehicle door

(Concluded on the next page.)

TABLE 4.1 (Concluded)

Item	Column 1 Provisions for Offences	Column 2 Number of Demerit Points	Column 3 Short Description of Offences for Convenience of Reference Only
29	Section 143 and subsection 144(9) of the *Highway Traffic Act* and any municipal by-law prohibiting turns	2	Prohibited turns
30	Section 160 of the *Highway Traffic Act*	2	Towing of persons on toboggans, bicycles, skis, etc., prohibited
31	Subsection 182(2) of the *Highway Traffic Act*	2	Failing to obey signs prescribed by regulation under subsection 182(1)
32	Subsection 106(2) of the *Highway Traffic Act*	2	Driver failing to wear complete seat belt assembly
33	Subclause 106(4)(a)(i) of the *Highway Traffic Act*	2	Driving while passenger under 16 fails to occupy position with seat belt
33.1	Subclause 106(4)(a)(ii) of the *Highway Traffic Act*	2	Driving while passenger under 16 fails to properly wear seat belt
34	Subsection 8(2) of Regulation 613 of the Revised Regulations of Ontario, 1990	2	Driver failing to ensure infant passenger is secured as prescribed
34.1	Subsection 8(3) of Regulation 613 of the Revised Regulations of Ontario, 1990	2	Driver failing to ensure toddler passenger is secured as prescribed
34.2	Subsection 8(4) of Regulation 613 of the Revised Regulations of Ontario, 1990	2	Driver failing to ensure child passenger is secured as prescribed
35	Subsection 159.1(1) of the *Highway Traffic Act*	3	Failing to slow down and proceed with caution when approaching stopped emergency vehicle
36	Subsection 159.1(2) of the *Highway Traffic Act*	3	Failing to move into another lane when approaching stopped emergency vehicle—if safe to do
37	Subsection 79(2) of the *Highway Traffic Act*	3	Motor vehicle equipped with or carrying a speed measuring warning device
38	Subsection 154.1(3) of the *Highway Traffic Act*	3	Improper use of high occupancy vehicle lane
39	Subsection 146.1(3) of the *Highway Traffic Act*	3	Failing to obey traffic control stop sign
40	Subsection 146.1(4) of the *Highway Traffic Act*	3	Failing to obey traffic control slow sign
41	Subsection 176(3) of the *Highway Traffic Act*	3	Failing to obey school crossing stop sign

Source: Demerit Point System, O. reg. 339/94, table.

CHAPTER SUMMARY

This chapter is designed to give the reader an overview of the rules of the road created under the HTA in part IX (speed) and part X (rules of the road), and makes further reference to some of the basic equipment requirements in part VI. Each rule is described in general terms, its exceptions and exemptions are noted, and the penalties for offences are noted where that information is provided in the HTA. For the specific elements of a charge, read the relevant section of the HTA that has been identified in the chapter and the relevant regulations.

KEY TERMS

equestrian

headway

NOTES

1. "Municipality," as used here, includes cities, towns, incorporated and unincorporated villages, and police villages. Note that the city of Toronto has been given separate powers in the HTA to regulate speed under the *Stronger City of Toronto for a Stronger Ontario Act*, SO 2006, c. 11.

2. SO 1994, c. 27, s. 138(14), amending s. 150 of the HTA by adding clause (f) to subsection (3).

3. Section 166 also refers to electric railways. This reference is to a form of streetcar referred to as an inter-urban car or radial railway. These were relatively high-speed streetcars, often on their own rights of way, that provided service to suburban areas in the first two decades of the 20th century. The fact that the reference is still there long after the last of the railways had disappeared, and after many statutory revisions, indicates that the HTA is a relatively old statute that has not been thoroughly revised in terms of language and content.

REVIEW QUESTIONS

Short Answer

1. A police officer may direct traffic when he or she considers it reasonably necessary to do so.

    a. Describe three situations in which a police officer would consider it necessary to direct traffic.

    To ensure orderly movement of traffic to prevent injury or damage 134(2)

    b. Could a pedestrian be prosecuted for disobeying a police officer's manual signal for traffic direction? Explain your answer.

    Yes a pedestrian could 134(3)

    c. May a police officer legally direct a motorist through an intersection against a red traffic light? Explain your answer.

    Yes, they are insuring the safety of all vehicles on the road

    d. Give the statutory references for a, b, and c.

2. a. Under what section of the HTA do the police have the authority to close a highway? *Yes a police officer has the power to close off a portion of the highway by posting signs or traffic signalling devices.*

   pg 27

   s 182(2) HTA

   b. What procedure should a police officer follow to close a highway lawfully?

   c. Identify the person or persons who are exempt from the prohibition of operating a vehicle on a closed highway. *Fire Trucks, police vehicles, and ambulances are exempt from operating a vehicle on a closed highway. pg 68*

   s. 128(13) HTA

   Emergency vehicles

3. a. Certain rules govern traffic at uncontrolled intersections (where there are no signs or signals). Describe the two rules that have to do with right of way that are imposed on drivers of vehicles approaching uncontrolled intersections. *A vehicle shall yeild to a car that has already entered in the intersection. If both vehicles enter at the same time, the vehicle on the right has the right of way. pg 72*

   s. 135 HTA

   b. Give the statutory reference.

4. a. The driver of any vehicle or streetcar, on approaching a stop sign at an intersection, is required to stop in one of three places. Identify these places and list them in the proper order.

1st is at stop line, if none then
2nd at cross walk and if neither crosswalk or stop line than
3rd immediately before entering the intersection. pg 72

b. Give the statutory reference.

S 136 HTA

5. After a driver has lawfully stopped at a stop sign, there is a lawful requirement for both the stopped driver and the traffic on the through highway.

a. Describe the requirements for the stopped driver.

To yeild and wait for traffic
Yeild for the right of way traffic

b. Describe the requirements for traffic on the through highway.

Has the requirements of being careful and watching the road

c. Give the statutory reference.

136

6. Section 144 of the HTA describes the rules regarding traffic signals.

   a. This section expands the definition of "intersection" to include an area beyond the area that is enclosed within the extension of the curb lines. What extra area is now included in this definition?

   A car turning right must yeild to all traffic on coming. If there is a crosswalk then the vehicle must wait until the pedestrian has crossed all the way

   b. Where must a driver of a vehicle stop when approaching an intersection, facing a red light?

   The driver must stop at the stop line no stop line stop at the crossline, if neither stop before entering the intersection.

   Same answer →

   c. Where must the driver of a vehicle stop when approaching a red traffic signal at a location other than at an intersection?

   The same applies the driver has to stop at a stop line.

   d. Section 144 describes the rules with regard to traffic signals other than red lights. List these other traffic signals and what they require or permit a driver to do.

   green signal - A driver may proceed through an intersection
   Amber signal - The driver shall stop is they are able to safely
   Red signal - The driver must stop

7. a. What responsibility is placed on the driver of a vehicle who is approaching an intersection and facing a yield sign?

Their responsibility is to yield and wait for any oncoming traffic to pass, and can proceed if its safe to do so.

b. Give the statutory reference.

S 138 HTA

8. a. What responsibility is placed on the driver of a vehicle intending to enter a highway from a private road or driveway?

When entering from a private drive, they must yield to any oncoming traffic and proceed if safe to do so.

b. Give the statutory reference.

S. 139(1)

9. a. List and describe the three duties imposed on a driver of a vehicle at a pedestrian crossover.

1. If someone is about to cross you must stop and wait for them to pass
2. If the person is going to pass from the opposite side of the street, you must stop and let them pass the entire way.
3. No car shall overtake another car waiting at a crosswalk.

b. Give the statutory reference.

S 140 HTA.

10. Section 141 sets out the correct method for making turns at an intersection.

   a. Describe the term "centre line," as it is used in this section.

   Centre line is the line that splits the two sides of the highway. centre of the road way.

   b. Describe the lawful requirements with regard to the position of a vehicle making a right turn at an intersection, including multiple-lane situations.

   The car will stay to the left then make a right turn into the next lane. Then after turn right on the intersection.

   c. Describe the lawful requirements with regard to the position of a vehicle making a left turn at an intersection, including multiple-lane situations.

   The vehicle shall turn to the left lane when it is safe to do so, then turn left on the intersection, when it is safe to do so. There are no oncoming vehicles coming from the other direction.

11. a. Two duties are imposed on the driver of a vehicle on a highway before turning left or right at an intersection, private drive, or from one lane to another. What are those two duties?

   The driver must signal and indicate which way they're going and the second is to apply the brake so they know when to stop.

   b. Give the statutory reference.

   S. 142 HTA

c. Is the driver of a vehicle that is parked or stopped on the highway always required to signal before setting the vehicle in motion? Explain.

Yes a signal is required because if there is a person coming, they need to know which way your going.

d. How may a driver commit an offence with regard to the use of directional signals for an improper purpose?

12. a. Under certain conditions, the driver of a vehicle on a highway is prohibited from turning his or her vehicle so that it proceeds in the opposite direction—that is, making a U-turn. List the conditions that prohibit U-turns.

- on a curve, where traffic approaches from both sides
- on or within 30m of a railway crossing
- on or near a crest of a grade
- within 150 m of a bridge, viaduct or tunnel

b. Under what conditions is a driver prohibited from making a U-turn, regardless of the view?

On the railway

c. Give the statutory references for a and b.

S. 143 HTA

13. a. Driving to the left of the centre of a roadway is prohibited under certain conditions. List these conditions.

view is obstructed
curb and a highway

b. When is a driver prohibited from driving left of the centre of a roadway, regardless of the driver's view?

c. Name the exceptions listed when it is not an offence to drive left of the centre of a roadway.

highway divided into lanes where more than one direction

d. Give the statutory references for a, b, and c.

S. 149

14. Certain duties are imposed on persons driving vehicles on highways when being met or overtaken by other vehicles.

a. Give the statutory reference.

S. 148

b. What must a driver do when meeting an oncoming vehicle?

must pull to the right so the person has the right of way

c. What two duties are imposed on the driver of a vehicle intending to overtake and pass another vehicle going in the same direction?

15. a. What duty is imposed on the driver of a vehicle that is being overtaken by a faster vehicle?

    b. Give the statutory reference.

16. a. The driver of a motor vehicle on a highway may overtake and pass to the right of another vehicle only where the movement can be made in safety and under certain circumstances. What are these circumstances?

    b. Give the statutory reference.

    c. Name two circumstances where it is permissible to pass on the right while going off the roadway.

    only if the shoulder is paved and the car overpassed has a signal on.

17. a. Certain duties are imposed on drivers of vehicles using highways that have been divided into clearly marked lanes. This means a highway with three or more clearly marked lanes, not a highway divided only by a centre line. What must the driver do before moving from one clearly marked lane to another? *maintain in your lane unless it is safe to change to the other lane.*

   b. Give the statutory reference.

   S. 154

   c. Is it permissible to drive straddling the lane markings? Explain.

   d. Give two examples of how lanes may be designated for use of certain traffic by erecting official signs for a particular movement of traffic.

   e. When may the driver of a vehicle lawfully use the centre lane of a highway divided into three lanes?

18. There are six instances in the HTA where the driver of a vehicle must stay on the right-hand side of the road, having regard to the direction in which the vehicle is being driven. Identify these six instances.

   a.

   b.

   c.

   d.

   e.

   f.

19. a. What are the duties imposed on the driver of a vehicle on the approach of an emergency vehicle that is sounding a bell or siren or has a flashing red light on the roof?

   Your responsibility is to pull over to the right

   b. Give the statutory reference.

   S. 159

   c. Under law, what is the minimum distance that a vehicle must remain behind a fire department vehicle responding to an alarm?

   less than 150 m

20. What sections of the HTA prohibit a person from clinging to a vehicle or from being towed on a bicycle, sled, or toboggan or from attaching himself or herself to the outside of a vehicle while riding a bicycle, sled, or toboggan?

21. a. Crowding the driver's seat so as to interfere with the proper management or control of the vehicle is prohibited. Give two examples of how this offence could be committed.

    b. Give the statutory reference.

22. a. The driver of a vehicle approaching a railway crossing must stop when an electrical or mechanical signal device or a flagperson is giving warning of an approaching train. Give the statutory reference.
    S. 163 driver shall stop 5 m from nearest rail.

    b. Where must the driver stop?

    c. When may the driver proceed?

23. a. Two duties are imposed on a person who opens the door of a motor vehicle on a highway. What are these two duties?

It has to be done when it is safe to do so

b. Give the statutory reference.

24. The driver of a motor vehicle on a highway is required to use the lower beam of a multiple-beam headlamp when lighted lamps are required under certain circumstances. Within what distance must the lower beams be used in the following instances?

a. When approaching another vehicle.

when approaching 150 m

b. When following another vehicle.

60 m

c. Give the statutory references for a and b.

S. 168

25. a. Three duties are imposed on the driver of a school bus when picking up or dropping off children or developmentally handicapped adults. What are these duties? *must be sober, must have signal lights on.*

   b. In what two locations on a roadway should the driver of a school bus not activate the flashing red lights when picking up or dropping off children or developmentally handicapped adults?
   60 m of an intersection.

   c. Describe where the driver of a vehicle or streetcar must stop in relation to a school bus when encountering a school bus that is stopped for the purpose of picking up or discharging children or developmentally handicapped adults in the following instances.

      i. When facing the bus.
      before reaching the bus

      ii. When following the bus.
      20 m behind

   d. Give the statutory references for a, b, and c.
   S. 175

26. a. What are the minimum exterior lamp requirements for passenger motor vehicles other than motorcycles?

    4 minimum exterior lights a car can have, seen at 150 m
    S 62 HTA

    b. Are you permitted to take your car to have the windows tinted?

    c. Must all passengers on motorcycles wear helmets?

    All passengers must wear approved head wear while driving
    S. 104 HTA

    d. Give the statutory references for a, b, and c.

27. Create a chart that lists distances (30 m, 150 m, and so on) set out in sections of the HTA that you have studied in this chapter. For each distance listed, summarize the various statutory requirements. (For example, under 30 m, you could describe various requirements governing U-turns and passing other vehicles.)

Discussion Questions

1. Anna is driving on a highway where the posted speed is 80 km/h. The roadway is clear, dry, and level. Anna hears a grinding sound whenever she puts her car into fourth gear, so she decides to leave it in third gear, which allows her to travel at about 55 km/h and no faster. Traffic is beginning to build up behind her, and some drivers are growing impatient, passing in relatively risky places (on curves and hills with limited visibility). Can Anna be charged with any offence? Should she be, in these circumstances? Discuss the pros and cons of charging her.

2. Describe how red light camera systems and photo-radar systems work. What are the arguments in favour of these kinds of systems, and what are the arguments against using them? Is there any evidence to show how effective these kinds of systems are? (This may require some research. You may wish to use a web browser's search engine, such as Google, to search for "photo radar" and "red light camera.")

3. You have been asked to write a code of road rules for bicyclists and users of motor-assisted bicycles. Use the rules of the road as the basis for providing practical guidelines for bicycle and motor-assisted bicycle riders, noting where the rules require drivers of these vehicles to act in certain ways and where these drivers need to adapt to some of the rules of the road that cannot easily be applied to bicycles (making left turns at a multilane intersection, for example).

4. You are assigned the job of writing a guide for the drivers of certain classes of vehicles, alerting them to the exemptions and exceptions to the rules of the road that apply to them and their vehicles. Examining the rules of the road, prepare a guide for drivers of the following vehicles:

    a. road-service vehicles, including self-propelled road-building machinery;

    b. school buses;

    c. ambulances; and

    d. fire trucks.

CHAPTER 5

Highway Traffic Act Offences

CHAPTER OBJECTIVES

After completing this chapter, you should be able to:

- Distinguish between a charge and an arrest, and know the circumstances where a police officer should either arrest and charge, or simply charge, an offender.
- Understand and be able to apply the ticketing procedure in the *Provincial Offences Act* (POA).
- Identify arrestable offences under the *Highway Traffic Act* (HTA).
- Recognize the circumstances that entitle an officer to seize permits, licences, equipment, and vehicles under the HTA.

INTRODUCTION

This chapter introduces the reader to safe stop and pursuit procedures, and some of the more common offences under the *Highway Traffic Act* (HTA). Particular attention is paid to identifying the essential elements of offences and the circumstances required in order to proceed with a charge or an arrest. In reading this chapter, you may wish to refer to a copy of the HTA for the specific language used in creating an offence and as a reference to defences, procedures, and penalties.

MOTOR VEHICLE STOPS

The general public comes into contact with police officers during motor vehicle stops. Public support for the police can be greatly enhanced if this contact is conducted professionally. Make all your vehicle stops **GREAT** stops.

The procedure outlined here provides a guide on how to handle the verbal interaction between the officer and the motorist in situations where there is no risk to the officer.

Greeting
- Greet the driver courteously.
- "Good morning, sir/ma'am" is sufficient.
- Do not make this greeting in the form of a question. "How are you this morning?" invites a sarcastic response.
- Do not ask the driver whether he or she knows why he or she was stopped—this is asking the driver to incriminate himself or herself, and you should already have the evidence needed for the moving violation or you would not have stopped the vehicle. This is not an investigative situation where you have no suspect.

Reason for the stop
- Immediately after the greeting, inform the driver of the reason for the stop: "The reason I stopped you is _____."
- The driver is going to ask you what the problem is anyway, so tell him or her promptly.

Explanation
- Pause *briefly* after telling the driver why you have stopped him or her.
- The pause permits the driver to offer an explanation if there is one.
- Sometimes the driver has a valid explanation and a police officer will look foolish in court if the officer showed no interest in an explanation that could have saved everyone concerned a lot of time and effort.

Accreditation
- After pausing briefly for an explanation, ask the driver to produce his or her driver's licence, vehicle permit, and evidence of insurance.
- If the driver takes the pause as an opportunity for verbal abuse, cut him or her off with your demand for accreditation that he or she must lawfully provide.
- If the driver continues the verbal abuse, sternly repeat your demand for the documents. *Do not engage in an argument.*

Tell the driver what you are going to do and what he or she must do.
- Tell the driver whether you are going to give him or her a ticket.

- If you do not tell the driver what you are going to do, he or she is likely to get out of the car and walk back to the cruiser to ask whether he or she is going to be given a ticket—this makes the stop much more dangerous.
- Tell the driver to stay in his or her car and that you will be approximately five minutes if there are no interruptions.
- When you return to the driver's window, courteously explain the driver's responsibilities with regard to the ticket.

If the above procedure is followed, the motorist often responds with "thank you." The motorist is obviously not thanking you for the ticket, but for the courteous and professional way that you treated him or her. This positive experience is much more beneficial than a stressful experience where the officer is verbally abused. Remember, it is important to pause for an explanation, but cut the driver off quickly with the demand for the driver's licence, vehicle permit, and insurance if the driver becomes verbally abusive.

Recognizing Driver Behaviour

If the police officer is subjected to some verbal abuse, then it is valuable to recognize the driver's pattern of behaviour. Recognizing the behaviour enables the officer to understand the interaction and not personalize the comments. The cumulative effect of personalizing verbal attacks can be devastating for the officer's mental health. The motorist is usually attacking what the officer represents and not the officer personally.

Negative driver's responses can be grouped into six categories.

1. **Indignant Response**

    "Is this all you've got to do?"

    "Why aren't you catching the rapists and murderers instead of stopping me for _____?"

2. **Influencing Response**

    "I'm a good friend of the chief."

    "Is _____ working today?"

3. **Denial of Responsibility**

    "You're absolutely wrong!"

    "I did no such thing!"

4. **Assertion of Discrimination**

    "You stopped me just because I'm _____!"

5. **Insulting Response**

    "You're just a _____!"

    "All you cops are the same!"

6. Emotional Response

"Officer, I can't afford a ticket, I have to feed my kids."

"Officer, my husband will kill me if I get a ticket!"

Other emotional responses by a driver include excessive crying and attempts at flirtation with the police officer.

SUSPECT APPREHENSION PURSUITS

Rather than totally banning police pursuits or allowing pursuits for any infraction, the government of Ontario allows pursuits when specific criteria are met. On January 1, 2000, a regulation under the *Police Services Act*, "Suspect Apprehension Pursuits," O. reg. 546/99, came into force. Highlights of the regulation are set out below.

Highlights of the Suspect Apprehension Pursuits Regulation

- Pursuits may be carried out if a criminal offence is committed or is about to be committed, or if it is necessary to identify a vehicle or a person in it.

- Before launching a pursuit, the officer must determine that there is no alternative method available to prevent an offence or identify a vehicle or person in it.

- An officer must determine that to protect public safety it is necessary to launch a pursuit and that this necessity outweighs risk to the public from the pursuit itself.

- This risk assessment is ongoing and continuous, and if the officer assesses that the risk to the public from continuing the pursuit outweighs the benefit of apprehending a person or vehicle, he or she is obliged to discontinue the pursuit.

- No pursuit should be continued for a non-criminal offence if the identity of the person is known and, once the motor vehicle or the fleeing person has been identified, the pursuit should cease.

- An officer is obliged to notify a dispatcher once a pursuit starts.

- The dispatcher is obliged to notify the communications supervisor and road supervisor, if there is one; either supervisor will further carry out the risk assessment to determine when and if to break off a pursuit.

- Every police service will establish its own pursuit rules that are consistent with this regulation and these rules must be in writing and describe the duties of the officers, dispatchers, and road and communications supervisors, and specify the equipment used in pursuits.

- Firearms should not be used for the sole purpose of stopping a fleeing vehicle.

- Where possible, pursuit in unmarked police vehicles should be avoided.

- A police vehicle may be used to physically stop a fleeing vehicle if the fleeing vehicle has lost control or collided and come to a stop, and is trying to escape after stopping.

- Police vehicles may be used to block a road on which a vehicle is escaping in order to block its escape.

- Police officers must undergo training in techniques of using police vehicles to physically stop fleeing vehicles.

- Where a pursuit involves more than one jurisdiction, the supervisor in the jurisdiction in which the pursuit begins is responsible for decisions about continuing the pursuit, but he or she may hand over responsibility to a supervisor in the other jurisdiction.

- An officer who decides not to initiate a pursuit, or who breaks one off, will not be deemed to have violated the code of conduct.

- All officers, dispatchers, and supervisors must receive pursuit training that is approved by the solicitor general, and all pursuits must be recorded on forms approved by the solicitor general.

The Suspect Apprehension Pursuits regulation is set out in appendix C.

HTA OFFENCES

Charge Versus Arrest

Under the HTA, offenders are usually charged and given a Provincial Offence Ticket, which is more formally known as a Provincial Offence Notice. Because the offender usually produces a driver's licence and vehicle permit, there is no need to **arrest** a person to establish his or her identity, and a ticket can be used for most offences. The procedure for ticketing is described in the *Provincial Offences Act* (POA).

arrest
results when a person's physical liberty is inhibited by conveying an intention to restrict the person's liberty; the actual restraint may involve physical force, although an arrest may occur without the use of force

POA Ticketing Procedure

Reproduced in figure 5.1 are three pages of a multi-layered Provincial Offence Ticket. The complete ticket is reproduced as appendix B at the back of the book. You can photocopy it and practise completing a ticket with the appropriate information and wording for the charge for any scenario you create.

Instructions for Completing a Provincial Offence Ticket

PERSONAL SERVICE OF NOTICE ON DATE OF OFFENCE

There are several pages to what is collectively called the Provincial Offence Ticket. The top page is the Certificate of Offence, which is the copy that is filed with the Provincial Offences Court. Printing firmly on this top page will mark all subsequent pages. The second page is the Offence Notice, which is served on the defendant.

FIGURE 5.1 Provincial Offence Ticket (Top Page)

ICON Location Code / *Code de Localisation RIII*

Offence Number / *N° D'Infraction*

Form 1 Provincial Offences Act Ontario Court of Justice
Formule 1 Loi sur les Infractions Provinciales Cour de Justice de L'Ontario

Certificate of Offence / *Procès-Verbal D'Infraction*

I/Je soussigné(e) ______
(Print name/*nom en lettres moulées*)

Believe and certify that on the day of / *Crois et atteste que le jour de*
Y/A 2 0 | M/M | D/J | Time/ *À (Heure)* M

Name / *Nom* ______
Family/*Nom de famille*

______
Given/*Prénom* Initials/*Initiales*

Address / *Adresse* ______
Number and street/*N° et rue*

______
Municipality/*Municipalité* P.O./*C.P.* Province Postal code/*Code postal*

Driver's licence No./*Numéro de permis de conduire*
PROV. ON

Birthdate/*Date de naissance* Y/A 1 9 | M/M | D/J
Sex/ *Sexe*
Motor vehicle involved/*Véhicule impliqué* ☐ Yes/*Oui* ☐ No/*Non*

At/*À* ______

______
Municipality/*Municipalité*

Did commit the offence of: / *A commis l'infraction suivante:* ______

Contrary to: / *Contrairement à:* ______

Sect./*Art.* ______

Plate number/ *N° de plaque d'immatriculation*	Year/ *Année*	Prov	Make/ *Marque*	Collision Involved/ *Collision Impliquée*	Witnesses/ *Témoins*	Code
		ON		☐ Y/O ☐ N	☐ Y/O ☐ N	

Commercial	CVOR/*CECVU*	CVOR number/ *N° du CECVU*
☐ Yes/*Oui*	☐ Yes/*Oui*	

And I further certify that I served an offence notice personally upon the person charged
Je certifie en outre que j'ai signifié un avis d'infraction en mains propres à l'accusé(e)
☐ On the offence date/*Le jour de l'infraction*
☐ Other/*Autre* ______

Signature of issuing Provincial Offences Officer / *Signature de l'agent des infractions provinciales*	Officer No. / *N° de l'agent*	Platoon/ *Peloton*	Unit/ *Unité*

Set fine of / *L'amende fixée de*	Total payable / *Montant total exigible*	Total payable includes costs and applicable victim fine surcharge / *Le montant total exigible comprend les frais et la suramende compensatoire qui s'applique*
$ $	$ $	

Summons issued. You are required to appear in court on
Assignation délivrée. *vous devez comparaître le*
Y/A 2 0 | M/M | D/J | Time / *À (Heure)* M

Ct. room/*Salle d'audience*
Ontario Court of Justice P.O.A. Office at / *Cour de Justice de l'Ontario bureau L.I.P. à*

Conviction entered. Set fine (including costs) imposed./*Condamnation inscrite. Amende fixée (y compris les frais) imposée*
Y/A 2 0 | M/M | D/J

______
Justice/*Juge de paix*

03-588

DATA BUSINESS FORMS S54496b S54497

FIGURE 5.1 Provincial Offence Ticket (Second Page)

ICON Location Code
Code de Localisation RIII

Offence Number
N° D'Infraction

Form 4 Provincial Offences Act Ontario Court of Justice
Formule 4 Loi sur les Infractions Provinciales Cour de Justice de L'Ontario

Offence Notice / *Avis d'Infraction*

(Print name/*nom en lettres moulées*)

Believes and certifies that on the day of
Crois et atteste que le jour de

Y/A 2 0 M/M D/J Time/ *À (Heure)* M

Name
Nom

Family/*Nom de famille*

Given/*Prénom* Initials/*Initiales*

Address
Adresse

Number and street/*N° et rue*

Municipality/*Municipalité* P.O./*C.P.* Province Postal code/*Code postal*

Driver's licence No./*Numéro de permis de conduire*

PROV ON

Birthdate/*Date de naissance*
Y/A 1 9 M/M D/J

Sex/ *Sexe*

Motor vehicle involved/*Véhicule impliqué*
☐ Yes/*Oui* ☐ No/*Non*

At/*À*

Municipality/*Municipalité*

Did commit the offence of:
A commis l'infraction suivante:

Contrary to:
Contrairement à:

Sect./*Art.*

Plate number/ *N° de plaque d'immatriculation*	Year/ *Année*	Prov	Make/ *Marque*	Collision Involved/ *Collision Impliquée*	Witnesses/ *Témoins*	Code
		ON		☐ Y/*O* ☐ N	☐ Y/*O* ☐ N	

Commercial ☐ Yes/*Oui*
CVOR/*CECVU* ☐ Yes/*Oui*
CVOR number/ *N° du CECVU*

And I further certify that I served an offence notice personally upon the person charged
Je certifie en outre que j'ai signifié un avis d'infraction en mains propres à l'accusé(e)

☐ On the offence date/*Le jour de l'infraction*
☐ Other/*Autre*

Signature of issuing Provincial Offences Officer
Signature de l'agent des infractions provinciales

Officer No. *N° de l'agent* | Platoon/ *Peloton* | Unit/ *Unité*

Set fine of
L'amende fixée de
$ $

Total payable
$ $
Montant total exigible

Total payable includes costs and applicable victim fine surcharge
Le montant total exigible comprend les frais et la suramende compensatoire qui s'applique

Summons issued.
You are required to appear in court on
Assignation délivrée.
vous devez comparaître le

Y/A 2 0 M/M D/J Time / *À (Heure)* M

Ct. room/*Salle d'audience*

Ontario Court of Justice P.O.A. Office at
Cour de Justice de l'Ontario bureau L.I.P. à

Date of service if other than offence date
Date de la signification de l'avis si elle diffère de celle de l'infraction

Y/A M/M D/J

FIGURE 5.1 Provincial Offence Ticket (Last Page)

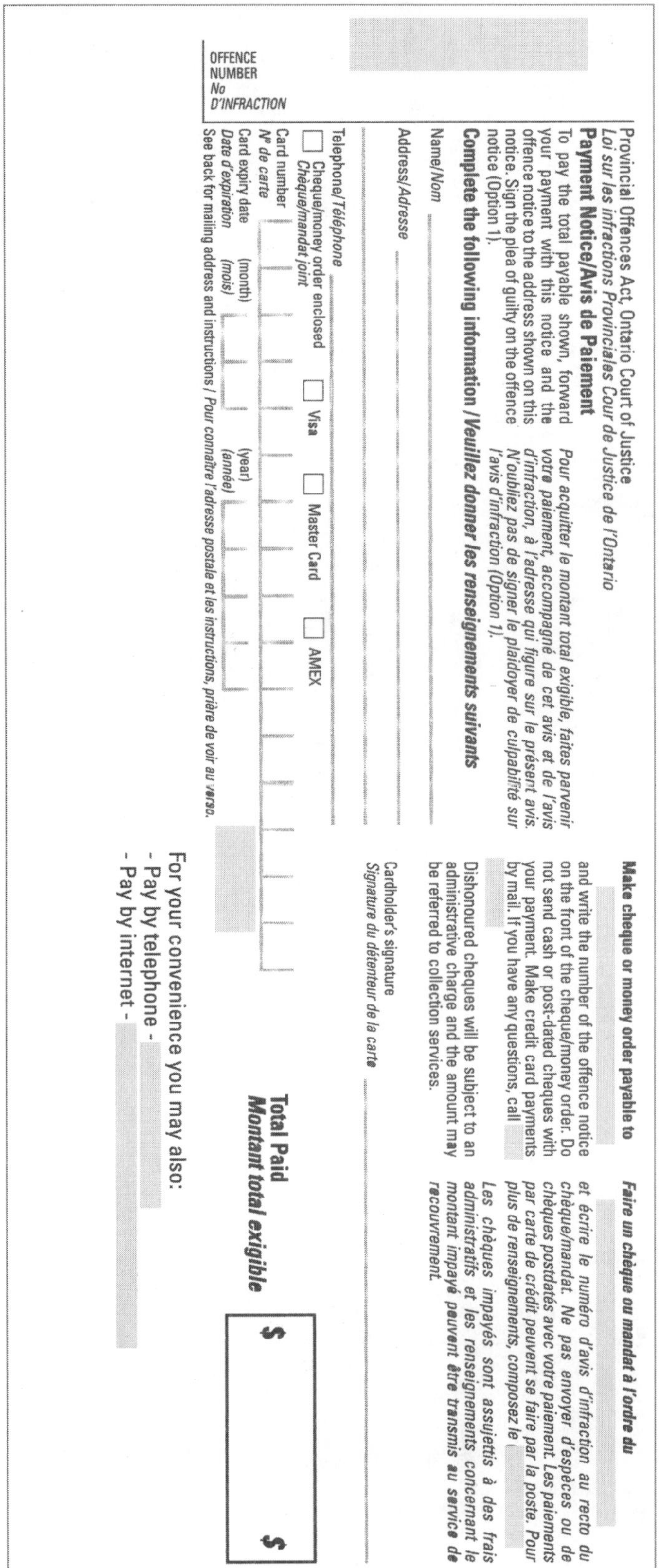

OFFENCE NUMBER
No D'INFRACTION

Provincial Offences Act, Ontario Court of Justice
Loi sur les infractions Provinciales Cour de Justice de l'Ontario

Payment Notice/Avis de Paiement

To pay the total payable shown, forward your payment with this notice and the offence notice to the address shown on this notice. Sign the plea of guilty on the offence notice (Option 1).

Pour acquitter le montant total exigible, faites parvenir votre paiement, accompagné de cet avis et de l'avis d'infraction, à l'adresse qui figure sur le présent avis. N'oubliez pas de signer le plaidoyer de culpabilité sur l'avis d'infraction (Option 1).

Complete the following information /*Veuillez donner les renseignements suivants*

Name/*Nom* ____________

Address/*Adresse* ____________

Telephone/*Téléphone* ____________

☐ Cheque/money order enclosed *Chèque/mandat joint* ☐ Visa ☐ Master Card ☐ AMEX

Card number *Nº de carte*

Card expiry date *Date d'expiration* (month) *(mois)* (year) *(année)*

See back for mailing address and instructions / *Pour connaître l'adresse postale et les instructions, prière de voir au verso.*

Make cheque or money order payable to

and write the number of the offence notice on the front of the cheque/money order. Do not send cash or post-dated cheques with your payment. Make credit card payments by mail. If you have any questions, call

Dishonoured cheques will be subject to an administrative charge and the amount may be referred to collection services.

Faire un chèque ou mandat à l'ordre du

et écrire le numéro d'avis d'infraction au recto du chèque/mandat. Ne pas envoyer d'espèces ou de chèques postdatés avec votre paiement. Les paiements par carte de crédit peuvent se faire par la poste. Pour plus de renseignements, composez le

Les chèques impayés sont assujettis à des frais administratifs et les renseignements concernant le montant impayé peuvent être transmis au service de recouvrement.

Cardholder's signature
Signature du détenteur de la carte ____________

Total Paid
Montant total exigible
$ $

For your convenience you may also:
- Pay by telephone -
- Pay by internet -

Note that the original signature of the issuing officer must appear on both the page that is filed with the court and the page that is served on the defendant.

- Complete the Certificate of Offence (top page) down to and including the certification area. The certification area is the area where the issuing officer certifies that he or she served the Offence Notice (second page) on the person charged. DO NOT sign the certification area yet.

- When describing the offence, make sure to use the short-form wordings for the offence as prescribed in the POA and reproduced in appendix A.

- Enter the set fine as prescribed in the POA.

- Remove the Offence Notice (second page) and the Payment Notice (last page, unlabelled). Now sign the certification area of the Offence Notice. This places an original signature on the Offence Notice that is served on the defendant. Serve both of these pages on the defendant.

- Return to the original Certificate of Offence (top page) and complete the Code Box (top left corner), if it is not preprinted.

- Sign the certification area on the Certificate of Offence (top page). Now an original signature appears on the Certificate of Offence that is filed with the court, and the court may use copies of the signature for other uses.

PERSONAL SERVICE OF SUMMONS ON DATE OF OFFENCE

When an offence has no set fine prescribed in the POA, an Offence Notice with an out-of-court settlement cannot be used. Instead, the defendant must be summoned to Provincial Offences Court and a justice of the peace will determine the fine at the conclusion of the trial.

In this case, a Summons will be served on the defendant instead of an Offence Notice and the Offence Notice will be discarded (see figure 5.2). A Summons can be found at the back of the ticket book that is issued to police officers. There are only three Summonses per book of 25 tickets because they are not used as often as tickets.

- Insert the Summons behind the Certificate of Offence (top page).

- Complete the Certificate of Offence down to and including the certification area. DO NOT sign the certification area yet.

- Enter the next applicable court date.

- Remove the Summons copy. Enter the Certificate of Offence number in the top right corner of the Summons. Enter the location code in the Code Box in the upper left corner, if applicable.

- Sign the Summons and serve it on the defendant.

- In the certification area of the Certificate of Offence, strike out "Offence Notice" and "Avis d'infraction," initial the change, and print "Summons" and "Assignation."

FIGURE 5.2 Provincial Offence Summons

ICON LOCATION CODE
CODE DE LOCALISATION
RIII

FORM 6 PROVINCIAL OFFENCES ACT ONTARIO COURT OF JUSTICE
FORMULE 6 LOI SUR LES INFRACTIONS PROVINCIALES COUR DE JUSTICE DE L'ONTARIO

SUMMONS / *ASSIGNATION*

BELIEVES AND CERTIFIES THAT ON THE DAY OF
CROIS ET ATTESTE QUE LE JOUR DE

Y/A M/M D/J TIME/*À (HEURE)* M

NAME
NOM

FAMILY/*NOM DE FAMILLE*

GIVEN/*PRÉNOM* INITIALS/*INITIALES*

ADDRESS
ADRESSE

NUMBER AND STREET/*N° ET RUE*

MUNICIPALITY/*MUNICIPALITÉ* P.O./*C.P.* PROVINCE POSTAL CODE/*CODE POSTAL*

DRIVER'S LICENCE NO./*NUMÉRO DE PERMIS DE CONDUIRE* PROV ON

BIRTHDATE/*DATE DE NAISSANCE* Y/A M/M D/J SEX *SEXE* MOTOR VEHICLE INVOLVED *VÉHICULE IMPLIQUÉ*

1 9 ☐ YES/*OUI* ☐ NO/*NON*

AT/*À*

MUNICIPALITY/*MUNICIPALITÉ*

DID COMMIT THE OFFENCE OF:
A COMMIS L'INFRACTION SUIVANTE :

CONTRARY TO:
CONTRAIREMENT À :

SECT./*ART.*

PLATE NUMBER
N° DE PLAQUE D'IMMATRICULATION

PROV ON

CODE

CVOR / *CECVU*
☐ YES/*OUI*

THIS IS THEREFORE TO COMMAND YOU IN HER MAJESTY'S NAME TO APPEAR BEFORE THE ONTARIO COURT OF JUSTICE
POUR CES MOTIFS, ORDRE VOUS EST DONNÉ, AU NOM DE SA MAJESTÉ, DE COMPARAÎTRE DEVANT LA COUR DE JUSTICE DE L'ONTARIO

OFFICER NO. *N° DE L'AGENT*	PLATOON *PELOTON*	UNIT *UNITÉ*

Y/A M/M D/J TIME/*À (HEURE)* M

CT.ROOM / *SALLE D'AUDIENCE*

ONTARIO COURT OF JUSTICE P.O.A. OFFICE AT/
COUR DE JUSTICE DE L'ONTARIO BUREAU - L.I.P. À

AND TO ATTEND THEREAFTER AS REQUIRED BY THE COURT IN ORDER TO BE DEALT WITH ACCORDING TO LAW. THIS SUMMONS IS SERVED UNDER PART 1 OF THE PROVINCIAL OFFENCES ACT.
ET D'Y ÊTRE PRÉSENT(E) PAR LA SUITE LORSQUE LE TRIBUNAL L'EXIGERA, DE FAÇON À ÊTRE TRAITÉ(E) SELON LA LOI. CETTE ASSIGNATION VOUS EST SIGNIFÉE AUX TERMES DE LA PARTIE 1 DE LA LOI SUR LES INFRACTIONS PROVINCIALES.

SIGNATURE OF PROVINCIAL OFFENCES OFFICER
SIGNATURE DE L'AGENT DES INFRACTIONS PROVINCIALES

- Enter the location code in the Code Box in the upper left corner, if applicable.
- Sign the certification area on the Certificate of Offence. Now an original signature appears on the Certificate of Offence that is filed with the court, and the court may use copies of the signature for other uses.
- Discard the Offence Notice.

In this case, the Payment Notice (last page, unlabelled) did not have to be served on the defendant because there is no set fine for an out-of-court settlement.

Part III Summons

Section 22 of the POA states:

> Where a provincial offences officer believes, on reasonable and probable grounds, that an offence has been committed by a person whom the officer finds at or near the place where the offence was committed, he or she may, before an information is laid, serve the person with a summons in the prescribed form.

This prescribed form is a part III summons and is used for more serious offences where an increased fine is expected, such as driving without insurance.

Part III Information

Following the serving of a part III summons, a part III information must be sworn to. Section 23(1) of the POA states:

> Any person who, on reasonable and probable grounds, believes that one or more persons have committed an offence, may lay an information in the prescribed form and under oath before a justice alleging the offence and the justice shall receive the information.

Note that an information may be sworn to by any person, whereas the part III summons must be served by a provincial offences officer. An information may be laid anywhere in Ontario.

Arrestable Offences Under the HTA

Some offences in the HTA are also arrestable. This means that the offender can be arrested as well as be charged with the offence. The HTA identifies those offences for which arrest is an option, and there is a list of those offences in this chapter. Usually, where a person is arrested for an HTA offence, he or she will be released once the offence has ceased and proper identification has been obtained so that the offender can be ticketed. As noted earlier, because most HTA offences are committed in the presence of an officer, it is sufficient to simply charge the offender using a ticket where proper identification is produced. Provincial policy is to avoid the more costly and time-consuming arrest procedure where possible. This is why the right to arrest is restricted to situations where there is uncertainty about the identity of a driver or vehicle, where there is the risk of the offence being repeated or continuing, or where further investigation may be required prior to a charge being laid. Who may arrest and under what circumstances is discussed below.

It is important to note that an arrest and a charge are not the same thing, but are separate actions taken against an offender. A charge occurs when an accused is issued a document that accuses the named person of committing an offence, sets out the offence, the location and time of the offence, and the requirement that the accused attend court at a named place and time to answer the charge. An arrest occurs when a person is taken into custody and is not released until certain conditions have been satisfied.

Under the HTA, a person can be charged without being arrested. If a person is arrested under the HTA, he or she is also likely to then be charged.

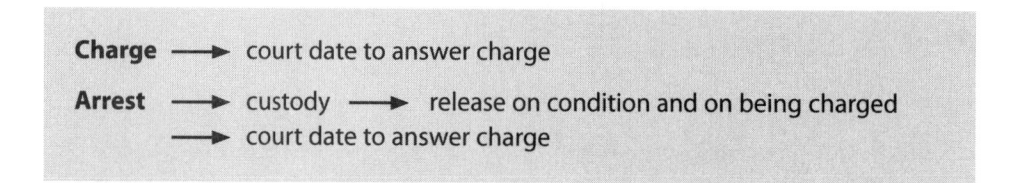

Charge ⟶ court date to answer charge

Arrest ⟶ custody ⟶ release on condition and on being charged
⟶ court date to answer charge

Arrest Authorities, HTA, Sections 217(2) and (3)

According to s. 217(2), the power to arrest a person for violation of specific offences is granted to the following people under certain conditions:

- Any person finding someone committing an offence listed under s. 217(2) may, under s. 217(3), arrest that person without a warrant. This arrest power is sometimes referred to as a "citizen's arrest." The person making the arrest is obliged to use no more force than is necessary to make the arrest, and to turn the person over to the police as soon as possible.

- A police officer, under s. 217(2), may arrest a person without a warrant whom the officer, on reasonable grounds, believes has committed an offence listed in s. 217(2).

The s. 217(2) offences for which an offender may be arrested are as follows:

s. 9(1)	Making a false statement.
s. 12(1)(a)	Defacing or altering a permit, number plate, or evidence of validation.
s. 12(1)(b)	Using or permitting the use of a defaced or altered permit, number plate, or evidence of validation.
s. 12(1)(c)	Removing a number plate without the authority of the owner.
s. 12(1)(d)	Using or permitting the use of a number plate on a vehicle other than the number plate authorized for use on that vehicle.
s. 12(1)(e)	Using or permitting the use of evidence of validation on a number plate other than the evidence of validation furnished by the Ministry of Transportation for that vehicle.
s. 12(1)(f)	Using or permitting the use of a number plate or evidence of validation other than in accordance with the HTA or its regulations.
s. 13(1)	Exposing a number other than that furnished by the ministry on a part of a motor vehicle or trailer in a position or manner that would confuse the identity of a number plate.

s. 33(3)	Failing to identify self on failing to surrender driver's licence.
s. 47(5)	Applying for, procuring, or having in his or her possession the plate portion of a permit issued to him or her while his or her permit is suspended or cancelled or while he or she is prohibited from owning a motor vehicle.
s. 47(6)	Applying for, procuring, or having in his or her possession a driver's licence while he or she is suspended or he or she is prohibited from operating a motor vehicle.
s. 47(7)	Applying for or procuring a Commercial Vehicle Operator's Registration Certificate (**CVOR certificate**) while his or her CVOR certificate is suspended.
s. 47(8)	Operating a commercial motor vehicle for which a CVOR certificate is required without a CVOR certificate in his or her possession or while his or her CVOR certificate is suspended.
s. 51	Operating a motor vehicle for which the permit has been suspended or cancelled.
s. 53	Driving a motor vehicle while his or her driver's licence is suspended.
s. 106(8.1)	Failing to wear a seat belt and failing to identify himself or herself when a police officer asks him or her to do so and believes he or she is 16 years of age or older.
s. 130	Careless driving.
s. 172	Racing on a highway.
s. 184	Removing, defacing, or interfering with any notice or obstruction lawfully placed on a highway.
s. 185(3)	Being a pedestrian on a highway where prohibited.
s. 200(1)(a)	Failing to remain at the scene of a collision.
s. 216(1)	Failing to stop when signalled or requested by a police officer.

CVOR certificate
the Commercial Vehicle Operator's Registration Certificate, which must be held by the operator of a commercial vehicle unless he or she is excluded or exempted under the HTA; requires commercial vehicle operators to comply with safety requirements under the HTA and other legislation

Seizure Authorities Under the HTA

The HTA authorizes the seizure of permits, validation tags, number plates, motor vehicles, driver's licences, and radar warning devices in circumstances set out in the HTA.

PERMITS, VALTAGS, AND NUMBER PLATES

Under s. 14(1), where a police officer has reason to believe that a permit, valtag, or number plate was obtained under false pretenses, is not authorized for use on a particular vehicle or furnished for a particular vehicle, or is defaced or altered, the officer may seize the permit, valtag, or number plate, as the case may be (or all of them, if the facts warrant), and retain them until the facts as to the issue of improper use have been determined.

RADAR WARNING DEVICE

Under ss. 79(3) and (4), a police officer who has reasonable grounds to believe that a motor vehicle is equipped with, or carries, a radar warning device may stop the vehicle, enter it, and search it without a warrant. If he or she finds a radar warning device, it may be seized. If the person accused of having such a device is convicted, the seized radar warning device is forfeited to the Crown. Note that the warrantless search under s. 79(3) does not extend to a search of the body of the driver or other occupants of the vehicle, unless the device is in plain sight of the officer or the search is incidental to an arrest. Searches of vehicles and drivers, generally, are discussed in chapter 6.

DRIVER'S LICENCES

Under s. 48(5), a police officer may take possession of a person's driver's licence when he or she is given a 12-hour suspension.[1] If the person fails to produce the licence or is unable to produce it, the licence is considered suspended and invalid. As well, if a court suspends a person's driver's licence on conviction for an offence where suspension is a possible penalty, s. 212 authorizes a police officer to seize the licence. A police officer may also seize the licence under s. 212 when the licensee is notified of suspension by a police officer.

MOTOR VEHICLES

A motor vehicle may be seized under s. 48(11) on a 12-hour suspension under s. 221(1) when it has been abandoned on or near a highway, and under s. 217(4), when the driver is arrested. The costs of the tow and subsequent storage charges are incurred by the owner of the vehicle.

CRIMINAL CODE DRIVING OFFENCES

In addition to the offences in the HTA, there are a number of driving offences in the *Criminal Code* (CC). Impaired driving, criminal negligence in the operation of a motor vehicle, and other CC driving offences have complex procedural requirements and are discussed in the next chapter, as is criminal procedure under the CC, which differs significantly from HTA procedures, particularly with respect to apprehension.

CHAPTER SUMMARY

This chapter examines HTA offences. It begins with suggestions on how to do a safe motor vehicle stop and conduct a motor vehicle pursuit. Once a decision has been made to charge a person with an HTA offence, the person may simply be charged, or charged and arrested. If a decision is made to charge a person with an HTA offence, the officer may issue a POA Offence Notice. The Offence Notice procedure and the requirements for completing the form are discussed in some detail. We note that some HTA offences are not arrestable offences, while some HTA offences are. The ones used most frequently are described here. The chapter concludes with a discussion of specific right to seize permits, valtags, licences, and even vehicles under the HTA.

KEY TERMS

arrest

CVOR certificate

NOTES

1. A 12-hour suspension may be given when a person blows "warn" on a roadside screening device, blows 50 mg or more on a breathalyzer, or refuses a screening device demand, breathalyzer demand, or demand for a blood sample. A 12-hour suspension and related charges are discussed in more detail in chapter 6.

REVIEW QUESTIONS

True or False?

Place a "T" next to the statement if it is true, or an "F" if it is false.

_____ 1. A summons is used when an offence has no set fine prescribed in the *Provincial Offences Act*, because a justice of the peace must determine the fine.

_____ 2. There is no difference between a charge and an arrest under the HTA.

_____ 3. Defacing or altering a permit, number plate, or evidence of validation (s. 12(1)(a)) is not an arrestable offence under the HTA.

_____ 4. A person whose Ontario driver's licence is suspended for unpaid fines and who is driving a car on a city street in Ontario is guilty of the offence of disqualified operation of a motor vehicle.

_____ 5. If you suspect that a person's number plate has been altered, you can seize it under s. 14(1) of the HTA.

_____ 6. A person whose driver's licence is suspended for demerit points in Ontario is guilty of a provincial offence if he or she drives his or her car on a highway in Ontario.

Short Answer

Briefly answer the following questions.

1. List five rules from the Suspect Apprehension Pursuits Regulation.

    a.

    b.

    c.

    d.

    e.

2. List five offences under the *Highway Traffic Act* for which an offender may be arrested.

    a.

    b.

    c.

    d.

    e.

3. List the five steps an officer should use when communicating with a motorist during a vehicle stop.

   a.

   b.

   c.

   d.

   e.

Discussion Question

Recognizing abusive driver behaviour is a method of depersonalizing it. Why is this important? What are some of the categories of driver reactions to a vehicle stop?

CHAPTER 6

Impaired Driving and Other Criminal Code and Highway Traffic Act Offences

CHAPTER OBJECTIVES

After completing this chapter, you should be able to:

- Understand the role of case law in lower courts involving provincial offences, and in courts involving *Criminal Code* (CC) offences.

- Know the essential elements of some of the more common driving offences in the CC.

- Identify and understand the essential elements of the offences of being impaired and being "over 80" that must be proved to obtain a conviction.

- Know the function and purpose of an approved screening device and a breathalyzer and the relationship between these two instruments in providing evidence of alcohol-related driving offences.

- Understand and appreciate the kind of evidence needed to support "reasonable suspicion" and "reasonable grounds to believe" that a driver is either impaired or "over 80."

- Know when a lawful demand may be made for a breath sample for an approved screening device or breathalyzer or for a blood sample in connection with alcohol-related driving offences.
- Know when the grounds exist for a blood warrant, and what facts must be proved to satisfy a justice of the peace that a warrant should be issued.
- On assessing evidence, determine whether an impaired or "over 80" charge can be laid.
- Know under what circumstances a 12-hour or 90-day suspension can be made under the *Highway Traffic Act* (HTA).
- Understand the essential elements of the offence of driving while disqualified and be able to apply that understanding to determine the various circumstances in which that charge can be laid.
- Understand the difference between an HTA suspension and a CC prohibition and the importance of that distinction.
- Know when a search warrant is required under the CC to search a vehicle.

OVERVIEW OF JURISDICTION OVER MOTOR VEHICLE LAW

General: Provincial Law and Criminal Law

Laws governing regulations and offences involving motor vehicles are contained in the Ontario *Highway Traffic Act* (HTA) and in regulations made under that Act, as we have noted in earlier chapters. Some of the more serious operating offences are contained in the *Criminal Code* of Canada (CC), a federal statute.

Laws governing the rights of citizens to sue for personal injury and property damage arising from a motor vehicle collision are governed by provincial negligence law and motor vehicle insurance law. Although negligence and insurance law are not concerns of this text, a police officer, like any other citizen, can be summonsed to give evidence at a trial in a civil action for negligence, and his or her oral evidence, the contents of the officer's notebook, and the contents of an accident report prepared by the officer may all be relevant to the issues in a civil trial. An officer who is served with a summons issued under the Ontario *Rules of Civil Procedure* should notify his or her superiors and follow department procedures for responding to a civil summons.

THE IMPORTANCE OF CASE LAW IN INTERPRETING CRIMINAL LAW STATUTES

Leaving aside negligence law, you should always be aware of whether the motor vehicle law you are dealing with is federal or provincial because the prosecution procedures are different. Another distinction has to do with how case law may change the interpretation of the HTA or the CC. Most HTA cases are heard by justices of the peace (JPs). A JP may give a decision, but rarely provides written reasons for that decision.

This is important because, in many cases, judges must follow the interpretations that previous judges have made in their written reasons. Consequently, there may be a good deal of variation in how a section of the HTA is interpreted from one JP's court to another. This problem is compounded by the fact that there are few appeals of JPs' decisions, which might result in written reasons being given, because an appeal is too expensive to be worth the bother in most cases. Given the absence of HTA case law as a guide to interpretation of the HTA, in some cases there is a risk of inconsistent decisions—one JP may be quite unaware of how another is ruling, particularly where there is little case law to serve as an interpretive aid.

Cases under the CC are another matter. Cases involving impaired driving or other criminal offences under the CC are usually heard by a judge of the Ontario Court of Justice, or, depending on the nature of the CC offence, by an Ontario Superior Court judge, with or without a jury. At this level, the court procedures are much more formal, and judges often give written reasons for judgment that other judges and lawyers read. Written reasons for judgment are important because

- they may become precedents (that is, court decisions made for the first time on new points of law) for interpreting the CC or other laws;

- they are treated as persuasive by other judges at the same court level—that is, the reasoning in the written reasons for judgment is likely to be followed by other judges in future cases in the same court; and

- if a decision is appealed at trial to an appellate court, the appellate court's decision and its reasons for judgment become not just persuasive but binding on lower trial courts hearing similar cases; this means that lower courts must follow the decision in an appellate court.

What all this means is that CC cases are more likely to involve situations where the meaning and interpretation of a section of the CC has been changed or affected by written reasons interpreting that section. The meaning of a section of the CC is therefore not static, but changes as new case law continues to interpret the meaning of the section. This means that you have to be aware that a case decision may affect how you deal with impaired drivers or other offenders. It is not your responsibility as an officer to research or interpret case law, but it is your responsibility to be aware of the effect of case law changes on what you have to do to secure convictions.

The area of impaired driving has been a fertile field for judges and lawyers in developing case law that interprets the various CC sections dealing with impaired driving. One reason for this is that CC driving offences are common in the courts, and involve a broader cross-section of the population than is the case for most criminal offences. Many of those charged with a CC driving offence have the resources to hire good lawyers and mount technical defences. The result is a tremendous amount of case law on drunk driving offences, much of which comes from provincial appellate courts and the Supreme Court of Canada. We will refer to some of the more important cases in the course of our discussion of CC drunk driving offences.

Criminal Code Procedure: An Overview

Offences under the CC, such as offences involving impaired driving, are not provincial offences; they are criminal offences. CC offences are dealt with through procedures and courts that are different from those used for HTA offences. Most CC offences, including impaired driving offences, are dual procedure offences (also called mixed or hybrid offences). This means that the Crown initially has the right to decide to try the offence as a summary conviction offence or as an indictable offence. If the Crown chooses to proceed summarily, as it usually does, the trial is held before a judge of the Ontario Court of Justice.

If the Crown elects to try the offence as an indictable offence, the procedural route depends on whether the offence falls under s. 553, 536, or 469 of the CC. The following list describes the procedure for a "553" offence, a "536" offence, and a "469" offence:

- If the offence is listed as a "553" offence, the trial procedure is the same as if the Crown had elected to proceed summarily, but the Crown can ask for a longer sentence than it could have asked for if it had proceeded summarily.

- If the offence is a "536" offence, the accused has the right to elect to be tried by an Ontario Court judge alone, or by a Superior Court judge alone, or by a Superior Court judge and jury.

- If the offence is a "469" offence—most of which are very serious, such as murder—the trial goes before a Superior Court judge and jury.

The procedural routes for CC offences are illustrated in figure 6.1.

CRIMINAL CODE MOTOR VEHICLE OFFENCES

As we have noted, laws about driving motor vehicles are within the jurisdiction of the province, under the division of powers set out in ss. 91 and 92 of the *Constitution Act, 1867*. All driving offences are provincial offences.

However, criminal offences involving drinking and driving or negligence causing serious injury or death using motor vehicles, vessels, aircraft, and railway equipment have been held to be constitutionally valid criminal law under the exercise of the federal power over criminal law and procedure as set out in s. 91(27) of the *Constitution Act, 1867*. This is because these offences are not merely about driving, but about behaviour deemed to be criminal. Furthermore, the offences in the CC are different from and generally broader than the offences in the HTA.

The definition of motor vehicle in these "operation" and "care and control" offences (CC, s. 253) is found in s. 2 of the CC. It is much broader than and quite different from the definition in the HTA. The CC definition includes any land vehicle that is drawn, propelled, or driven by any means other than muscular power, except railway equipment. The CC definition, therefore, includes snowmobiles, farm tractors, self-propelled implements of husbandry (that is, reapers and combines), road-building machines, and traction engines, whether operated on a highway or not.

This means that a person can be convicted of impaired operation of a farm tractor in his or her own back field, although such a charge would be unusual in the absence of a complaint related to danger to other persons or property. Another way of putting this is that the CC offences are "anywhere" offences—that is, they can be committed anywhere.

Definitions of "Motor Vehicle"

CC: A motor vehicle, as defined in the CC, includes any land vehicle that is drawn, propelled, or driven by any means other than muscular power,

Except railway equipment.

HTA: A motor vehicle, as defined in the HTA, includes automobiles, motorcycles, motor-assisted bicycles (unless otherwise indicated), and any other vehicle propelled or driven by power other than muscular power,

Except motorized snow vehicles,
farm tractors,
self-propelled implements of husbandry,
road-building machines,
streetcars or motor vehicles on rails, and
traction engines.

FIGURE 6.1　Procedural Routes for CC Offences

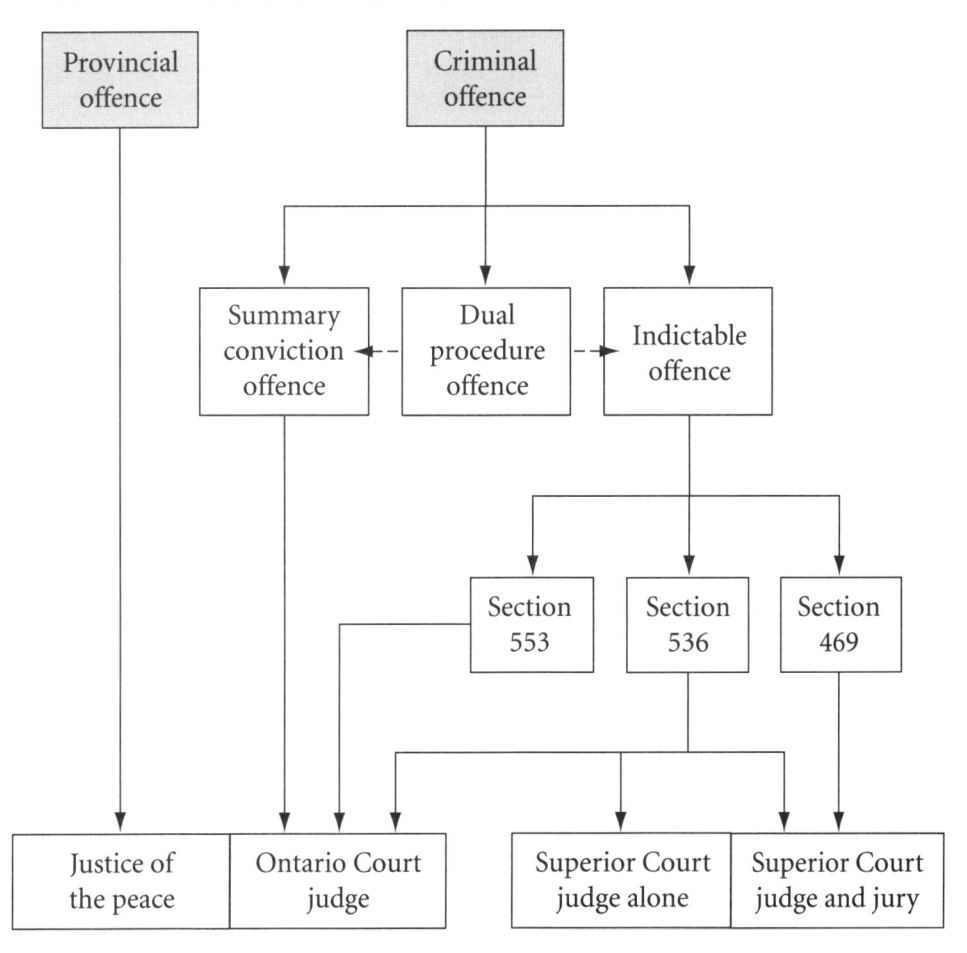

```
                Provincial              Criminal
                 offence                offence
                    │                      │
                    │            ┌─────────┼─────────┐
                    │            ▼         ▼         ▼
                    │      ┌──────────┐ ┌──────┐ ┌──────────┐
                    │      │ Summary  │ │ Dual │ │Indictable│
                    │      │conviction│◄─┤proc. ├─►│ offence │
                    │      │ offence  │ │offence│ │          │
                    │      └──────────┘ └──────┘ └──────────┘
                    │            │                    │
                    │            │        ┌───────────┼───────────┐
                    │            │        ▼           ▼           ▼
                    │            │    ┌────────┐ ┌────────┐ ┌────────┐
                    │            │    │Section │ │Section │ │Section │
                    │            │    │  553   │ │  536   │ │  469   │
                    │            │    └────────┘ └────────┘ └────────┘
                    ▼            ▼                    ▼           ▼
              ┌──────────┐ ┌──────────┐         ┌──────────┐ ┌──────────┐
              │Justice of│ │ Ontario  │         │ Superior │ │ Superior │
              │ the peace│ │  Court   │         │  Court   │ │  Court   │
              │          │ │  judge   │         │judge alone│ │judge and jury│
              └──────────┘ └──────────┘         └──────────┘ └──────────┘
```

Criminal Negligence, Dangerous Driving, and Other Criminal Code Offences Involving Motor Vehicles

As you will see later in this chapter, offences concerned with impaired driving involve especially complex procedures for investigating, apprehending, and charging someone. For that reason, impaired driving offences are discussed separately from other CC driving offences. Some of the other CC offences that drivers can commit in motor vehicles are discussed in the box below.

> ## Common CC Motor Vehicle Driving Offences
>
> - criminal negligence causing bodily harm and criminal negligence causing death, ss. 220 and 221
> - dangerous operation of a motor vehicle, s. 249
> - flight from a pursuing peace officer causing death or bodily harm, s. 249.1
> - failure to stop at the scene of an accident, s. 252
> - street racing, ss. 249.2-249.4

CRIMINAL NEGLIGENCE CAUSING BODILY HARM AND CRIMINAL NEGLIGENCE CAUSING DEATH, CC, SECTIONS 220 AND 221

Criminal negligence is defined in s. 219 as an act, or omission to perform a duty imposed by law, that shows reckless disregard for the lives or safety of other persons. Section 220 sets out the penalty for causing death by criminal negligence, and s. 221 sets out the penalty for causing bodily harm. Both offences are indictable, and can carry lengthy prison sentences, including life imprisonment for criminal negligence causing death. It is clear that the breach of a provincially imposed duty is not itself sufficient to support a charge of criminal negligence. Nor is mere civil negligence—the failure to meet the standard of care expected of a reasonably prudent person. Instead, indifference is the standard: the accused knew or ought to have known that the act or omission could threaten the life or safety of another person but acted without regard for the consequences. It is not necessary to prove that the act was willful or deliberate; indifference is sufficient. However, it is not clear from the cases whether indifference is an objective standard (determining whether a reasonable person would assume that the accused acted wilfully in light of all the circumstances) or a subjective one (proving that the accused was in fact indifferent in deciding to act or failing to act).[1] In addition to the mental element, the accused's behaviour must constitute a marked departure from that expected of a reasonable person in the circumstances.

Although these two offences often arise in cases involving the operation of a motor vehicle, they do not require the accused to be driving a motor vehicle or have a motor vehicle in his or her care or control. The offence is much broader than that, encompassing all kinds of situations.

DANGEROUS OPERATION OF A MOTOR VEHICLE, CC, SECTION 249

An accused commits the offence of dangerous operation of a motor vehicle, or dangerous driving, when he or she operates a motor vehicle in a manner that is dangerous to the public. Determining whether the operation of the vehicle is dangerous to the public requires consideration of the surrounding circumstances:

- the nature, condition, and use of the place at which the motor vehicle is being operated, and
- the amount of traffic that at the time is, or might reasonably be expected to be, at that place.

Dangerous driving is a mixed or hybrid offence if no one is injured, but, if the accused causes bodily harm or death, the offence is deemed to be indictable and carries correspondingly greater penalties. Dangerous driving is deemed to be a lesser and included offence in charges of criminal negligence causing death (CC, s. 220), bodily harm (CC, s. 221), or manslaughter (CC, s. 236). There is a specific and related offence for impaired driving causing death or bodily harm (CC, s. 255).

To obtain a conviction for dangerous driving, there is no need to prove that anyone was harmed. It is sufficient to show that someone might have been harmed.[2] However, the conduct required for conviction must be proven to be a marked departure from prudent conduct, not just mere carelessness or negligence, which might be enough for conviction on an HTA offence such as careless driving, or for a finding of negligence in a civil case for damages.[3]

FLIGHT FROM A PURSUING PEACE OFFICER CAUSING DEATH OR BODILY HARM, CC, SECTION 249.1

An accused commits this offence when he or she operates a motor vehicle while being pursued by a peace officer in a motor vehicle. If the accused, in order to escape the pursuit, fails to stop as soon as practicable, then the offence is complete. It does not matter whether the accused stopped at a later point if he or she failed to stop at the first reasonable opportunity. The offence is a mixed or hybrid offence, unless the accused has caused death or bodily harm, in which case the offence is indictable and carries increased penalties. A driving prohibition order may also be imposed. It is a lesser and included offence for criminal negligence causing bodily harm or death, and also for manslaughter.

FAILURE TO STOP AT THE SCENE OF AN ACCIDENT, CC, SECTION 252

An accused commits this offence if he or she has the care or control of or is in charge of a motor vehicle that is involved in an accident with a person, vehicle, aircraft, vessel, or cattle in the charge of someone. If the accused fails to stop, provide identification, and, where any person has been injured or appears to require assistance, offer assistance, the offence is complete. For this offence, if the accused knows that a person has been injured or appears to require assistance, the offence is a mixed offence. However, the offence is indictable if the accused knows that bodily harm has occurred, or knows that someone involved in the accident is dead, or knows that bodily harm has occurred and the accused is reckless as to whether death might occur and it, in fact, does occur. The accused can be convicted once it is shown that he or she failed to perform the duties described above (stop, identify himself or herself, and offer assistance when necessary). However, in the case of an indictable offence, a conviction will not follow if the prosecution proves only that the accused should have known that someone suffered bodily harm or death. To obtain a conviction, the prosecution must show that the accused knew that someone had suffered bodily harm or death. Some cases also indicate that the accused will not be convicted of failing to stop if the act causing the collision was deliberate rather than accidental; in such cases, other charges, including assault or manslaughter, could be laid.[4]

STREET RACING

Street racing is now a CC offence, with greater penalties if there are convictions for dangerous driving, criminal negligence causing death, or criminal negligence causing bodily harm. The penalties also increase for repeat offenders. Driving prohibition orders can also be imposed on repeat offenders, up to and including a lifetime ban. Street racing is discussed in conjunction with a similar HTA offence in chapter 4.

Impaired Driving: Some Basic Terms and Concepts

We now turn to those sections of the CC that address the issue of impaired driving. Before we examine the law associated with impaired operation of a motor vehicle, it is necessary to understand the following concepts.

Ability Impaired

Proof of impairment is established through a *description of a person's condition* due to the consumption of alcohol or a drug. The description must convince the court that the person so described does not have the ability to operate a motor vehicle safely because he or she has been drinking or because he or she ingested a drug. The degree of impairment depends on a person's tolerance to alcohol. Some people are impaired after consuming just a couple of drinks or a small amount of a drug, while others require many drinks or larger amounts of a drug before they become impaired.

> **NOTE**
> There is a crucial distinction between impairment generally and impairment of a person's ability to operate a motor vehicle. When a person has a drink, his or her ability to drive is not necessarily impaired. The alcohol might impair his or her ability to, say, thread a needle but not impair his or her ability to drive: *R v. Andrews* (1996), 104 CCC (3d) 192 (Alta. CA).

Over 80 Milligrams

This is a *measure* of the amount of alcohol in 100 ml of a person's blood. It is unlawful to operate a motor vehicle with more than 80 mg of alcohol per 100 ml of blood.

This measurement simply proves whether you are over the legal limit and should not be confused with proof of impairment. It is possible to be "over 80" and not be impaired, or be impaired and not be "over 80."

> **NOTE**
>
> It is not necessary to prove that the accused knew or ought to have known that he or she was or might be "over 80." Criminal intent is proved if it is shown that the accused voluntarily consumed alcohol: *R v. Murray* (1985), 22 CCC (3d) 502 (Ont. CA).

Operating

Operating means that the person is *driving* a motor vehicle, steering a boat, or piloting an aircraft—that is, the vehicle is under way with the person directing its movement.

Care or Control

"Care or control" means that the person is not operating the motor vehicle, vessel, or aircraft, but is *using* the vehicle or its equipment, or is involved in some activity that risks putting the vehicle in motion. For example, a person who gets into the driver's seat of a car, puts the key in the ignition, and turns the engine on, but does not drive it, would be considered to have the care or control of the vehicle.

> **NOTE**
>
> The mere fact that a person has custody of a vehicle is not sufficient to convict the accused. There must be some risk that the vehicle could be set in motion: *R v. Decker* (2002), 162 CCC (3d) 503 (Nfld. CA).

Reasonable Suspicion

Reasonable suspicion refers to a hunch or suspicion for which there is some rational basis to suspect that someone has been consuming alcohol. The odour of an alcoholic beverage on someone's breath is sufficient evidence to form reasonable suspicion.

> **NOTE**
>
> Reasonable suspicion applies only to the issue of whether the accused has alcohol in his or her body, and not to operation or control of a vehicle; the latter element must be proved as a fact: *R v. Swetiorzecki* (1995), 97 CCC (3d) 285 (Ont. CA).

Reasonable Grounds to Believe

Reasonable grounds to believe refers to a set of circumstances that would satisfy an ordinary, cautious, and prudent person that there is reason to believe that certain facts are true, and which goes *beyond mere suspicion*. In other words, establishing reasonable grounds to believe requires much more evidence than the evidence that would establish reasonable suspicion. For example, in addition to smelling alcohol on a driver's breath, an officer would need to make other observations, such as the driver's difficulty keeping his or her balance when getting out of the car, in order to have reasonable grounds to believe that the driver is impaired. Observations of more than one of these behaviours or acts are usually required.

> **NOTE**
>
> Reasonable grounds to believe need not be based on the accused's operation of a vehicle. They may be based on the officer's observance of the accused's condition, or on information supplied by third parties: *R v. Strongquill* (1978), 43 CCC (2d) 232 (Sask. CA).

Belief Versus Suspicion

A police officer will often be challenged in court about his or her reasonable grounds to believe. The challenge will usually be about whether the officer had enough evidence to have "reasonable grounds for believing" or whether there was only enough evidence to support a "reasonable suspicion."

Reasonable suspicion is not usually enough to provide a lawful authority for police officers to take action. Reasonable suspicion is limited to the authority to demand a breath sample using an approved screening device. Police officers cannot arrest someone on reasonable suspicion that he or she committed an indictable offence.

Recall that reasonable grounds to believe refers to a set of facts or circumstances that would satisfy an ordinary, cautious, and prudent person that there is reason to believe those facts are true, and which goes beyond mere suspicion. This definition indicates that belief is more than suspicion, and should be based on more information. Defence counsel will always question whether the police officer had enough evidence to convince an average person, other than himself or herself.

Defence counsel will also challenge the officer on the truthfulness of the evidence that supports reasonable grounds to believe. This evidence often consists of a police officer's subjective impressions (odour of alcohol or slurred speech) and is easier to attack.[5] The officer's testimony needs to include very specific and detailed examples of how the accused exhibited those characteristics. However, the more objective evidence gathered from the approved screening device, breathalyzer, or blood test will corroborate the officer's subjective impressions.

Approved Screening Device, CC, Section 254

An approved screening device is an instrument that indicates whether there are reasonable grounds to believe that a person is "over 80." In order to demand a breath sample for the screening device, a police officer must have a reasonable suspicion that a person has been consuming alcohol. If the person fails the screening device test, the officer can turn reasonable suspicion that a person has been drinking into reasonable grounds to believe that the person is "over 80." This instrument does not indicate the exact amount of alcohol in the blood, but places the person in a "pass," "warn," or "fail" category.

> **NOTE**
>
> It is not necessary to lead expert evidence on the capabilities of an approved screening device. It is sufficient if a certified technician can explain what it does and can testify that it was in good working order: *R v. Delorey* (2004), 188 CCC (3d) 372 (NSCA).

Breathalyzer, CC, Section 258

The breathalyzer is a more sophisticated instrument than the screening device. The breathalyzer accurately measures the amount of alcohol in a person's blood, whereas the screening device merely identifies drivers who may be "over 80." In order for a police officer to demand breath samples for a breathalyzer, he or she must have reasonable grounds to believe either that a person is "over 80" or that a person's ability is impaired. See figures 6.2 and 6.3.

FIGURE 6.2 Measuring Reasonable Suspicion and Reasonable Grounds to Believe

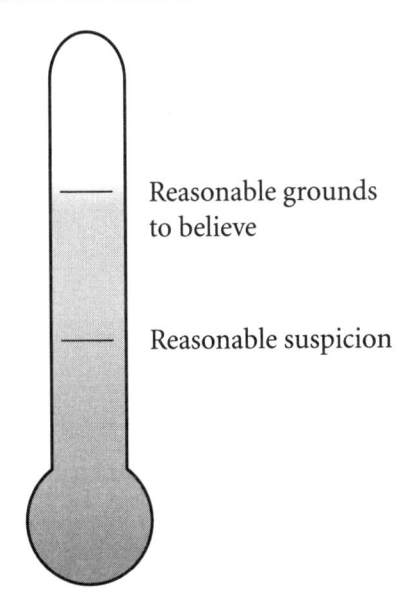

FIGURE 6.3 Stages of Alcoholic Influence/Intoxication

Blood Alcohol Concentration (mg per 100 ml)	Stage of Alcoholic Influence	Clinical Signs/Symptoms
10-50	Sobriety	◆ Influence/effects usually not apparent or obvious ◆ Behaviour nearly normal by ordinary observation
30-120	Euphoria	◆ Mild euphoria, sociability, talkativeness ◆ Increased self-confidence; decreased inhibitions ◆ Diminished attention, judgment, and control ◆ Some sensory-motor impairment ◆ Slowed information processing
90-250	Excitement	◆ Emotional instability; loss of critical judgment ◆ Impairment of perception, memory, and comprehension ◆ Decreased sensory response; slower reaction time ◆ Reduced visual acuity and peripheral vision; slow glare recovery ◆ Sensory-motor incoordination; impaired balance; slurred speech; vomiting; drowsiness
180-300	Confusion	◆ Disorientation, mental confusion; vertigo; dysphoria ◆ Exaggerated emotional states (fear, rage, grief, etc.) ◆ Disturbances of vision (double vision, etc.) and of perception of colour, form, motion, dimensions ◆ Increased pain threshold ◆ Increased muscular incoordination; staggering gait; loss of full control over body movements ◆ Apathy, lethargy
250-400	Stupor	◆ General inertia; approaching loss of motor functions ◆ Markedly decreased response to stimuli ◆ Marked muscular incoordination; inability to stand or walk ◆ Vomiting; incontinence of urine and feces ◆ Impaired consciousness; sleep or stupor
350-500	Coma	◆ Complete unconsciousness; coma; anesthesia ◆ Depressed or abolished reflexes ◆ Subnormal temperature ◆ Impairment of circulation and respiration ◆ Possible death
450+	Death	◆ Death from respiratory arrest

Source: Based on Kurt M. Dubowski, University of Oklahoma, Stages of Acute Alcoholic Influence/Intoxication (table). Available online at www.indiana.edu/~lawactn/faculty/dubowski/dub_STAGES.doc. Copyright © 2006 by Dr. Kurt M. Dubowski. All rights reserved. Reprinted by permission.

Grounds for a Lawful Demand for an Approved Screening Device Test, CC, Section 254(2)

Before a police officer[6] can demand that a breath sample be blown into a screening device, the officer must have a "reasonable suspicion" that the operator or person who has care or control of a motor vehicle, a vessel, an aircraft, or railway equipment has alcohol in his or her body.

Reasonable suspicion can arise when

- the officer smells the odour of an alcoholic beverage on the person's breath;
- the operator admits that he or she has consumed alcohol; or
- the officer sees the operator consume an alcoholic beverage and climb into his or her car and drive away.

Turning "Reasonable Suspicion" into "Reasonable Grounds to Believe"

When an officer demands a breath sample for the approved screening device and the person fails the screening device test, the officer has "reasonable grounds to believe" that the person is "over 80." Failure of the screening device test is the only way for an officer to obtain the reasonable grounds to believe that the person is "over 80." It is unacceptable to the court that an officer could look at a person and reasonably determine with accuracy that the person is "over 80," because the officer does not know the person's tolerance for alcohol.

Grounds for a Lawful Demand for a Breathalyzer Test, CC, Section 254(3)(a)

Before a police officer can lawfully demand that breath samples (two samples at least 15 minutes apart) be provided by breathing into a breathalyzer instrument, the officer must have reasonable grounds to believe that the operator or person with care or control of a motor vehicle, a vessel, an aircraft, or railway equipment is "over 80" or that his or her ability is impaired by alcohol. Reasonable grounds arise under either of the following conditions:

- when, on reasonable suspicion, a person breathes into an approved screening device and fails the test; or
- when a person's behaviour and demeanour provide the officer with reasonable grounds to believe, beyond reasonable suspicion, that the person's ability is impaired by alcohol.

Driver Evaluation

When a police officer approaches the driver of a motor vehicle that he or she has just stopped, there are three possible scenarios:

1. The officer quickly appreciates that the driver has not been drinking and continues with the procedure for the driving offence for which the driver was stopped.

2. The officer forms reasonable suspicion that the driver has alcohol in his or her system. The officer can now lawfully make a demand that the driver provide a breath sample for an approved screening device.

3. The officer forms reasonable grounds to believe that the driver's ability to operate a motor vehicle is impaired by alcohol. The officer can now arrest the driver on reasonable grounds to believe that he or she has committed an indictable offence (see figure 6.4). The officer will advise the suspect of the right to counsel and make the breathalyzer demand. The suspect is usually taken to the police station for the breathalyzer test.

FIGURE 6.4 Breath Demands

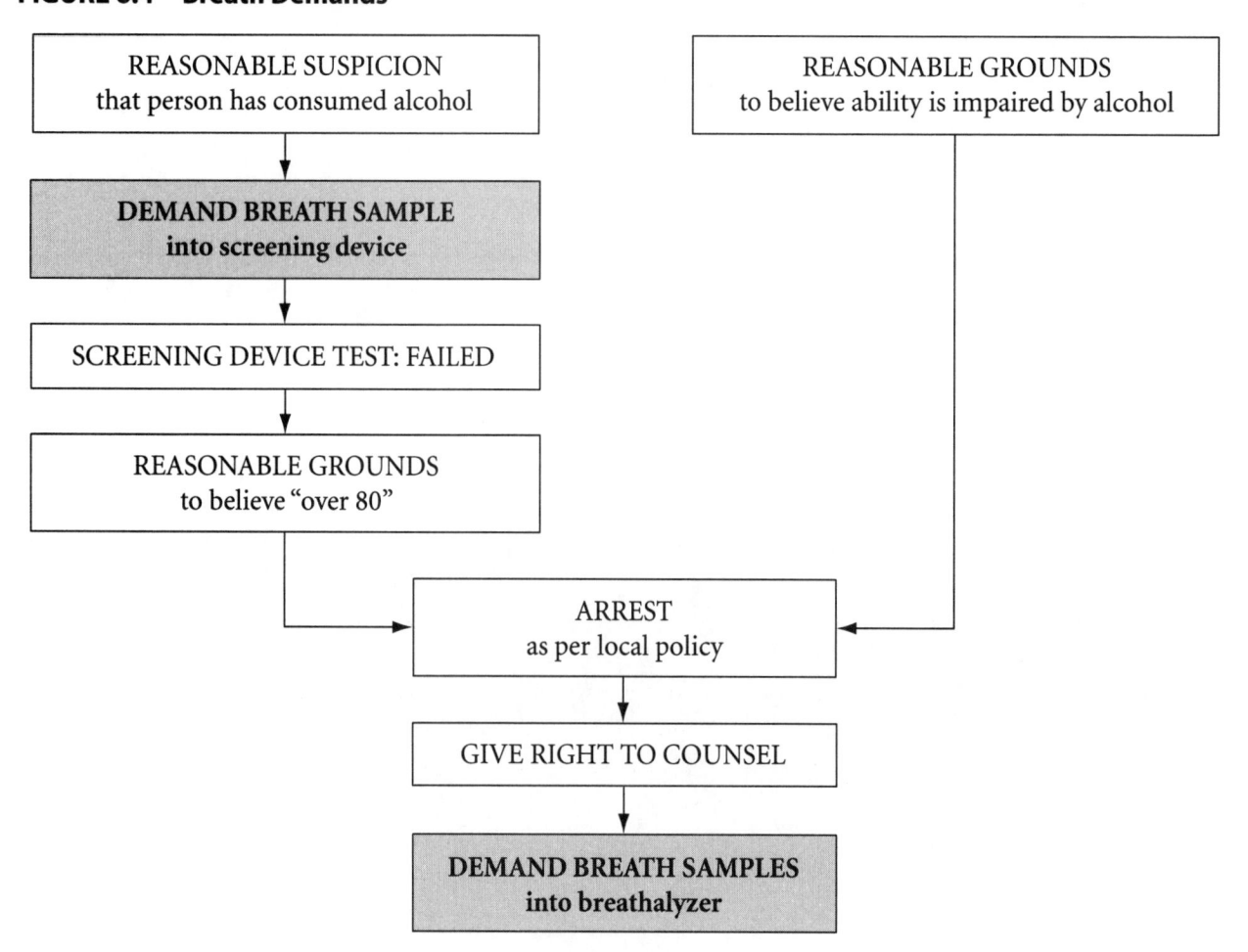

```
REASONABLE SUSPICION                    REASONABLE GROUNDS
that person has consumed alcohol        to believe ability is impaired by alcohol
            │                                       │
            ▼                                       │
   DEMAND BREATH SAMPLE                             │
     into screening device                          │
            │                                       │
            ▼                                       │
  SCREENING DEVICE TEST: FAILED                     │
            │                                       │
            ▼                                       │
    REASONABLE GROUNDS                              │
    to believe "over 80"                            │
            │                                       │
            └──────────►  ARREST  ◄─────────────────┘
                       as per local policy
                             │
                             ▼
                   GIVE RIGHT TO COUNSEL
                             │
                             ▼
                   DEMAND BREATH SAMPLES
                      into breathalyzer
```

Grounds for a Lawful Demand for Blood, CC, Sections 254(3)(b) and (4)

In cases where a lawful breathalyzer demand could be made but the person is incapable of providing a breath sample or it is impractical to obtain breath samples, a police officer can demand blood samples. A person may be *incapable* of providing breath samples because he or she has sustained an injury to the face, mouth, or lungs. It might be *impractical* to take breath samples because the person has been injured and needs immediate medical attention; the safety of the person is more important than performing a breathalyzer test. However, before determining incapacity or impracticability, the officer must have reasonable grounds to believe a person is either "over 80" or impaired.

> **NOTE**
>
> The blood samples must be taken by or under the supervision of a qualified medical practitioner who must be satisfied that it will not endanger the life and health of the person. Failure to do this constitutes a violation of the security of the person under s. 7 of the *Canadian Charter of Rights and Freedoms*, and an unlawful search under s. 8: *R v. Green*, [1992] 1 SCR 614.

Grounds for a Blood Warrant, CC, Section 256

In some circumstances, instead of demanding breath samples or blood samples, the police officer may apply to a justice of the peace for a warrant to obtain blood samples, whether or not the person consents. However, there are some prerequisites that must be met before a blood warrant can be sought:

- there must have been a collision resulting in the death of another person or bodily harm to another person or to the alleged offender;
- the police officer has lawful grounds for a blood demand, but the person is unable to consent to the blood demand because of a mental or physical condition arising from the consumption of alcohol or from the collision.

An example of a mental condition that could prevent a person from consenting to a blood demand is shock. A person in shock would probably not hear the blood demand or understand it, and therefore could not properly consent to or refuse the demand. An example of a physical condition that could prevent a person from consenting to a blood demand is unconsciousness. Note that in charging a person with impaired operation causing bodily harm, the harm must be to a person other than the driver, although injury to the driver qualifies as a ground for a blood warrant. The person must be conscious and able to understand the blood demand made by a police officer. If the person refuses, he or she can be charged with "refusal" under s. 254(5). If the person consents, blood samples can be taken.

If the subject is unconscious or unable to understand the blood demand, the police officer must go before a JP to get permission to seize blood samples from the person. The JP acts as an independent adjudicator to determine whether the police have sufficient grounds to justify issuing a warrant to seize blood from a person who cannot respond to a lawfully made blood demand. The JP's function is to protect the rights of the person, so that the police do not proceed at will to seize blood samples without the subject's knowledge or consent. The officer has four hours from the time of the offence to obtain the warrant. However, even though the officer has four hours to obtain the warrant, if the samples are not taken within three hours of the offence, the blood alcohol concentration (BAC) presumption is lost. (The concept of legal presumption is discussed under the heading "Three-Hour Limit on Obtaining Breath or Blood Samples," below.) In this case, whatever the blood alcohol reading, expert evidence will have to be given to show the rate at which the BAC was decreasing, and to give some idea of what the BAC was likely to have been at the time of the offence. If the officer is not sure when the person was driving the vehicle, he or she can always proceed with the arrest on the basis of the person's having the care or control of the vehicle, because this can usually be established.

The reason for the blood warrant is often incorrectly presumed to be for situations where the person refuses a blood demand. This is not the case. If the person refuses a blood demand, he or she will simply be charged with refusal to supply a blood sample. The penalty is the same as for a conviction for being impaired or being "over 80."

As mentioned above, another reason for obtaining a blood warrant rather than simply making a blood demand is a collision that results in an injury.

> **NOTE**
>
> Information about blood alcohol content from a blood sample taken for medical purposes other than determining blood alcohol content may not be used in evidence without obtaining a warrant for the blood sample: *R v. Dersch*, [1993] 3 SCR 768.

Three-Hour Limit on Obtaining Breath or Blood Samples, CC, Sections 254 and 258

The demand for the first of the breathalyzer or blood samples must be made within three hours of the commission of the offence of being impaired while operating or having the care or control of a motor vehicle, or being "over 80." In any case, the demand should be made immediately, or as soon as is practicable, once the officer has concluded that he or she has reasonable grounds to believe that the person's ability is impaired by alcohol or that the person has over 80 mg of alcohol per 100 ml of blood.

Time Limits for Breath and Blood Samples

Although the federal government has changed the time limit within which the demands for breath or blood samples must be made to be lawful, it did not change the time limit within which the BAC presumption applies. This lack of compatibility seems to be an oversight and will probably be corrected with the next revision of the *Criminal Code*. If a lawful demand for breathalyzer samples is made at 2 hours and 30 minutes after the offence, the subject is still lawfully required to provide the samples, but the presumption is lost. The Crown attorney must now decide whether he or she wishes to subpoena an expert from the Centre of Forensic Sciences to provide evidence of the BAC at the time of the offence.

The first of the two breath samples for breathalyzer analysis must be taken within three hours of the offence, or an important presumption in law is lost. The **legal presumption** is that the breathalyzer analysis indicates the BAC at the time of the offence, even though the test may be taken up to three hours after the offence. This can be important because as the body metabolizes alcohol, the BAC begins to drop.

legal presumption
the proof of one fact by the Crown means that a second fact is presumed to be true without the Crown having to adduce evidence to prove the second fact; however, the accused may present evidence to disprove the second fact, thereby rebutting the presumption

For a Breathalyzer Demand to Be Lawful
- The officer must have reasonable grounds to believe that the subject's ability is impaired by alcohol, or
- the officer must have reasonable grounds to believe that the subject has over 80 mg of alcohol per 100 ml of blood in his or her system, and
- the demand must be made within **three hours** of the offence (not the arrest).

For the BAC Presumption to Be Lawful
- The police officer must have had lawful grounds for a breathalyzer demand,
- the breathalyzer demand must have been made within **two hours** of the offence, and
- the first of two breathalyzer tests must have been made within **two hours** of the offence, or both blood tests must have been made within **two hours** of the offence.

The second breath sample, unlike the first, does not have to be taken within the three-hour limit for the presumption to hold. The second sample must be taken at least 15 minutes later, although 20 minutes is the usual practice (to make sure that it is more than 15 minutes after the first sample was taken). The breathalyzer technician reports the lower of the two readings to the court. Failure to justify to the court's satisfaction any delay in taking the breath or blood samples can lead to their exclusion as evidence. The court does not consider an inconvenience to police procedure to be a justifiable excuse.

BAC at time of test = BAC at time of offence

Once a police officer believes that he or she has reasonable grounds to believe that a person has committed the indictable offences of operating or having care or control of a motor vehicle while impaired or while being "over 80," the police officer can arrest the person immediately. The officer should then advise the person of his or her right to counsel and make a breathalyzer or blood demand. If the samples are obtained within three hours of the offence, the police have the benefit of the presumption that the blood alcohol concentration at the time of the offence is the same as at the time of the test. If the demand for breathalyzer or blood samples has been made within two hours of the offence, but the first of the two breath samples, or both blood samples, cannot be obtained within two hours of the offence, the person still has to provide the samples. However, the presumption that the BAC at the time of the offence is the same as at the time of the test is lost.

Impairment by Drugs

The offence of being impaired refers to impairment by alcohol or drugs. However, a lawful demand for a breath sample for an approved screening device or breathalyzer can only be made if alcohol is involved, not drugs.

A person can be arrested for operating a motor vehicle while impaired by drugs. The police officer must obtain an admission from the person as to the reason for the "impaired behaviour" or obtain a voluntary urine sample for analysis.

Impaired and "Over 80" Charges

When a person fails the approved screening device test and is arrested on the basis that there are reasonable grounds to believe that he or she has committed the offence of being "over 80," he or she can be charged only with being "over 80."

As stated previously, when a person's ability is assessed as being impaired by alcohol, the person may be arrested because there are reasonable grounds to believe that the person has committed the offence of being impaired. If the subsequent breathalyzer tests prove that the person is "over 80," he or she can be charged with being both impaired and "over 80." Charging with both offences is only possible when the person is both impaired and "over 80." Remember that someone can be "over 80" and not show any signs of being impaired.

Twelve-Hour Suspensions in Alcohol-Related Driving Matters, HTA, Section 48

The 12-hour suspension is a useful tool for a police officer who encounters a driver who has enough alcohol in his or her system to cause concern, but not enough to charge the driver with being impaired or "over 80." It can also be used where a driver refuses to provide breath or blood samples. A 12-hour suspension involves taking the driver's licence from the driver of a motor vehicle and holding it for a 12-hour period. The province issues driver's licences under the HTA and authorizes their suspension. Because driving is a privilege and otherwise within the jurisdiction of the province, no court hearing is required when a licence is suspended. When a 12-hour suspension is in effect, the person may not drive a motor vehicle. A 12-hour suspension may be imposed when

- a driver blows "warn" on an approved screening device,
- a driver blows 50 mg or more on a breathalyzer, or
- a driver refuses
  - an approved screening device breath sample demand,
  - a breathalyzer breath sample demand, or
  - a blood sample demand.

When the results of a breathalyzer test indicate a BAC of *less* than 50 mg, no 12-hour suspension can be imposed lawfully, even if the person is charged with being impaired solely on the strength of the officer's subjective observations of the driver.

A police officer can have the motor vehicle seized and towed away at the expense of the owner if the officer believes that the car should be removed and that the owner cannot arrange for its removal.

Ninety-Day Suspensions, HTA, Section 48.3

If a person blows "over 80" on both breathalyzer tests, or refuses to supply a breath sample for the breathalyzer, the police can immediately fax the Ontario Ministry of Transportation licensing office, which will fax back a 90-day suspension order. The driver must hand over the licence to the officer, who must forward the licence and other documents as required under the regulations to the registrar of motor vehicles. This will occur after an arrest but before trial, and is in addition to any penalty that the court might impose if the person is found guilty. If the person is found not guilty, there is no compensation for the suspension. As with the 12-hour suspension, the officer can have the vehicle towed away at the owner's expense, unless the owner can arrange for its removal.

The 90-day suspension has been strongly criticized because a person is punished before he or she is found guilty. And the punishment is severe; it can cause real hardship for an accused who may lose his or her job because he or she is unable to get to work. A similar provision has withstood a court challenge in Manitoba, in part because the suspension is seen as protection for the public, not punishment for the accused (HTA, s. 48.3(10)).

Ignition Interlock Programs: CC, Section 259 and HTA, Section 41.2

Of the approximately 15,000 drinking and driving offences in Ontario in each year, approximately 75 percent involve first offenders. The other 25 percent involve repeat offenders and have been the focus of intense efforts to deter the repetition of the offence. These efforts include increased suspension periods, mandatory assessment for alcohol abuse, education and treatment, increased fines, and impoundment of vehicles.

In addition, in 2001, Ontario introduced its Ignition Interlock Program. Section 41.2 of the HTA provides the authority for the establishment and operation of an ignition interlock program in Ontario. Likewise, section 259 of the CC authorizes a court to allow an offender to drive during a period in which driving would be otherwise prohibited, provided that the driver registers in an ignition interlock program.

An ignition interlock device is an in-car alcohol breath screening device that locks the ignition and prevents a driver from starting a car if the device detects a blood alcohol level that exceeds the preset limit. Before starting the vehicle, the driver must blow into the device, and must also provide additional breath samples at random, preset times, while the engine is running. If a sample is not provided, or if the BAC exceeds the limit, the device issues a warning, records the event, and activates the alarm systems on the vehicle until the engine is turned off.

After having penalties imposed under the CC and HTA, a driver eligible to have a driver's licence reinstated will have an ignition interlock condition placed on their licence for at least one year. This means that the driver must have an interlock device installed on his or her own vehicle at his or her own expense or choose not to drive at all until the condition is removed from the driver's licence.

Currently, first-time offenders will have a one-year condition imposed following the reinstatement of the licence, second-time offenders will have a minimum of three years imposed, and third-time offenders will have a lifetime condition imposed. All persons who drive the vehicle must provide breath samples, because the device does not distinguish between the offender and other drivers.

A driver who tries to circumvent the interlock device by driving a vehicle that is not equipped with an interlock device, or who tampers with the device, will face fines of up to $20,000 in the case of a commercial vehicle, and $1,000 in the case of other motor vehicles. In addition, if a driver is apprehended while driving a vehicle that is not equipped with a device, or if tampering is reported by the interlock device service provider, the interlock condition on the licence will be extended for a further period. If a vehicle owner knowingly allows a driver with an interlock condition on his or her licence to drive the vehicle owner's car, the vehicle owner may be subject to penalties under the HTA.

Once the period of the ignition interlock condition has expired, the driver must apply for removal of the condition; otherwise, it remains on the licence.

An officer doing a traffic stop will readily discover on a licence check whether there is a condition. If there is, the officer should check to see that the vehicle has an operating ignition interlock device.

Operating a Motor Vehicle While Disqualified, CC, Section 259(4)

This provision provides a penalty in some, but not all, cases where a person operates a motor vehicle while disqualified from doing so. The disqualification may be either a prohibition from driving or a licence suspension that arose from

- a conviction for being impaired,
- a conviction for being "over 80," or
- an absolute or conditional discharge for being impaired or being "over 80" (the person is discharged but the court still imposes the penalty of a prohibition from driving for a specified period of time).

Case Illustration

In October 1995, a Fredericton, New Brunswick man was fined $300 for operating a motor vehicle while his ability was impaired by alcohol. The motor vehicle was an electric-powered wheelchair. The convicted man, Raymond MacDonald, suffers from muscular dystrophy and is unable to operate a manual wheelchair.

Any conviction for impaired operation of a motor vehicle carries a mandatory prohibition from operating any motor vehicle for a minimum of three months. This prohibition is imposed by the *Criminal Code* and it applies throughout Canada on any road or areas where motor vehicles are permitted access. This conviction, therefore, prevented Mr. MacDonald from being able to move without assistance for three months on roads or other areas where motor vehicles are permitted access. He was effectively barred from those places by the prohibition order.

Although the criminal offence of operating a motor vehicle while ability is impaired by alcohol can occur anywhere, the resulting criminal prohibition usually applies to drivers of automobiles, and the offender can usually find other ways of getting around. But Mr. MacDonald was unable even to move around his own community because his sole source of mobility was taken away from him. Although the prohibition is lawful on its face, it might not survive a challenge under the *Canadian Charter of Rights and Freedoms*, because it could be construed as a violation of the right not to be subjected to cruel or unusual punishment, under s. 12, or as discrimination on the basis of disability, prohibited by s. 15.

"Disqualified" means that either a judge has made a prohibition order or the province has suspended the licence.

A 12- or 90-day suspension under the HTA, or a suspension for unpaid parking tickets, cannot be the basis for a charge of driving while disqualified. For these HTA violations, there is the s. 53(1) HTA offence of driving while suspended.

A **prohibition order** prohibits the operation of a motor vehicle as defined in the CC on a street, road, highway, or other area where the public is permitted to operate a motor vehicle (for example, in a private parking lot). A prohibition order is imposed by a judge for a driving offence under the CC.

A **suspension** of a driver's licence is done by the authority of a province under its traffic laws. For example, in Ontario the suspended driver cannot drive a motor vehicle (as defined in the HTA) on a highway (as defined in the HTA). The driver can be suspended for a CC conviction or for an HTA offence.

A prohibition order is more extensive than a suspension because it covers all kinds of motor vehicles, except railway equipment. The HTA definition excludes several types of motor vehicles that would be included by the CC. The prohibition order also covers practically any place that a motor vehicle could physically operate in or on. A suspension under the HTA only affects highways, which is a narrower definition.

It is possible for a person to be both "prohibited" and "suspended" at the same time. When this situation arises, the prohibition order is more significant because it is broader and more inclusive.

prohibition order
made on conviction for a CC driving offence and disqualifies a person from driving a motor vehicle as defined in the CC

suspension
may be made under the authority of the HTA for either a CC offence or an HTA offence; disqualifies a driver from driving a motor vehicle as defined in the HTA on a highway as defined in the HTA

FIGURE 6.5 Drunk Driving Offence Procedure at a Glance

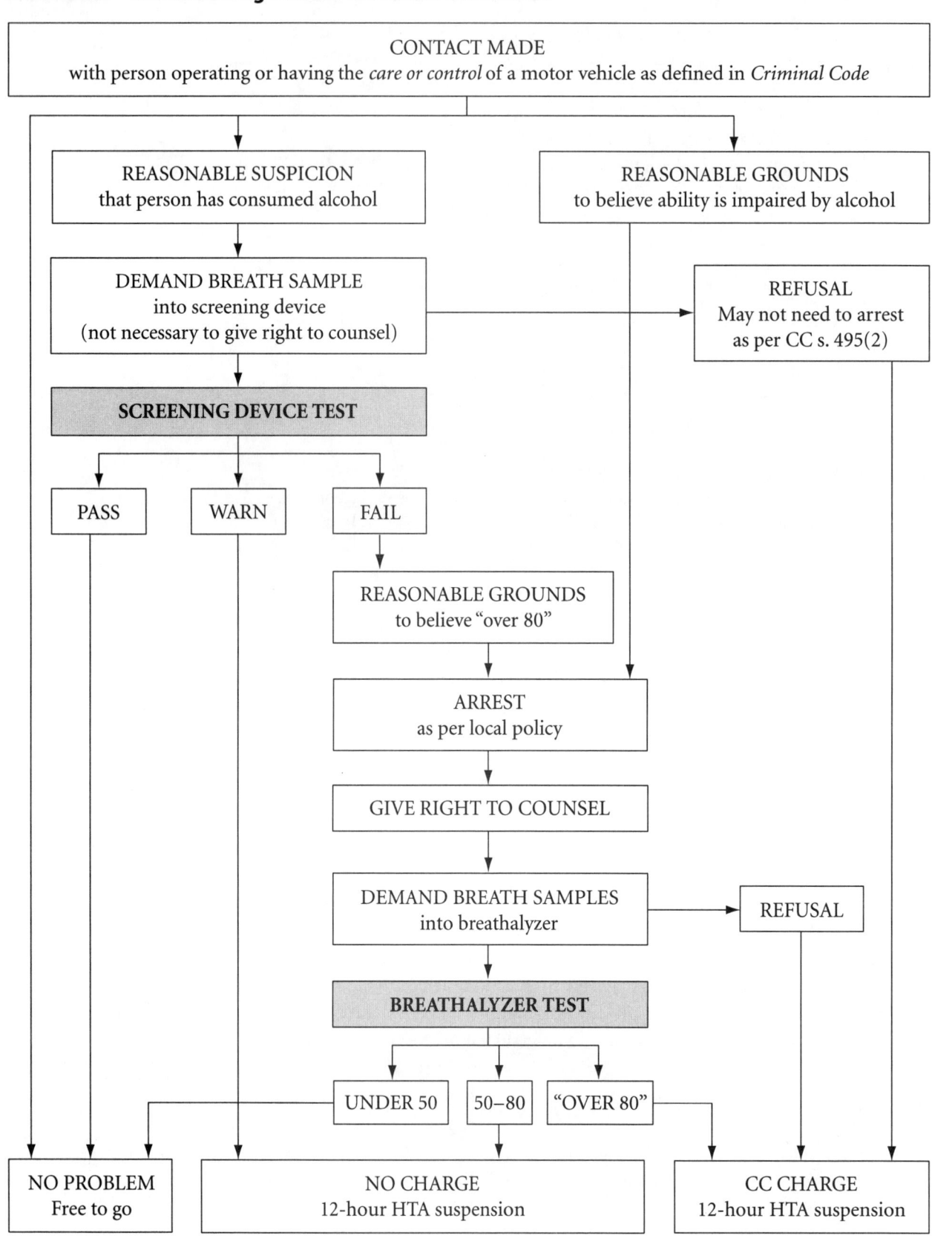

```
                          CONTACT MADE
        with person operating or having the care or control of a motor vehicle as defined in Criminal Code
                                    │
         ┌──────────────────────────┴──────────────────────────┐
         ▼                                                     ▼
   REASONABLE SUSPICION                              REASONABLE GROUNDS
   that person has consumed alcohol                  to believe ability is impaired by alcohol
         │
         ▼
   DEMAND BREATH SAMPLE  ─────────────────────────▶  REFUSAL
   into screening device                             May not need to arrest
   (not necessary to give right to counsel)          as per CC s. 495(2)
         │
         ▼
   SCREENING DEVICE TEST
         │
   ┌─────┼─────┐
   ▼     ▼     ▼
  PASS  WARN  FAIL
                │
                ▼
         REASONABLE GROUNDS
         to believe "over 80"
                │
                ▼
             ARREST
         as per local policy
                │
                ▼
         GIVE RIGHT TO COUNSEL
                │
                ▼
         DEMAND BREATH SAMPLES  ─────▶  REFUSAL
         into breathalyzer
                │
                ▼
         BREATHALYZER TEST
                │
        ┌───────┼───────┐
        ▼       ▼       ▼
    UNDER 50  50–80  "OVER 80"

   NO PROBLEM        NO CHARGE              CC CHARGE
   Free to go        12-hour HTA suspension  12-hour HTA suspension
```

VEHICLE SEARCHES

The case law on vehicle searches falls into two categories: search incidental to arrest and search of a vehicle as a place.

Search Incidental to Arrest

The courts have long held that when an individual is arrested, an officer may search the suspect's body on arrest without first obtaining a search warrant. The courts have also held that where the suspect is arrested in a vehicle, or emerges from one at the time of or shortly after his or her arrest, the vehicle may also be searched without a warrant. Some cases have gone further, and stated that if a vehicle was in the vicinity of the arrest, there is no reason not to include the vehicle in the accused's vicinity as part of a search incidental to arrest. Some cases indicate that the warrantless search may be conducted hours after the arrest if there is a reasonable explanation for the delay. The search may extend to the vehicle's interior, including the trunk, and possibly under the hood. However, if parts of the car have to be taken apart as part of the search, a warrant may be required.

Search of a Vehicle as a Place

In some circumstances, a vehicle may be considered a place, like a house or an office. In this case, a warrant must be obtained under s. 487(1) of the CC. To obtain a warrant, an officer must, at the time that the warrant is sworn, have reasonable grounds to believe that an identified tangible thing that is evidence of an offence will be found in the vehicle. If a vehicle is found in a place for which a search warrant has been issued, then it may be searched, in the same way that a room or a container in the place may be searched. However, the situation is different if the vehicle is on the same property as the place named in the warrant but not contained within it. For example, if the warrant clearly describes a house that may be searched, the search will not include a vehicle parked on the property on which the house is located, but not contained within the house. If the vehicle were parked in a garage that forms part of the house, then it could be searched because the warrant indicates that the house is the place to be searched and the garage is part of the house. The proper approach here is to obtain a separate warrant to search the vehicle.

Because a vehicle, unlike a house, has wheels and can be moved beyond the reach of law enforcement officials, there are some circumstances where a warrantless search may be conducted. Here, there must be grounds to obtain a search warrant, but due to **exigent** circumstances, it is impractical to obtain a warrant. In this case, a warrantless search may be conducted if it can be shown that

- the vehicle was lawfully stopped or the occupants were lawfully detained (although not necessarily arrested);
- the officer conducting the search had reasonable grounds to believe that an offence had been, was being, or was about to be committed and a search would disclose evidence relevant to that offence; and

exigent
requiring immediate aid or action

- exigent circumstances existed, such as imminent loss, removal, or destruction of the evidence so that it was not feasible to obtain a search warrant.

CHAPTER SUMMARY

This chapter identifies some of the more common motor vehicle offences under federal and provincial law that a police officer is likely to encounter. The distinction between a charge and an arrest under the HTA is made, and the circumstances are identified where an officer can proceed with either a charge or an arrest. The procedures for both a charge and an arrest are explained. Particular attention is paid to HTA offences for which a person may be arrested, and where licences, vehicles, and equipment may be seized.

The chapter examines driving-related criminal offences in the CC concerning offences that involve drinking and driving. Basic terms and concepts related to CC definitions of "motor vehicle," "impaired driving," being "over 80," "operating" a vehicle, and "having care or control of a vehicle" are defined, as are the various standards of proof required to use the approved devices and methods to determine a person's blood alcohol level. The chapter discusses the circumstances where a lawful demand for breath samples can be made or a warrant obtained for blood samples, and indicates how the evidence so obtained can be properly used to obtain a conviction. In this context, particular attention is paid to the time limits for these procedures and the investigative procedure to be followed. Finally, the different types of suspension and prohibition orders are explored with respect to the consequences for each type of order.

KEY TERMS

legal presumption

prohibition order

suspension

exigent

NOTES

1. *R v. Waite*, [1989] 1 SCR 1436; *R v. Tutton*, [1989] 1 SCR 1392.

2. *R v. Edland* (1990), 23 MVR (2d) 37.

3. *R v. Rajic* (1993), 80 CCC (3d) 533 (Ont. CA); leave to appeal to the SCC refused.

4. *R v. O'Brien* (1987), 39 CCC (3d) 528 (Nfld. SCTD).

5. Counsel will also focus on whether the police were scrupulous in affording the right to counsel and whether the testing procedures were

carried out properly. Because drunk driving is an offence that crosses class and income divisions, there are more offenders who have the money and resources to support an aggressive and imaginative defence than is the case for most criminal charges. For this reason, a disproportionately large number of reported criminal cases are "drunk driving" cases.

6. The CC uses the more encompassing term "peace officer."

REVIEW QUESTIONS

Short Answer

Briefly answer the following questions.

1. a. What is the difference between the definitions of "motor vehicle" in the HTA and the CC?

   b. Why is the difference important?

2. How could you be "over 80" and not be impaired?

3. What is the difference between "reasonable suspicion" and "reasonable grounds to believe"?

4. Explain what the differences are between a breathalyzer and an approved screening device in terms of function and purpose.

5. What are the grounds for a lawful demand for the following?

   a. A breath sample for an approved screening device.

   b. A breath sample for a breathalyzer.

   c. A blood sample.

6. Explain the importance of the two-hour limit and the three-hour limit in determining the BAC.

7. May a police officer make a breathalyzer demand for someone he or she has grounds to believe is impaired by drugs? Explain your answer.

8. Cite the statute and section number that authorizes the following:

    a. A demand for a breath sample for an approved screening device.

    b. A demand for a breath sample for a breathalyzer.

    c. A demand for a blood sample.

    d. An application for a warrant to obtain a blood sample.

e. Suspension of a driver's licence for 12 hours.

f. Suspension of a driver's licence for 90 days.

9. Explain what events must occur or what factors must be present before the police may validly take the steps described in question 8.

Discussion Questions

1. Rank the following four topics in the order in which they would occur sequentially and describe the basis for your ordering.

   a. blood warrant

   b. blood demand

   c. breathalyzer demand

   d. approved screening device demand

2. "In drunk driving cases, timing is everything." Discuss this statement in terms of the nature of the offences, the requirements of the law, and any other relevant matter.

3. Discuss the following statements:

   a. Breathalyzer evidence is only corroborative evidence for a charge of operating a motor vehicle while ability is impaired by alcohol, but is essential evidence for a charge of operating a motor vehicle with over 80 mg of alcohol per 100 ml of blood.

   b. Failing an approved screening test is not sufficient evidence by itself for a charge of operating a motor vehicle with over 80 mg of alcohol per 100 ml of blood.

   c. If a peace officer has the lawful grounds to make a breathalyzer demand, he or she also has the lawful grounds to make an arrest.

   d. If a person is arrested on the basis that there are reasonable grounds to believe that he or she is "over 80," an additional charge of being impaired is not possible, but if the subject is arrested on reasonable grounds to believe that he or she is impaired, an additional charge of "over 80" is possible.

CHAPTER 7

Collision Investigation

CHAPTER OBJECTIVES

After completing this chapter, you should be able to:

- Describe the steps for investigating a collision.
- Develop a safe driving strategy for responding to emergency calls.
- Recognize and understand the significance of the signs and symbols for dangerous goods.
- Understand your duty with respect to assisting injured persons.
- Understand when and how to close off and safeguard a collision scene.
- Understand what to do if there are downed hydro lines at a scene.
- Understand what steps to take if there is a vehicle fire.
- Understand what steps to take to safeguard the public if the road is icy.
- Understand how to handle fighting or argumentative drivers.
- Recognize situations where a cautioned statement is required.
- Take a cautioned statement that will stand up to court scrutiny.
- Obtain information from a driver who has been cautioned and opted to remain silent.
- Deal with unruly spectators.

INTRODUCTION

This chapter introduces you to basic collision investigation practices and techniques. The focus here is on arriving safely at the scene, surveying it, and prioritizing emergencies so as to be able to secure and manage the collision scene. Managing the scene includes dealing with injuries, dangerous goods, fires, and other hazards. The officer also must effectively interview persons at the scene to try and determine what happened, using various interview techniques.

COLLISION INVESTIGATION AND RECONSTRUCTION

The police are required to investigate or receive a report of a collision from drivers involved in every motor vehicle collision in Ontario where a personal injury occurs or there is property damage valued at more than $1,000 (reg. 596, as amended by O. reg. 537/97, s. 11). Because even minor damage to motor vehicles is expensive to repair, the $1,000 reporting threshold is easily reached in most cases and, as a result, the police investigate virtually every motor vehicle collision in Ontario.

Some collisions will receive additional attention. Besides an investigation, a serious collision may also require a collision reconstruction. If it appears that criminal or provincial charges may be laid, civil litigation is likely, or a coroner's inquest may be called.

There are many reasons why police officers attend motor vehicle collisions. Police officers must record the identification of all persons involved, the type of injuries sustained, the registration of the vehicles involved, the insurance particulars of the vehicle owners, the type and amount of damage to vehicles and property, and the location and time of the collision. This information, recorded and saved by the police, is necessary to prevent incorrect or fraudulent claims, to provide a basis for statistical analysis by the Ontario Ministry of Transportation and to provide evidence for prosecutions and inquests.

Note that although police officers must investigate any violations of the law and collect evidence relevant to a prosecution, this is not necessarily the same as finding fault. A driver may be "at fault" for the purposes of a civil suit for negligence, but the conduct of the driver may fall far short of what is required for a prosecution under provincial legislation or under the *Criminal Code* of Canada (CC). "Fault" is a term of interest to insurance companies dealing with civil liability for negligence; it is not a term of interest to the police.

STEPS IN A COLLISION INVESTIGATION

The steps described here are general in nature and do not apply to all situations. The steps that make up this approach to collision investigation should be considered a good starting framework that you can develop further as you become more experienced. The steps are set out and discussed below.

Mental Role Playing

Psychologists have determined that in some circumstances the mind cannot tell the difference between an imagined experience and a real one. Russian sports psychologists have exploited this idea by having their figure skaters and gymnasts visualize their routines repeatedly so that the pattern becomes imprinted in their minds; the athletes thus act more instinctively when performing their routines. This visualization technique also allows the athletes to practise much more in their minds than their bodies could manage physically.

A police officer can employ this mental role-playing technique to condition himself or herself to act more instinctively when confronting a collision scene. During quiet times on his or her shift, a police officer can imagine a collision scenario and then think of the correct response to the scene. The brain becomes used to the pattern of response and the officer will then act instinctively under the pressure of a collision situation.

Officers can further improve their response over time if they "debrief" themselves. After each collision, officers must ask themselves how they could improve their performance. Debriefing is an important way to reinforce and refine the skills used in carrying out a procedure.

Approaching the Scene

OBTAIN AS MUCH INFORMATION AS POSSIBLE

Prior to arrival, obtain as much information as possible to expedite an efficient and effective handling of the collision scene.

Find out the exact location of the collision, and determine the lane and lane direction, if it is a divided highway. Find out where the closest cross street is from your approach.

Ascertain whether there are any injuries and, if there are, ask whether medical personnel have been dispatched. Ask whether any other emergency services are needed and, if they are, ask whether they have been dispatched. These could include hydro personnel (if there are downed wires), the fire department, officers for traffic control, or environmental protection personnel.

GUARANTEE YOUR ARRIVAL

At the Ontario Police College, new police recruits were given the task of driving a given route to a collision scene as fast as possible. Each recruit was timed with a stopwatch, and his or her time was recorded. The recruits invariably turned this exercise into a competition with other students. The recruits drove at excessive speeds and hit many of the pylons along the route and also had to brake and slow down suddenly and frequently. They were then asked to drive the same route again, using a car that could not exceed a predetermined speed limit. Each recruit was again timed with a stopwatch and his or her time recorded. The recruits were surprised to discover that the second controlled run was always faster. The moral of this story is: *If you slow down and drive at a more controlled speed, you will actually get there faster and more safely.*

A section of the *Highway Traffic Act* (HTA) that deals with rate of speed exempts police officers in the lawful performance of their duties from the speed limits imposed in the HTA or any speed bylaw. Responding to a motor vehicle collision is within the lawful performance of a police officer's duty, so police officers may exceed the speed limit when en route to a collision scene. However, considering the experiment at the Ontario Police College, driving *excessively* over the speed limit is inefficient and unnecessarily risky.

The HTA also authorizes the driver of an emergency vehicle, after stopping the vehicle at a red light, to proceed through the red light, if it is safe to do so. Emergency vehicles do not, however, have blanket authority to run through a red light. If the driver of an emergency vehicle is involved in a collision while proceeding through a red light, there is a presumption that it was not safe to run the light. The burden of proving that it was safe is always on the driver of the emergency vehicle.

The HTA defines an emergency vehicle as a vehicle used by a police officer in the lawful performance of his or her duties on which a siren is continuously sounding, and from which intermittent flashes of red light are visible from all directions. This definition means that a police officer cannot lawfully proceed through a red light in an emergency situation unless the flashing red lights are on and the siren is continuously sounding. In the event that an officer is involved in a collision while proceeding through a red light, there could be civil liability issues for the officer and the police service.

The HTA also permits a police department vehicle to drive off the roadway to overtake another vehicle. Passing on the shoulder is sometimes necessary when traffic stops on the roadway and no other lane is open. If the shoulder is unpaved, care should be taken in the event that it is a "soft shoulder" to prevent a possible rollover.

In the event that a motorist fails to pull over to permit an emergency vehicle to pass, there is not much that can be done at the time by the officer responding to a collision. However, all other police officers can enforce the law when they see such an obstruction of other emergency vehicles. The HTA states that the driver of a vehicle, on the approach of an ambulance, fire, or police department vehicle on which a bell or siren is sounding or on which a lamp located on the roof of the vehicle is producing intermittent flashes of red light, shall immediately bring such a vehicle to a standstill, as near as practicable to the right-hand curb or edge of the roadway and parallel to it and clear of any intersection. If the vehicle is on a roadway that has more than two lanes for traffic and is designated for the use of one-way traffic, the driver shall stop as near as practicable to the nearest curb or edge of the roadway, parallel to it, and clear of any intersection.

Prioritizing Emergencies

When officers arrive at a collision scene, they must stop to evaluate what they are confronting. If there is more than one emergency, they need time to determine which emergency, if left unattended, would cause the most serious consequences. You can remember this important step by using the mnemonic "be safe":

B	Before
E	Entering
S	Stop
A	And
F	First
E	Evaluate

When considering what action to take, the officer should be mindful of the priorities at all collision scenes: YOU, THEM, IT. Your first priority should be your own safety. If you rush into a collision scene where there is a spill of dangerous goods or downed hydro lines, you may become another casualty. In order for you to be effective, you cannot become one of the injured. You may need to close the road to protect yourself as you enter the scene and to prevent the situation from becoming worse. Second, if there are injured persons, attend to them. Last, concern yourself with property damage.

Situations that could cause the most serious consequences if left unattended are:

- the presence of dangerous goods,
- injuries,
- an unprotected collision scene and unprotected evidence,
- downed hydro lines,
- vehicle fires,
- dangerous road conditions,
- property at risk of being stolen, and
- fighting drivers.

DANGEROUS GOODS

Transport Canada has developed a system of dangerous-goods placards to be placed on all vehicles transporting dangerous goods, and a similar system of dangerous-goods labels to be placed on containers of dangerous goods. The purpose of these placards and labels is to alert emergency response crews, who can quickly identify the dangerous goods in question so that appropriate action can be taken. Prompt and appropriate action minimizes damage and saves lives when these goods are involved in a collision.

If emergency personnel are unsure of the dangers, there are emergency phone numbers at both the federal and provincial levels of government to obtain information about the appropriate response. Police officers should record these numbers for quick access.

The dangerous-goods placards and labels use a three-part system to identify the goods:

- colour,
- symbols, and
- class numbers.

The first officer at a collision scene, when evaluating the situation from a distance, may recognize the category of dangerous goods by colour first. Colour is easily recognizable from afar. For example, the colour of the placard could warn of poison, explosives, or radioactive material. Symbols on the placards assist in interpreting the meaning of the colour of the placard. For example, a red placard is enhanced by a symbol of a flame to convey the message that the goods are flammable. Be aware that in poor light conditions, it is harder to recognize and to distinguish one colour from another. A strong flashlight and a closer look may be necessary.

Binoculars may be necessary to identify the class number printed on the bottom of the placard. For example, a number 2 at the bottom of the placard tells the emergency personnel that the goods involve a compressed gas. This information, along with the condition of the vehicle or the containers, needs to be immediately relayed to the communications centre, which in turn should notify the appropriate authorities. If a tanker truck is ruptured and the compressed gas is poisonous, only emergency personnel with protective clothing and breathing apparatus may approach. They may be able to obtain the **bill of lading** from the cab of the vehicle to identify the specific cargo. Their job will also be to neutralize any danger, so that investigation and cleanup can be done safely and effectively. The responsibility of the police will be to secure the scene and evacuate the area downwind of the collision to minimize injury and damage.

Obviously, police officers need to know the meaning of the colour symbols and class numbers used on dangerous-goods placards and labels to prevent injury to themselves and others and to prevent further damage to property.

As stated above, dangerous-goods placards can be initially identified from afar by colour. The table below provides a list of these colours and the type of dangerous goods they identify:

Orange	Explosives
Red	Anything flammable
Green	Non-flammable compressed gases
Blue	Substances that are dangerous when wet
Yellow	**Oxidizers**
White	Poisonous and infectious substances
Yellow over white	Radioactive materials
White over black	Corrosives

Dangerous-goods placards and labels employ the use of nine symbols that assist in the interpretation of the colour. See figure 7.1 for a breakdown.

---

bill of lading
a receipt for merchandise that accompanies the merchandise when it is being transported from one place to another; it should provide detailed information about the cargo carried by a commercial vehicle

oxidizer
a substance that combines with oxygen, which may be quite volatile, flammable, or otherwise chemically active and therefore dangerous

Collision Investigation CHAPTER 7 177

FIGURE 7.1   Dangerous-Goods Symbols

Explosive	Flammable	Infectious
(exploding bomb)	(flame)	(biomedical symbol)
Compressed Gas	**Radioactive**	**Poison**
(gas cylinder)	(trefoil)	(skull and crossbones)
Corrosive	**Oxidizers**	**Miscellaneous**
(acid attacking hand or metal)	(burning "O")	(black stripes)

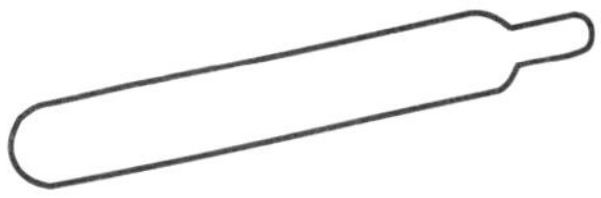

Dangerous goods are divided into nine classes. The class number is printed at the bottom of the placard or label. Transport Canada's chart of dangerous goods is reproduced in colour on the inside front and inside back covers of this book. The nine classes of dangerous goods are listed below, together with their corresponding colours and symbols:

Class	Colour	Symbol
Class 1: Explosives	Orange	Exploding bomb
Class 2: Compressed gases	Red Green White	Flame Gas cylinder Skull
Class 3: Flammable liquids	Red	Flame
Class 4: Flammable solids	Red and white stripes White over red Blue	Flame Flame Flame
Class 5: Oxidizers	Yellow	Burning "O"
Class 6: Poisonous/ infectious substances	White White	Skull Biomedical symbol
Class 7: Radioactives	Yellow over white	Trefoil
Class 8: Corrosives	White over black	Acid on hand or metal
Class 9: Miscellaneous	Black stripes over white	

Note that the flammable compressed gas placard and the flammable liquid placard are both red and carry the flame symbol. They differ only in their class number.

> **HINT** To remember the class number for class 2, 3, and 4 dangerous goods, use the following mnemonic: the higher the class number, the denser the substance.
>
> Class 2   Compressed gas
> Class 3   Liquids (more dense than gas)
> Class 4   Solids (most dense)

INJURIES

Injured persons should not be moved if there is a risk of aggravating the injury, but they may have to be moved if there is a danger of more serious consequences.

If a live victim needs to be removed from a vehicle, stabilization is required. Stabilization of the scene, stabilization of the vehicle, and stabilization of the victim must all be considered before a victim is moved. Ambulance and fire personnel are best equipped to treat and move injured persons, so it is imperative to have these experts on scene as soon as possible.

Only medical practitioners (doctors) can pronounce someone dead. Police officers, however, can assume death in three circumstances:

1. decapitation,
2. transection (cutting in half) of the body, or
3. decomposition of the body.

According to the Ontario *Coroners Act*, no person, including police officers, shall interfere with or move a dead body without a "warrant to take possession of the body of a deceased person" signed by the coroner. When a police officer can assume death, he or she should cover the body and its parts with a blanket until the coroner arrives.

There will be times when police officers will not be able to assume that death has occurred. Because police officers are qualified in first aid and CPR, they are obligated (if emergency medical personnel are not on the scene) to render first aid to every victim whom they cannot assume is dead. Failure to provide first aid can lead to a charge of neglect of duty under the Ontario *Police Services Act* and possibly a charge of criminal negligence causing death under the CC. There is also the possibility of a civil action by the victim or his or her family.

Officers should make sure that each victim is identified before the victims are removed from a collision scene. Obviously, discretion is required to make sure that the attempt to identify the victim does not interfere with those persons rendering emergency medical services. Officers should also make sure that they know the name of the hospital where each victim is being taken and who is transporting the victim.

In a collision with multiple victims where there is a lack of emergency medical personnel, a police officer will have to prioritize who needs treatment first. Officers will have to group victims into three categories:

1. Victims whose injuries are life threatening and require immediate treatment.
2. Victims whose injuries are not life threatening and who can wait for treatment.
3. Victims whose injuries are so severe that death is imminent, and survival is unlikely.

Note that category 1 victims are the officer's top priority.

Hopefully, an officer will never have to make these kinds of decisions, but by clarifying the decision-making process, and using the mental role-playing technique, an officer can prepare himself or herself for such a situation.

If the collision involves only property damage, a police officer should make sure not to trivialize the collision. The collision may be routine for the police officer, but it is a dramatic life event for the victim. A little sympathy can go a long way to enhancing the image of the police service. Remember, the officer's report is important, but it is not more important than public support.

PROTECTING THE SCENE

The HTA authorizes a police officer to close a highway or any part thereof to ensure the orderly movement of traffic, to prevent injury or damage to persons or property, or to permit proper action in an emergency. Every person shall obey the officer's directions (HTA, s. 134). Emergency and service vehicles are exempt from road-closure rules. For the purposes of closing a highway or any part of it, a police officer may post or cause to be posted signs to that effect, or may place or cause to be placed traffic control devices as prescribed by the regulations.

The regulations prescribe the use of a "Do Not Enter" sign and not fewer than three orange cones, or not fewer than two rectangular shapes with horizontal orange and black stripes mounted on posts, or not fewer than two barricades that are orange or orange with with black bars. See figure 7.2.

The HTA also authorizes police officers to direct traffic to ensure the orderly movement of traffic, to prevent injury or damage to persons or property, or to permit proper action in an emergency.

With these powers comes the responsibility to ensure that no further injury or damage occurs at a collision scene. This responsibility means that officers attending a collision scene must warn other traffic approaching the scene so that the traffic has time to slow down and stop, if necessary. Flares are usually used for this purpose and must be placed far enough ahead of the collision scene according to the circumstances. On a long straight road with no view obstructions, only the speed limit is a factor in determining how far from the collision to place the flares. On a road with curves, hills, bridges, or other view obstructions of the collision scene, the flares may have to be placed much farther ahead.

Until the proper road or lane closure devices are in place, or if none are available, officers will have to direct traffic manually. This may require several police officers. If other officers are not available, a police cruiser, with the red lights activated, may be used to close a lane. Especially at night, officers directing traffic should ensure that they are wearing the appropriate reflective vests to avoid personal injury.

DOWNED HYDRO LINES

If hydro lines are down at a collision scene, hydro distribution companies recommend that the police officers stay in the police cruiser until the power can be shut off. If the road is wet, stepping onto the road could result in death by electrocution. The investigating officer should also take steps to keep other persons away from the collision scene and tell those involved in the collision to stay in their cars until the power has been shut off. Once the power has been shut off, the officer can continue to deal with other emergencies arising from the collision.

VEHICLE FIRES

If there are no dangerous goods involved, and a vehicle is on fire, the ignition should be turned off, if possible, and all people kept away until the fire department arrives. If the fire is small and can be extinguished, a dry-chemical extinguisher should be used. If no extinguisher is available, the fire should be smothered with dirt or a blanket, not water. The officer should remember his or her priorities when trying to save a car that is on fire. The officer's personal safety has priority over property. If occupants are still in the vehicle, rescue the occupants, if possible.

> **HINT**
>
> In extinguishing a car fire, use a fire extinguisher when one is available.
>
> Do not attempt to extinguish a car fire with water.

Figure 7.2 Barricades

Do Not Enter Sign
(60 cm × 60 cm)

- Red reflective circle
- White reflective background and bar
- Black border
- 6.5
- 44 cm
- 50 cm
- 5
- 5

Orange Cone

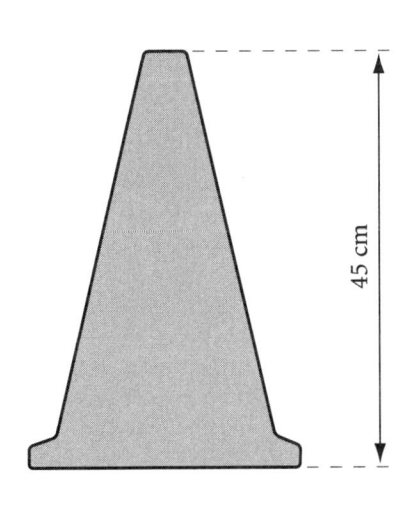

- 45 cm

Post

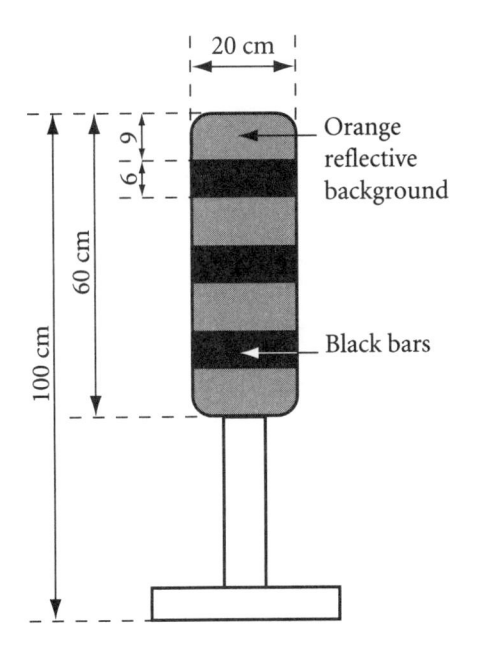

- 20 cm
- Orange reflective background
- 9
- 6
- 60 cm
- 100 cm
- Black bars

Barricade

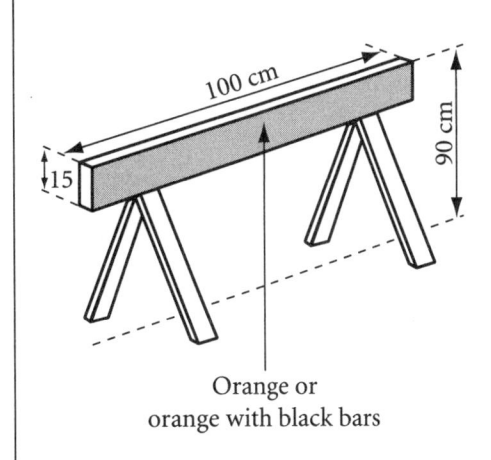

- 100 cm
- 15
- 90 cm
- Orange or orange with black bars

ROAD CONDITIONS

Often after an ice storm, the road conditions, if left unattended, may cause a serious collision. When investigating a serious collision due to icy roads, notify the communications centre to dispatch the road-sanding and road-salting equipment to the scene to reduce the likelihood of further collisions. Failure to do this may result in a charge of neglect of duty and exposure to civil liability.

THEFT PROTECTION

Sometimes valuable cargo is spilled on the road, and looting ensues. In this case, the investigating officer should immediately call for assistance to help secure the scene. If the first officer on the scene runs after someone who has stolen some cargo, the scene is left unprotected. At least one officer must protect the cargo while the investigating officer attends to other aspects of the collision.

If the road must be closed to prevent other collisions and injuries, or if the present collision has resulted in injuries, protecting the cargo is obviously secondary to attending to the injured. It would be unjustifiable, not to mention extremely unprofessional, for an officer to chase someone who has stolen a VCR or a case of beer from a spilled cargo if the driver is unconscious from injuries. Remember the motto YOU, THEM, IT; property is the last priority. An officer's first instinct may be to chase someone who is running from the scene with some cargo, but the officer must concern himself or herself first with the safety of others.

FIGHTING DRIVERS

The first officer on the scene must immediately call for backup if drivers are fighting. After doing so, the officer must stop the fight and keep the drivers apart. It will be necessary to place each driver in the back of separate police cruisers until the officer finds out what happened. Criminal charges may need to be laid, and neither driver should be allowed to leave until the incident is fully understood by the officer on the scene. This temporary incarceration will allow each driver to cool down. The authority to arrest in this case is granted to prevent a continuing breach of the peace. If there are no other charges pending, each driver may be released when he or she has calmed down. No charges may be laid for breach of the peace.

Management of People at the Scene

All dealings with the public must be done in a manner that enhances the professionalism of the police service. Collision investigations are one of the most common situations when ordinary members of the public come into contact with the police. The police officer must not make a bad impression if the police service seeks to gain or maintain public support. The officer must be seen to be courteous, sympathetic, and fair.

Four Questions to Ask at a Collision Scene

1. "IS ANYONE HURT?"

When approaching people at a collision scene, the police officer should first ask if anyone is hurt. This initial question shows concern for people first, and demonstrates that the police are not just there to lay charges or assign blame. This question also has investigative merit because the investigating officer may be challenged by an insurance company at a later date about why the officer did not initiate medical treatment for an injured person. If a person later claimed that he or she had sustained neck or back problems, the investigating officer can truthfully state that no one reported any injuries when questioned at the outset of the investigation.

The question also has the indirect value of helping to sort out the crowd that may have gathered. The crowd will usually direct the officer to the injured person(s) and react in other ways that give the officer clues about who is involved in the collision and who is just a spectator.

2. "WHO IS THE DRIVER OF THIS VEHICLE?"

If there are no injuries, the police officer should walk over and touch one of the vehicles and ask, "Who is the driver of this vehicle?" The voluntary answer to this investigative question is admissible in court because there is no mention of any charges at this stage. The question is also of such a nature that there is no dispute that the response is voluntary and not forced or coerced. The admission is important because it may be the only evidence of who was driving the vehicle. Once the driver is identified, the officer should ask the driver for his or her driver's licence, registration, and evidence of insurance. The officer should develop the habit of placing these documents together in a predetermined place, such as a right-hand pocket. This will save the officer the embarrassment of not being able to find the documents when he or she is ready to return them to the driver.

The officer could then ask the driver whether he or she was wearing a seat belt. Again, the confession is admissible in court if there is no dispute that the response is voluntary. The officer should then direct the driver to stay with his or her vehicle, or in another location if it is safer, until the officer returns.

If another vehicle is involved in the collision, the officer should walk over and touch that vehicle and ask, "Who is the driver of this vehicle?" Again, the voluntary answer is admissible in court because there is no mention of any charges at this stage. The officer should ask this driver for his or her licence, registration, and evidence of insurance, and place those documents in a predetermined place, such as a left-hand pocket (so as not to mix them up with the other driver's documents). The officer should ask whether the driver was wearing his or her seat belt and direct the driver to stay with his or her vehicle, or at another location if it is safer, preferably away from the other driver, to avoid a confrontation. The officer now has all of the documents of both drivers; this reduces the likelihood that either driver will leave the scene, and provides the officer with basic information for accident reports and charges, if charges are necessary.

3. "DID ANYONE WITNESS THE COLLISION?"

The identification of the drivers must not take very long because it is important to speak to any witnesses before they leave. The testimony of independent witnesses in court carries a lot of weight. The officer should approach the crowd and ask whether anyone witnessed the collision. If witnesses come forth, the officer should thank them for their assistance. The officer should tell the witnesses that it should only take a few minutes to record their statements, and then the officer should speak to each witness separately. If one witness says that he or she must leave immediately because of a scheduled meeting or for some other urgent reason, record his or her name and a number where he or she can be reached by phone. Insisting that he or she stay will only produce a hostile witness, who is likely to give a poor-quality statement and to be less helpful.

It is very important for the officer to listen to what each witness has to say before he or she asks for personal data. If the officer starts by asking for the witness's name, date of birth, address, phone number, place of employment, work phone number, and so on, the witness will likely fall into a question-and-answer mode, and may not offer information until he or she is asked for it. A better technique is for the officer to ask where the witness was in relation to the collision scene, and then ask the witness to recount, chronologically, what he or she saw. The officer should refrain from interrupting the witness with too many questions during the narrative, because it will disrupt the spontaneous flow of the witness's account and put the witness back into question-and-answer mode.

One technique to avoid interruptions, yet impose a logical order to the witness statement, is for the officer to hand the witness a card, and then ask the witness to please explain what he or she saw, following the order of the items on the card:

- Description of the vehicle.
- Direction of travel.
- Name of street.
- Lane of travel.
- Approximate speed.
- What happened?

> **HINT**
> People will talk when you listen.

It is always best to appear attentive when listening to a person who is speaking. People feel encouraged to talk if they see that you are listening. This point is very important to remember when taking any statement. The officer's interest and facial expressions will encourage a more detailed answer than would otherwise be obtained.

Listening means making continual eye contact and responding with facial expressions—not staring at your notebook and writing madly. If the investigating officer is looking only at his or her notebook, racing to record the witness's statement, and not paying attention to the witness, the witness becomes focused on the officer's writing and actually speaks at the pace of the officer's handwriting speed. Concentrating on the officer's problem will distract the witness and cause him or her to omit details in the statement. To avoid this problem, the officer should listen to the statement first, and then ask the witness to repeat the statement as the officer writes it down. Then the officer knows what to expect and can record the statement more effectively. Although this two-step procedure may appear to take more time, it really does not, because it reduces the time that it takes the officer to interrupt the witness to get the required details. There are other advantages to this approach: the statement is in the witness's own words, and in telling the story twice, the witness has the opportunity to consider the accuracy of his or her statement more carefully.

These statements can be handled as formal statements or as **"will say" statements**, depending on the policy of the police service and the severity of the collision. The witness should be invited to read the statement, to make any changes that he or she wishes, and to sign the statement. Because the Crown and defence counsel are likely to see the document, and it may be questioned in court, some attention should be paid to grammar, spelling, and clarity of language.

"will say" statements
a brief description or summary from an officer's notebook of what the witness will say in court; its primary audience is the Crown attorney and defence counsel, who will likely see the statement under evidentiary disclosure rules

4. "WAS ANYONE ELSE INVOLVED IN THE COLLISION?"

It usually is not necessary to take statements from passengers in the vehicles involved in the collision. These statements do not carry much weight because they are considered to be biased. Usually, the officer requires only information about a passenger's identity, position in the vehicle, seat belt use, and injury. If a person admits that he or she was not wearing a seat belt, this voluntary answer to an investigative question is admissible in court because there was no mention of any charges before the question was asked. The question must be asked in a manner that ensures there is no dispute that the response is voluntary.

Caution Statements

If the physical evidence is overwhelming or if independent witnesses supplied statements, the investigating officer may know beyond a reasonable degree of certainty that a violation of the HTA or CC has occurred. The officer should interview the non-offending driver first. The procedure for taking a statement from this driver is the same as for other witnesses. Get the driver's story first, and record the information from the driver's licence, registration, and insurance card last.

When the officer approaches the suspect driver, the officer should follow the **Judge's Rules** and read a prepared caution to him or her. The officer should read the caution before questioning the suspect because this driver is suspected of a violation and the giving of the caution may be necessary to prosecute a case against the suspect. The suggested language for the caution is as follows:

> You are to be charged with _____. Do you wish to say anything in answer to the charge? You are not obliged to say anything in answer to the charge unless you wish to do so, but whatever you do say may be given in evidence.

If, in response to the reading of the caution, the suspect driver does make a statement—known as a "cautioned statement"—it may be tendered as evidence at the trial. Prior to giving the contents of the statement as evidence, there will usually be a **voir dire** to ensure that the statement was voluntary and made without any inducements. The caution will go a long way to demonstrate that any subsequent statement was given voluntarily. Having the suspect driver read his or her statement over and make corrections before signing it also supports the case that the statement was given voluntarily.

Judge's Rules
rules that were developed by the English courts in the early 20th century, which govern the questioning of suspects; they have generally been applied in Canada and some of the rules have been incorporated into the *Canadian Charter of Rights and Freedoms*, particularly s. 10, which requires that a suspect be cautioned and advised of a right to counsel

voir dire
a "trial within a trial" conducted by a trial judge to determine whether evidence to be tendered is admissible in the main proceeding; an officer may have to give evidence on whether the accused was given a warning and whether his or her statement was voluntary and not compelled or coerced

If the driver refuses to make a statement after being cautioned, the officer may still charge the driver on the strength of physical evidence, on the evidence of the other driver, and on the evidence of independent witnesses. If there are no independent witnesses, the statement of the driver may be more important. Extra care should be exercised in taking this cautioned statement because its admission in court may be vital to the case.

Statements Required by Statute

If the suspect driver does not wish to make a cautioned statement at that time, he or she should be told of the statutory requirement in the HTA (ss. 199-200) to supply evidence necessary for the completion of the accident report. Failure to supply this information could result in a charge of failing to report a collision. However, care should be taken to explain to the driver that the statutory requirement invalidates the statement for use in court as evidence against the driver because it is a forced statement, not a voluntary one. Anything the driver says in providing information to complete the accident report cannot be used in court against the driver, but is required by the Ministry of Transportation for the planning of public safety. However, although the statement itself is not admissible in evidence against the driver, the information may provide useful insights that will assist the officer in gathering evidence that is admissible.

If the collision occurred at an intersection controlled by traffic lights and there is not enough physical evidence or statements from any independent witnesses, statements by statutory requirement will at least help determine the truth. In these cases, no charges are feasible. Remember that the investigating officer should be more concerned with determining what happened than with laying charges.

Unruly Spectators

If spectators become unruly, it is necessary to dispatch other police officers to the scene to assist. If spectators obstruct the officer in the lawful execution of his or her duty, a criminal charge of obstructing the police (CC, s. 129) is possible, although this detracts from the primary purpose of the investigation and is best handled by other officers.

Moving spectators back onto the sidewalk can be accomplished with an authoritative command. If people do not instantly obey the officer, an explanation of the consequences, given in a professional manner, is required. People who do not comply with this order are not necessarily "obstructing a peace officer"; there must be more evidence of interference with the collection of evidence or with other duties related to the collision investigation. Officers must not be overzealous in their wish to have everyone jump to their commands and immediately arrest those who do not. Arrests for this purpose diminish the professionalism of the police service and give the public the impression that the police are capricious and abuse their power.

CHAPTER SUMMARY

This chapter considers the role played by police officers at a motor vehicle collision scene, and provides information on how an officer manages a collision scene. Once an officer is dispatched to a collision, he or she must obtain as much advance information as possible, and then take steps to arrive quickly but safely at the scene. On arrival at the scene, the officer prioritizes emergencies, if there is more than one. The officer may have to deal with the presence of dangerous goods, injuries, downed hydro lines, fighting drivers, and vehicle fires. The officer also needs to take steps to ensure the protection of the collision scene, preserve evidence, and safeguard goods.

One of the officer's most important tasks is "people management." The officer must determine whether anyone is hurt, who the drivers are, who the witnesses are, and if necessary, obtain cautioned statements and witness statements, using various interview techniques designed to elicit accurate information efficiently and effectively.

KEY TERMS

bill of lading

oxidizer

"will say" statements

Judge's Rules

voir dire

REVIEW QUESTIONS

Short Answer

Briefly answer the following questions.

1. What would you do if you arrived at a collision scene and discovered

    a. that hydro lines were down?

    Close down the road, so that you or anyone else will not get hurt. First stay in the cruiser until the power can be shut off. If wet must stay inside vehicle and tell everyone involved to stay inside aswell.

    b. that a damaged tanker truck has a placard coloured red, with a flame and a number 3?

    Close down the streets and call the firefighters because all of those are flammable signs. red - anything flammable 3 - flame. The officers main priority is himself, so do not put out the fire if not safe to do so. Help all those who are in the vehicle.

    c. that two drivers are punching each other in the middle of the road?

    must immediately call for back up. Afterwards have to break up the fight and keep them separate.

d. that an injured person is badly cut, has bled profusely, and has no pulse, and a second person is sitting dazed on the side of the road, and appears to be in shock?

2. Explain what the following colours represent on dangerous-goods placards:

   a. yellow is an oxidizer, and the symbol is "O". A substance that combines with oxygen, and may be very volatile.

   b. white poisonous and infectious substances

   c. yellow over white Radioactive material Trefoil.

   d. green Non-flammable compressed gas.

e. blue — substances that are dangerous when wet

f. white over black — corrosive

3. Briefly describe the nine classes of dangerous goods.

   a. Explosive - orange
   exploding bombs

   b. compressed gas
   red green white
   anything that is poisonous
   when blown

   c. Flammable liquids
   Red liquid
   anything that will
   combust into flammes

   d. Flammable solid
   Red and white stripes
   white over red
   blue
   any solid that would combust
   into flammes.

e. oxidizers.
   yellow

f. poisonous/infectious
   white white
   anything that will kill if consumed.

g. Radioactivity
   Yellow over white
   Any chemical based poison

h. corrosive
   white over black
   will melt your skin

i. miscellaneous
   Black stripes over white

4. In what circumstances may an officer presume that a person at a collision scene is dead?

5. If the officer cannot presume that an injured person is dead, what must he or she do?

6. Suppose the collision scene is on a two-lane road, with one lane in each direction. Both lanes are blocked by the collision. Describe what you would do to close the road, and indicate the tools or devices you would use to do it.

7. What are the four questions you should ask at most collision scenes?

   a.

   b.

   c.

   d.

8. If a driver declines to answer your questions after being cautioned, is there any way to get information from that driver? Can that information be used in court?

Discussion Question

Given the following facts, explain what steps you would take as the first officer on the scene, in order.

You arrive at the scene of a collision at the intersection of two provincial highways in cottage country on a Friday night at 10 p.m. in summer. It is dark and beginning to rain. The intersection is controlled by traffic signals and is lit by two overhead street lights. There appear to be three vehicles involved. On the shoulder is a 48-passenger public commercial bus, with the front end demolished. The engine is still running, and a number of passengers appear to be injured. Some passengers are still on the bus, unable to get out through the doors on the smashed front end. About 15 people are gathered around the bus, some bleeding and dishevelled, and others appearing to be unhurt. The driver, it appears, is still in his seat, but he appears to be unconscious, and his clothing is covered with blood.

The second vehicle is a transport truck. It is in the intersection, lying on its side. It has completely blocked the roadway of both highways. Some of its cargo of red canisters has spilled. On the side of the truck you can see a red placard with a flame and the number 2 on it.

Lastly, there is a van behind the truck. Its front end is badly damaged. A man, woman, and two small children are standing next to the van. None of them appear to be injured.

The summer weekend traffic is snarled because vehicles cannot get through the intersection. Some vehicles are pulling onto the shoulder to try to inch past, others are trying to turn around and find an alternate route, and others are pulling onto the grass to stop, either to help or merely to watch. Your communications centre only told you that there was a collision for which they had no details. You and an ambulance are the only emergency vehicles dispatched to answer this call.

APPENDIX A

Short-Form Wordings and Set Fines from the Provincial Offences Act

The short-form wordings of charges as set out in the *Provincial Offences Act* are an aid in locating topics in the *Highway Traffic Act*. Users of this device must be aware that only charges are listed here. If police officers use the list of short-form wordings as a device for determining an appropriate charge, they must recognize that the short-form wordings do not adequately reflect all the facts in issue for an offence. The actual section, subsection, and clause should be referenced to determine whether a specific charge is appropriate. As long as users understand the limitations of this device, the short-form wordings are invaluable as an overview of all charges in the Act.

PROCEEDINGS COMMENCED BY CERTIFICATE OF OFFENCE, RRO 1990, REG. 950

SCHEDULE 43
HIGHWAY TRAFFIC ACT

Item	Column 1	Column 2 Section	Set Fine (Includes Costs)
1.	Drive motor vehicle, no permit	7(1)(a)	$85.00
2.	Drive motor vehicle, no currently validated permit	7(1)(a)	$85.00
3.	Drive motor vehicle, no plates	7(1)(b)(i)	$85.00
4.	Drive motor vehicle, fail to display two plates	7(1)(b)(i)	$85.00
5.	Drive motor vehicle, plate improperly displayed	7(1)(b)(i)	$85.00
6.	Drive motor vehicle, no validation on plate	7(1)(c)(i)	$85.00
7.	Drive motor vehicle, validation improperly affixed	7(1)(c)(i)	$85.00
8.	Draw trailer, no permit	7(4)(a)	$85.00
9.	Draw trailer, no plate	7(4)(b)	$85.00
10.	Draw trailer, plate improperly displayed	7(4)(b)	$85.00
11.	Fail to surrender permit for motor vehicle	7(5)(a)	$85.00
12.	Fail to surrender permit for trailer	7(5)(b)	$85.00
13.	Have more than one permit	7(15)	$85.00
14.	Drive motor vehicle, not in accordance with permit limitations	8	$140.00
15.	Permit driving of motor vehicle, not in accordance with permit limitations	8	$140.00
16.	REVOKED		
17.	Fail to notify change of address	9(2)	$85.00
18.	Fail to notify change of name	9(2)	$85.00
19.	Fail to notify change of address—lessee	9(3)	$85.00
20.	Fail to notify change of name—lessee	9(3)	$85.00
21.	Drive motor vehicle, no vehicle identification number	10(1)	$85.00
22.	Permit driving of motor vehicle, no vehicle identification number	10(1)	$85.00
23.	Draw trailer, no identification number	10(2)(a)	$85.00
24.	Permit drawing of trailer, no identification number	10(2)(a)	$85.00
25.	Draw conversion unit, no identification number	10(2)(b)	$85.00
26.	Permit drawing of conversion unit, no identification number	10(2)(b)	$85.00
27.	Draw converter dolly, no identification number	10(2)(c)	$85.00
28.	Permit drawing of converter dolly, no identification number	10(2)(c)	$85.00
29.	Fail to remove plates on ceasing to be owner	11(1)(a)	$85.00
30.	Fail to remove plates on ceasing to be lessee	11(1)(a)	$85.00
31.	Fail to retain plate portion of permit	11(1)(b)	$85.00
32.	Fail to give vehicle portion of permit to new owner	11(1)(c)(i)	$85.00
33.	Fail to give vehicle portion of permit to lessor	11(1)(c)(ii)	$85.00
34.	Fail to apply for permit on becoming owner	11(2)	$85.00

Item	Column 1	Column 2 Section	Set Fine (Includes Costs)
34.1	Fail to provide valid information package for inspection	11.1(1)	$140.00
34.2	Fail to deliver valid information package at time of vehicle transfer	11.1(1)	$140.00
35.	Deface plate	12(1)(a)	N.S.F.*
36.	Deface validation	12(1)(a)	N.S.F.
37.	Alter plate	12(1)(a)	N.S.F.
38.	Alter validation	12(1)(a)	N.S.F.
39.	Deface permit	12(1)(a)	N.S.F.
40.	Alter permit	12(1)(a)	N.S.F.
41.	Use defaced plate	12(1)(b)	N.S.F.
42.	Use defaced validation	12(1)(b)	N.S.F.
43.	Use altered plate	12(1)(b)	N.S.F.
44.	Use altered validation	12(1)(b)	N.S.F.
45.	Permit use of defaced plate	12(1)(b)	N.S.F.
46.	Permit use of defaced validation	12(1)(b)	N.S.F.
47.	Permit use of altered plate	12(1)(b)	N.S.F.
48.	Permit use of altered validation	12(1)(b)	N.S.F.
49.	Use defaced permit	12(1)(b)	N.S.F.
50.	Permit use of defaced permit	12(1)(b)	N.S.F.
51.	Remove plate without authority	12(1)(c)	N.S.F.
52.	Use plate not authorized for vehicle	12(1)(d)	N.S.F.
53.	Permit use of plate not authorized for vehicle	12(1)(d)	N.S.F.
54.	Use validation not furnished by Ministry	12(1)(e)	N.S.F.
55.	Use validation not furnished for vehicle	12(1)(e)	N.S.F.
56.	Permit use of validation not furnished by Ministry	12(1)(e)	N.S.F.
57.	Permit use of validation not furnished for vehicle	12(1)(e)	N.S.F.
58.	Use plate not in accordance with Act	12(1)(f)	$140.00
59.	Use plate not in accordance with regulations	12(1)(f)	$140.00
60.	Use validation not in accordance with Act	12(1)(f)	$140.00
61.	Use validation not in accordance with regulations	12(1)(f)	$140.00
62.	Permit use of plate not in accordance with Act	12(1)(f)	$140.00
63.	Permit use of plate not in accordance with regulations	12(1)(f)	$140.00
64.	Permit use of validation not in accordance with Act	12(1)(f)	$140.00
65.	Permit use of validation not in accordance with regulations	12(1)(f)	$140.00
66.	Confuse identity of plate	13(1)	$85.00
67.	Obstruct plate	13(2)	$85.00
68.	Dirty plate	13(2)	$85.00
69.	Entire plate not plainly visible	13(2)	$85.00
69.0.1	Obstruct plate, preventing accurate photograph by red light camera system	13(3.0.1)	$85.00

---

* "N.S.F." means no set fine.

Item	Column 1	Column 2 Section	Set Fine (Includes Costs)
69.1	Obstruct plate preventing accurate photograph	13(3)	$85.00
69.2	Obstruct plate preventing identification by toll system	13(3.1)	$85.00
70.	Operate commercial motor vehicle—no valid CVOR certificate	16(2)	$260.00
71.	Drive commercial motor vehicle—no valid CVOR certificate	16(2)	$175.00
72.	Fail to carry fleet limitation certificate	16(3)	$175.00
73.	Fail to carry CVOR certificate	16(3)(a)	$85.00
74.	Fail to carry vehicle lease	16(3)(b)	$85.00
75.	REVOKED		
76.	Fail to surrender CVOR certificate	16(4)	$85.00
77.	Fail to surrender vehicle lease	16(4)	$85.00
78.	REVOKED		
79.	Fail to surrender fleet limitation certificate	16(4)	$175.00
80.	Fail to notify change of officer's name	18	$175.00
81.	Fail to notify change of officer's address	18	$175.00
82.	Fail to notify change of officers	18	$175.00
83.	Fail to retain copy of lease	20(1)	$175.00
83.0.1	Provide fictitious, altered or fraudulently obtained CVOR certificate	21(4)	$400.00
83.0.2	Use fictitious, altered or fraudulently obtained CVOR certificate	21(4)	$400.00
83.0.3	Permit the use of fictitious, altered or fraudulently obtained CVOR certificate	21(4)	$400.00
83.0.4	Improperly use CVOR certificate	21(4)	$400.00
83.1	Operate commercial motor vehicle—improper insurance	23(1)	N.S.F.
83.2	Driver of commercial motor vehicle—fail to carry proof of insurance	23(3)	$175.00
83.3	Driver of commercial motor vehicle—fail to surrender proof of insurance	23(3)	$175.00
83.4	Inadequate cargo insurance	23.1	$85.00
83.5	No evidence of cargo insurance in vehicle	23.1	$85.00
84.	Drive motor vehicle—no licence	32(1)	$260.00
84.1	Drive commercial motor vehicle—no licence	32(1)	$310.00
85.	Drive motor vehicle—improper licence	32(1)	$260.00
85.1	Drive commercial motor vehicle—improper licence	32(1)	$310.00
86.	Drive streetcar—no licence	32(2)	$260.00
87.	Drive vehicle with air brakes—no endorsement	32(3)	$200.00
87.1	Drive commercial motor vehicle with air brake—no endorsement	32(3)	$310.00
88.	Drive motor vehicle in contravention of conditions	32(9)	$85.00
88.1	Drive commercial motor vehicle in contravention of conditions	32(9)	$310.00
89.	Permit unlicensed person to drive motor vehicle	32(10)	$200.00
89.1	Permit unlicensed person to drive commercial motor vehicle	32(10)	$310.00
90.	Permit person with improper licence to drive motor vehicle	32(10)	$200.00
90.1	Permit person with improper licence to drive commercial motor vehicle	32(10)	$310.00
91.	Permit unlicensed person to drive	32(10)	$200.00
91.1.	Permit operation of vehicles with air brakes—no endorsement on licence	32(11)	$200.00
91.2.	Permit novice driver to drive in contravention of condition or restriction	32(11.1)	$200.00

Item	Column 1	Column 2 Section	Set Fine (Includes Costs)
92.	Driver fail to surrender licence	33(1)	$85.00
92.1.	Accompanying driver fail to surrender licence	33(2)	$85.00
93.	Driver fail to give identification	33(3)	$85.00
93.1.	Accompanying driver fail to give identification	33(3)	$85.00
94.	Possess illegal licence	35(1)(a)	N.S.F.
95.	Use illegal licence	35(1)(a)	N.S.F.
96.	Possess non-Photo Card portion of cancelled, revoked or suspended licence	35(1)(b)	N.S.F.
97.	Use non-Photo Card portion of cancelled, revoked or suspended licence	35(1)	N.S.F.
98.	Permit another person to use all or part of licence or part of licence	35(1)(c)	N.S.F.
98.1.	Use other person's licence	35(1)(d)	N.S.F.
98.2.	Apply for more than one licence	35(1)(e)	N.S.F.
98.3.	Secure more than one licence	35(1)(e)	N.S.F.
98.4.	Possess more than one licence	35(1)(e)	N.S.F.
98.5.	Fail to surrender suspended, revoked or cancelled licence	35(1)(f)	N.S.F.
99.	Driving under licence of other jurisdiction while suspended in Ontario	36	N.S.F.
100.	Employ person under 16 to drive	37(2)	N.S.F.
101.	Permit person under 16 to drive	37(2)	N.S.F.
102.	Let unlicensed driver hire vehicle	39(1)	N.S.F.
103.	Fail to produce licence when hiring vehicle	39(3)	$85.00
103.1	Pick up passenger for compensation without authority	subsection 39.1(1)	$300.00
103.2	Owner—allow use of vehicle to pick up passenger for compensation without authority	subsection 39.1(2)	$300.00
103.3	Arrange for passenger pick-up for compensation without authority	subsection 39.1(3)	$300.00
103.4	Offer to arrange for passenger pick-up for compensation without authority	subsection 39.1(3)	$300.00
103.5	Fail to carry authority to pick up passengers for compensation	clause 39.1(4)(a)	$300.00
103.6	Fail to surrender authority to pick up passengers for compensation	clause 39.1(4)(b)	$300.00
103.7	Fail to identify self	subsection 39.1(6)	N.S.F.
104.	Apply for permit while prohibited	47(5)	N.S.F.
105.	Procure permit while prohibited	47(5)	N.S.F.
106.	Possess permit while prohibited	47(5)	N.S.F.
107.	Apply for licence while prohibited	47(6)	N.S.F.
108.	Procure licence while prohibited	47(6)	N.S.F.
109.	Possess licence while prohibited	47(6)	N.S.F.
110.	Procure CVOR certificate while suspended or cancelled	47(7)	$260.00
111.	Apply for CVOR certificate while suspended or cancelled	47(7)	$260.00

Item	Column 1	Column 2 Section	Set Fine (Includes Costs)
112.	Operate commercial motor vehicle—fleet limitation certificate not carried	47(8)(a)	N.S.F.
113.	Operate commercial motor vehicle—CVOR certificate	47(8)(b)	N.S.F.
113.1	Novice driver fail to provide breath sample	48.1(3)	$85.00
113.2	Novice driver refuse to provide breath sample	48.1(4)	$85.00
113.3	Novice driver fail to provide breath sample	48.1(4)	$85.00
113.4	Novice driver refuse to provide breath sample	48.1(4)	$85.00
113.5	Novice driver fail to surrender licence	48.1(5)	$85.00
113.6	Accompanying driver fail to provide breath sample	48.2(2)	$85.00
113.7	Accompanying driver refuse to provide breath sample	48.2(2)	$85.00
114.	Operate vehicle for which permit suspended	51	N.S.F.
115.	Operate vehicle for which permit cancelled	51	N.S.F.
116.	Driving while under suspension	53	N.S.F.
116.1	Passenger fail to identify self	57.1.1(1)	$85.00
116.2	Passenger fail to give required information	57.1.1(2)	$85.00
117.	No licence to operate vehicle business	59(1)	N.S.F.
118.	Interfere with officer inspecting vehicle business	59(6)	N.S.F.
119.	Fail to keep records	60(1)	N.S.F.
120.	Deal with vehicle identification number altered	60(2)	N.S.F.
121.	Deface vehicle identification number	60(3)	N.S.F.
122.	Remove vehicle identification number	60(3)	N.S.F.
123.	Fail to notify re vehicle stored more than 2 weeks	60(4)	$60.00
124.	Fail to report damaged vehicle	60(5)	$140.00
124.1	Give false report	60(6)	N.S.F.
125.	Drive without proper headlights—motor vehicle	62(1)	$85.00
125.1	Drive without proper headlights—commercial motor vehicle	62(1)	$200.00
126.	Drive without proper rear light—motor vehicle	62(1)	$85.00
126.1	Drive without proper rear light—commercial motor vehicle	62(1)	$200.00
127.	Drive without proper headlight—motorcycle	62(2)	$85.00
128.	Drive without proper rear light—motorcycle	62(2)	$85.00
129.	Drive without proper headlights—motorcycle with sidecar	62(3)	$85.00
130.	Drive without proper rear light—motorcycle with side car	62(3)	$85.00
131.	Drive with improper headlights	62(6)	$85.00
131.1	Drive with improper headlights—commercial motor vehicle	62(6)	$200.00
132.	Drive with headlamp coated	62(7)	$85.00
132.1	Drive with headlight coated—commercial motor vehicle	62(7)	$200.00
133.	Drive with headlamp covered	62(7)	$85.00
133.1	Drive with headlamp covered—commercial motor vehicle	62(7)	$200.00
134.	Drive with headlamp modified	62(7)	$85.00
134.1	Drive with headlamp modified—commercial motor vehicle	62(7)	$200.00
135.	More than 4 lighted headlights	62(9)	$85.00
135.1	More than 4 lighted headlights—commercial motor vehicle	62(9)	$200.00

Item	Column 1	Column 2 Section	Set Fine (Includes Costs)
136.	Improper clearance lights	62(10)	$85.00
136.1	Improper clearance lights—commercial motor vehicle	62(10)	$200.00
137.	Fail to have proper identification lamps	62(11)	$85.00
137.1	Fail to have proper identification lamps—commercial motor vehicle	62(11)	$200.00
138.	Fail to have proper side marker lamps	62(13)	$85.00
138.1	Fail to have proper side marker lamps—commercial motor vehicle	62(13)	$200.00
139.	Use lamp producing intermittent flashes of red light	62(14)	$85.00
139.1	Use lamp producing intermittent flashes of red light—commercial motor vehicle	62(14)	$200.00
140	Red light at front	62(15)	$85.00
140.1	Red light at front—commercial motor vehicle	62(15)	$200.00
141.	Use V.F.F. lamp improperly	62(16)	$85.00
141.1	Use V.F.F. lamp improperly—commercial motor vehicle	62(16.1)	$200.00
142.	Improper bicycle lighting	62(17)	$20.00
143.	Improper lighting on motor assisted bicycle	62(17)	$20.00
144.	Improper number plate light	62(19)	$85.00
145.	Use parking light while vehicle in motion	62(20)	$85.00
146.	Have more than one spotlamp	62(22)	$85.00
146.1	Have more than one spotlamp—commercial motor vehicle	62(22)	$200.00
147.	Improper use of spotlamp	62(22)	$85.00
147.1	Improper use of spotlamp—commercial motor vehicle	62(22)	$200.00
148.	Improper lights on traction engine	62(23)	$85.00
149.	No red light on rear of trailer	62(24)	$85.00
149.1	No red light on rear of trailer—commercial motor vehicle	62(24)	$200.00
150.	No red light on rear of object	62(24)	$85.00
150.1	No red light on rear of object—commercial motor vehicle	62(24)	$200.00
151.	No proper red lights—object over 2.6 metres	62(25)	$85.00
151.1	No proper red light—object over 2.6 m—commercial motor vehicle	62(25)	$200.00
152.	No lamp on left side	62(26)	$85.00
152.1	No lamp on left side—commercial motor vehicle	62(26)	$200.00
153.	Improper lights on farm vehicle	62(27)	$85.00
154.	No directional signals	62(29)	$85.00
154.1	No directional signals—commercial motor vehicle	62(29)	$200.00
155.	No brake lights	62(29)	$85.00
155.1	No brake lights—commercial motor vehicle	62(29)	$200.00
156.	No blue flashing light on snow removal vehicle	62(31)	$85.00
157.	Improper use of blue flashing light	62(32)	$85.00
158.	No sign—"right hand drive vehicle"	63	$85.00
159.	Improper braking system	64(1)	$85.00
159.1	Improper braking system—commercial motor vehicle	64(1)	$400.00
160.	Improper brakes on motorcycle	64(2)	$85.00

Item	Column 1	Column 2 Section	Set Fine (Includes Costs)
161.	Improper brakes on motor assisted bicycle	64(2)	$85.00
161.1	Improper brakes on bicycle	64(3)	$85.00
162.1	Improper brakes on trailer—commercial motor vehicle	64(5)	$400.00
162.	Improper brakes on trailer	64(5)	$85.00
163.	Defective brakes	64(7)	$85.00
163.1	Defective brakes—commercial motor vehicle	64(7)	$400.00
164.	Defective braking system	64(7)	$85.00
164.1	Defective braking system—commercial motor vehicle	64(7)	$400.00
165.	Sell improper brake fluid	65(1)(a)	N.S.F.
166.	Offer to sell improper brake fluid	65(1)(a)	N.S.F.
167.	Install improper brake fluid	65(1)(a)	N.S.F.
168.	Sell improper hydraulic oil	65(1)(b)	N.S.F.
169.	Offer to sell improper hydraulic oil	65(1)(b)	N.S.F.
170.	Install improper hydraulic oil	65(1)(b)	N.S.F.
171.	Improper windshield wiper	66(1)(a)	$85.00
171.1	Improper windshield wiper—commercial motor vehicle	66(1)(a)	$200.00
172.	No windshield wiper	66(1)(a)	$85.00
172.1	No windshield wiper—commercial motor vehicle	66(1)(a)	$200.00
173.	Improper mirror	66(1)(b)	$85.00
173.1	Improper mirror—commercial motor vehicle	66(1)(b)	$200.00
174.	No mirror	66(1)(b)	$85.00
174.1	No mirror—commercial motor vehicle	66(1)(b)	$200.00
175.	Improper mudguards	66(3)	$85.00
175.1	Improper mudguards—commercial motor vehicle	66(3)	$200.00
176.	No mudguards	66(3)	$85.00
176.1	No mudguards—commercial motor vehicle	66(3)	$200.00
177.	No odometer	66(5)	$85.00
177.1	No odometer—commercial motor vehicle	66(5)	$200.00
178.	Defective odometer	66(5)	$85.00
178.1	Defective odometer—commercial motor vehicle	66(5)	$200.00
179.	Operate motor vehicle—mirrors more than 305 mm	67	$85.00
180.	No speedometer on bus	68	$85.00
181.	Defective speedometer on bus	68	$85.00
182.	Improper tire—damage to highway	69(1)	$85.00
183.	Device on wheels—injure highway	69(2)	$85.00
184.	No lock shoe—animal drawn vehicle	69(3)	$85.00
185.	Improper tires	70(3)(a)	$85.00
185.1	Improper tires—commercial motor vehicle	70(3)(a)	$200.00
186.	Improper tires—drawn vehicle	70(3)(a)	$85.00
186.1	Improper tires—drawn vehicle—commercial motor vehicle	70(3)(a)	$200.00

Short-Form Wordings and Set Fines from the Provincial Offences Act — APPENDIX A

Item	Column 1	Column 2 Section	Set Fine (Includes Costs)
187.	Improperly installed tires	70(3)(b)	$85.00
187.1	Improperly installed tires—commercial motor vehicle	70(3)(b)	$200.00
188.	Improperly installed tires—drawn vehicle	70(3)(b)	$85.00
188.1	Improperly installed tires—drawn vehicle—commercial motor vehicle	70(3)(b)	$200.00
189.	Fail to mark rebuilt tire	71(2)	N.S.F.
190.	Sell unmarked rebuilt tire	71(3)	N.S.F.
191.	Offer to sell unmarked rebuilt tire	71(3)	N.S.F.
192.	Sell new vehicle—no safety glass	72(2)	N.S.F.
193.	Register new vehicle—no safety glass	72(2)	N.S.F.
194.	Install non-safety glass	72(3)	N.S.F.
195.	Window obstructed	73(1)(a)	$85.00
196.	Windshield obstructed	73(1)(a)	$85.00
197.	Have object obstructing view	73(1)(b)	$85.00
198.	Drive with window coated—view obstructed	73(2)	$85.00
199.	Drive with windshield coated—view obstructed	73(2)	$85.00
200.	Colour coating obscuring interior	73(3)	$85.00
201.	No clear view to front	74(1)(a)	$85.00
202.	No clear view to sides	74(1)(a)	$85.00
203.	No clear view to rear	74(1)(b)	$85.00
204.	No muffler—motor vehicle	75(1)	$85.00
205.	No muffler—motor assisted bicycle	75(1)	$85.00
206.	Improper muffler—motor vehicle	75(1)	$85.00
207.	Improper muffler—motor assisted bicycle	75(1)	$85.00
208.	Excessive fumes	75(3)	$85.00
209.	Unreasonable noise—signalling device	75(4)	$85.00
210.	Unreasonable smoke	75(4)	$85.00
211.	Unnecessary noise	75(4)	$85.00
212.	No horn—motor vehicle	75(5)	$85.00
213.	No horn—motor assisted bicycle	75(5)	$85.00
214.	No horn—bicycle	75(5)	$85.00
215.	Defective horn—motor vehicle	75(5)	$85.00
216.	Defective horn—motor assisted bicycle	75(5)	$85.00
217.	Defective horn—bicycle	75(5)	$85.00
218.	Have a siren	75(6)	$85.00
219.	No slow moving vehicle sign	76(1)	$85.00
219.1	Slow moving vehicle sign not attached to rear of vehicle or trailer	76(1)	$85.00
219.2	Slow moving vehicle sign not attached in accordance with regulations	76(1)	$85.00
219.3	Slow moving vehicle sign placed on fixed object	76(4)	$85.00
219.4	Prohibited use of slow moving vehicle sign	76(6)	$85.00
220.	No sleigh bells	77(1)	$25.00

Item	Column 1	Column 2 Section	Set Fine (Includes Costs)
221.	Television in front seat	78(1)(a)	$85.00
222.	Television visible to driver	78(1)(b)	$85.00
223.	Television operating in front seat	78(2)	$85.00
224.	Television operating—visible to driver	78(2)	$85.00
225.	Drive motor vehicle with speed measuring warning device	79(2)	$140.00
225.1	Drive motor vehicle with pre-empting traffic control signal device	79.1(1)	$140.00
226.	Improper means of attachment	80	$85.00
226.1	Improper means of attachment—commercial motor vehicle	80	$200.00
227	Refuse or fail to stop and move vehicle to a safe location	82(9)	$140.00
227.1	Refuse or fail to submit vehicle to examinations and tests	82(9)	$140.00
227.2	Refuse or fail to have vehicle repaired and submitted to further examinations and tests	82(9)	$140.00
227.3	Refuse or fail to have vehicle repaired and submit evidence of compliance	82(9)	$140.00
227.4	Refuse or fail to assist with examinations and tests of vehicle	82(9)	$140.00
227.5	Refuse or fail to place vehicle in safe condition	82(9)	$140.00
227.6	Refuse or fail to remove unsafe vehicle from highway	82(9)	$140.00
227.7	Operate unsafe vehicle on highway contrary to officer's prohibition	82(9)	$140.00
227.8	Permit operation of unsafe vehicle on highway contrary to officer's prohibition	82(9)	$140.00
227.9	Refuse or fail to stop and move vehicle to a safe location—commercial motor vehicle	82(10)	$400.00
227.10	Refuse or fail to submit vehicle to examinations and tests—commercial motor vehicle	82(10)	$400.00
227.11	Refuse or fail to have vehicle repaired and submitted to further examinations and tests—commercial motor vehicle	82(10)	$400.00
227.12	Refuse or fail to have vehicle repaired and submit evidence of compliance—commercial motor vehicle	82(10)	$400.00
227.13	Refuse or fail to assist with examinations and tests of vehicle—commercial motor vehicle	82(10)	$400.00
227.14	Refuse or fail to place vehicle in safe condition—commercial motor vehicle	82(10)	$400.00
227.15	Refuse or fail to remove unsafe vehicle from highway—commercial motor vehicle	82(10)	$400.00
227.16	Operate unsafe vehicle on highway contrary to officer's prohibition—commercial motor vehicle	82(10)	$400.00
227.17	Permit operation of unsafe vehicle on highway contrary to officer's prohibition—commercial motor vehicle	82(10)	$400.00
228.	Operate unsafe vehicle	84	N.S.F.
228.1	Operate unsafe vehicle—commercial motor vehicle	84	N.S.F.
229.	Operate unsafe streetcar	84	N.S.F.
230.	Operate unsafe combination of vehicles	84	N.S.F.
230.1	Operate unsafe combination of vehicles—commercial motor vehicle	84	N.S.F.
231.	Permit operation of unsafe vehicle	84	N.S.F.

Item	Column 1	Column 2 Section	Set Fine (Includes Costs)
231.1	Permit operation of unsafe vehicle—commercial motor vehicle	84	N.S.F.
232.	Permit operation of unsafe streetcar	84	N.S.F.
233.	Permit operation of unsafe combination of vehicles	84	N.S.F.
233.1	Permit operation of unsafe combination of vehicles—commercial motor vehicle	84	N.S.F.
234.	Operate vehicle—fail to display device	85(1)	$200.00
235.	Permit operation of vehicle fail to display device	85(1)	$200.00
236.	Issue SSC not provided by Ministry	86	N.S.F.
237.	Affix vehicle inspection sticker not provided by Ministry	86	N.S.F.
238.	Unauthorized person issue SSC	90(1)	N.S.F.
239.	Unauthorized person affix vehicle inspection sticker	90(2)	$200.00
240.	Issue SSC without proper inspection	90(3)(a)	N.S.F.
241.	Affix vehicle inspection certificate with out proper inspection	90(3)(a)	N.S.F.
242.	Issue SSC—vehicle not complying	90(3)(a)	N.S.F.
243.	Affix vehicle inspection sticker—vehicle not	90(3)(a)	N.S.F.
244.	SSC not made by inspection mechanic	90(3)(b)(i)	N.S.F.
245.	Vehicle inspection record not made by inspection mechanic	90(3)(b)(i)	N.S.F.
246.	SSC not countersigned	90(3)(b)(ii)	N.S.F.
247.	Unlicensed inspection station	91(1)	$400.00
248.	Corporation fail to notify change of officer or director	91(7)	N.S.F.
249.	Unregistered mechanic certify SSC	92(1)	N.S.F.
250.	Unregistered mechanic sign vehicle inspection record	92(1)	N.S.F.
251.	Obstruct inspector	98(6)	N.S.F.
252.	False statement in SSC	99(2)	N.S.F.
253.	Sell new vehicle not complying with standards	102(3)	N.S.F.
254.	Offer for sale new vehicle not complying with standards	102(3)	N.S.F.
255.	Expose for sale new vehicle not complying with standards	102(3)	N.S.F.
256.	Sell new vehicle not marked or identified	102(3)	N.S.F.
257.	Offer for sale new vehicle not marked or identified	102(3)	N.S.F.
258.	Expose for sale new vehicle not marked or identified	102(3)	N.S.F.
259.	No name on commercial vehicle	103(1)	$85.00
260.	Less than two reflectors—commercial vehicle	103(2)	$85.00
261.	Less than two reflectors—trailer	103(2)	$85.00
262.	Sell new commercial vehicle without two red rear lights	103(3)(a)	N.S.F.
263.	Offer to sell new commercial vehicle without two red rear lights	103(3)(a)	N.S.F.
264.	Sell trailer without two red rear lights	103(3)(a)	N.S.F.
265.	Offer to sell trailer without two red rear lights	103(3)(a)	N.S.F.
266.	Sell new commercial vehicle without two rear red reflectors	103(3)(b)	N.S.F.
267.	Offer to sell new commercial vehicle without two rear red reflectors	103(3)(b)	N.S.F.
268.	Sell trailer without two rear red reflectors	103(3)(b)	N.S.F.
269.	Offer to sell trailer without two rear red reflectors	103(3)(b)	N.S.F.

TRAFFIC MANAGEMENT

Item	Column 1	Column 2 Section	Set Fine (Includes Costs)
270.	No name and address on road-building machine	103(4)	$85.00
271.	Fail to wear proper helmet on motorcycle	104(1)	$85.00
272.	Fail to wear proper helmet on motor assisted bicycle	104(1)	$85.00
273.	Carry passenger under 16 not wearing proper helmet	104(2)	$85.00
273.1	Fail to wear proper helmet on bicycle	104(2.1)	$60.00
273.2	Permit person under 16 not wearing proper helmet on bicycle	104(2.2)	$60.00
273.3	Equestrian rider—fail to use proper equipment	104.1(1)	$60.00
273.4	Authorize or permit equestrian rider under 16 to ride without proper equipment	104.1(3)	$60.00
274.	Dealing with vehicle not confirming to standard	105(1)	N.S.F.
275.	Dealing with motor assisted bicycle—no document of compliance	105(2)	N.S.F.
276.	Drive with seat belt removed	106(1)	$85.00
277.	Drive with seat belt inoperative	106(1)	$85.00
278.	Drive with seat belt modified	106(1)	$85.00
279.	Driver—fail to properly wear seat belt	106(2)	$85.00
280.	Passenger—fail to occupy position with seat belt	106(3)(a)	$85.00
281.	Passenger—fail to properly wear seat belt	106(3)(b)	$85.00
282.	Drive while passenger under 16 fails to occupy position with seat belt	106(4)(a)(i)	$85.00
283.	Drive while passenger under 16 fails to properly wear seat belt	106(4)(a)(ii)	$85.00
284.	REVOKED		
285.	REVOKED		
286.	REVOKED		
287.	REVOKED		
287.1.	Driver—fail to ensure child passenger occupies seat belt assembly equipped position	106(7)	$85.00
288.	Fail to establish system to periodically inspect, repair and maintain commercial motor vehicles	107(2)	$310.00
289.	Fail to inspect commercial motor vehicle or cause inspection	107(3)	$310.00
290.	Fail to repair commercial motor vehicle or cause repair	107(3)	$310.00
291.	Fail to maintain commercial motor vehicle or cause it to be maintained	107(3)	$310.00
292.	Fail to instruct driver to inspect commercial motor vehicle or cause inspection of it	107(4)	$310.00
293.	Drive commercial motor vehicle without prescribed inspection	107(5)	$310.00
294.	Tow trailer without prescribed inspection	107(5)	$310.00
295.	Fail to report vehicle defect	107(6)	$310.00
296.	Fail to report trailer defect	107(6)	$310.00
297.	Drive defective vehicle	107(7)	$310.00
298.	Tow defective trailer	107(7)	$310.00
299.	Permit operation of defective vehicle	107(8)	$310.00
300.	Permit towing of defective trailer	107(8)	$310.00
301.	Fail to maintain documents or cause them to be maintained	107(9)	$310.00

Item	Column 1	Column 2 Section	Set Fine (Includes Costs)
302.	Fail to carry inspection report	107(10)	$310.00
303.	Fail to surrender inspection report	107(10)	$310.00
304.	Overwidth vehicle	109(1)	$310.00
305.	Overwidth load	109(2)	$310.00
306.	Overlength vehicle	109(6)	$310.00
307.	Overlength combination of vehicles	109(7)	$310.00
307.1	Operate overlength combination of vehicles	109(8)	$310.00
308.	Overlength semi-trailer	109(10)	$310.00
309.	Overlength bus	109(11)	$310.00
310.	Overheight vehicle	109(14)	$310.00
311.	Fail to carry permit in vehicle	110(6)	$310.00
312.	Fail to produce permit	110(6)	$310.00
313.	Oversize vehicle—violate permit	110(7)	$310.00
314.	Overweight vehicle—violate permit	110(7)	$200.00 + Schedule A
314.1	Fail to comply with condition of permit	110(7)	$310.00
314.2	Violate non-weight condition of special permit	110.2(3)(a)	$310.00
314.3	Violate weight condition of special permit	110.2(3)(b)	Schedule A
314.4	Violate weight condition of special permit—liftable axle lifted	110.2(3)(b)	$200.00+ Schedule A
314.5	Violate weight condition of special permit—liftable axle deployed improperly	110.2(3)(b)	$200.00 + Schedule A
314.6	Violate more than one condition, including a weight condition, of special permit	110.2(3)(c)	$200.00 + Schedule A
314.7	Violate more than one condition, including a weight condition, of special permit—liftable axle lifted	110.2(3)(c)	NSF
314.8	Violate more than one condition, including a weight condition, of special permit—liftable axle deployed improperly	110.2(3)(c)	NSF
315.	Fail to mark overhanging load	111(1)	$130.00
315.1	Fail to mark overhanging load—commercial motor vehicle	111(1)	$200.00
316.	Insecure load	111(2)	$130.00
316.1	Insecure load—commercial motor vehicle	111(2)	$310.00
316.2	Operate vehicle with load not secured as prescribed	111(2.1)	$130.00
316.3	Operate commercial motor vehicle with load not secured as prescribed	111(2.1)	$310.00
316.4	Permit operation of vehicle with load not secured as prescribed	111(2.1)	$130.00
316.5	Permit operation of commercial motor vehicle with load not secured as prescribed	111(2.1)	$310.00
316.6	Drive commercial motor vehicle without conducting inspections	111(2.2)	$310.00
317.	Overweight on tires … kg. … less than 150 mm.	115(1)(a)	Schedule A
317.1	Overweight on tires … kg.—liftable axle lifted	115(1)(a)	$200.00 + Schedule A

Item	Column 1	Column 2 Section	Set Fine (Includes Costs)
317.2	Overweight on tires … kg.—liftable axle deployed improperly	115(1)(a)	$200.00 + Schedule A
318.	Overweight on tires … kg. … 150 mm or over	115(1)(b)	Schedule A
318.1	Overweight on tires … kg.—liftable axle lifted	115(1)(b)	$200.00 + Schedule A
318.2	Overweight on tires … kg.—liftable axle deployed improperly	115(1)(b)	$200.00 + Schedule A
319.	Overweight single axle (single tires) … kg. Class A Highway	116(1)(a)	Schedule A
319.1	Overweight single axle (single tires) … kg. Class A Highway—liftable axle lifted	116(1)(a)	$200.00 + Schedule A
319.2	Overweight single axle (single tires) … kg. Class A Highway—liftable axle deployed improperly	116(1)(a)	$200.00 + Schedule A
320.	Overweight single axle (dual tires) … kg. Class A Highway	116(1)(a)	Schedule A
320.1	Overweight single axle (dual tires) … kg. Class A Highway—liftable axle lifted	116(1)(b)	$200.00 + Schedule A
320.2	Overweight single axle (dual tires) … kg. Class A Highway—liftable axle deployed improperly	116(1)(b)	$200.00 + Schedule A
321.	Overweight dual axle … kg. Class A Highway	116(1)(c)	Schedule A
321.1	Overweight dual axle … kg. Class A Highway—liftable axle lifted	116(1)(c)	$200.00 + Schedule A
321.2	Overweight dual axle … kg. Class A Highway—liftable axle deployed improperly	116(1)(c)	$200.00 + Schedule A
322.	Overweight triple axle … kg. Class A Highway	116(1)(d)	Schedule A
322.1	Overweight triple axle … kg. Class A Highway—liftable axle lifted	116(1)(d)	$200.00 + Schedule A
322.2	Overweight triple axle … kg. Class A Highway—liftable axle deployed improperly	116(1)(d)	$200.00 + Schedule A
323.	Overweight dual axle (single tires) … kg. Class A Highway	116(2)	Schedule A
323.1	Overweight dual axle (single tires) … kg. Class A Highway—liftable axle lifted	116(2)	$200.00 + Schedule A
323.2	Overweight dual axle (single tires) … kg. Class A Highway—liftable axle deployed improperly	116(2)	$200.00 + Schedule A
324.	Overweight triple axle (single tires) … kg. Class A Highway	116(3)	Schedule A
324.1	Overweight triple axle (single tires) … kg. Class A Highway—liftable axle lifted	116(3)	$200.00+ Schedule A
324.2	Overweight triple axle (single tires) … kg. Class A Highway—liftable axle deployed improperly	116(3)	$200.00 + Schedule A
325.	Overweight single front axle … kg. No verification. Class A Highway	116(4)	Schedule A
325.1	Overweight single front axle … kg. No verification. Class A Highway—liftable axle lifted	116(4)	$200.00 + Schedule A
325.2	Overweight single front axle … kg. No verification. Class A Highway—liftable axle deployed improperly	116(4)	$200.00 + Schedule A
326	Overweight single front axle … kg. Exceed rating. Class A Highway	116(6)	Schedule A

Item	Column 1	Column 2 Section	Set Fine (Includes Costs)
326.1	Overweight single front axle ... kg. Exceed rating. Class A Highway—liftable axle lifted	116(6)	$200.00 + Schedule A
326.2	Overweight single front axle ... kg. Exceed rating. Class A Highway—liftable axle deployed improperly	116(6)	$200.00 + Schedule A
327	Overweight two axle group ... kg. Class A Highway	117(1)(a)	Schedule A
327.1	Overweight two axle group ... kg. Class A Highway—liftable axle lifted	117(1)(a)	$200.00 + Schedule A
327.2	Overweight two axle group ... kg. Class A Highway—liftable axle deployed improperly	117(1)(a)	$200.00 + Schedule A
328	Overweight three axle group ... kg. Class A Highway	117(1)(b)	Schedule A
328.1	Overweight three axle group ... kg. Class A Highway—liftable axle lifted	117(1)(b)	$200.00 + Schedule A
328.2	Overweight three axle group ... kg. Class A Highway—liftable axle deployed improperly	117(1)(b)	$200.00 + Schedule A
329	Overweight four axle group ... kg. Class A Highway	117(1)(c)	Schedule A
329.1	Overweight four axle group ... kg. Class A Highway—liftable axle lifted	117(1)(c)	$200.00 + Schedule A
329.2	Overweight four axle group ... kg. Class A Highway—liftable axle deployed improperly	117(1)(c)	$200.00 + Schedule A
330	Overweight vehicle ... kg. Class A Highway	118	Schedule A
330.1	Overweight vehicle ... kg. Class A Highway—liftable axle lifted	118	$200.00 + Schedule A
330.2	Overweight vehicle ... kg. Class A Highway—liftable axle deployed improperly	118	$200.00 + Schedule A
331	Overweight vehicle during freeze-up ... kg.	119(4)	Schedule A
331.1	Overweight vehicle during freeze-up ... kg.—liftable axle lifted	119(4)	$200.00 + Schedule A
331.2	Overweight vehicle during freeze-up ... kg.—liftable axle deployed improperly	119(4)	$200.00 + Schedule A
332	Overweight on axle ... kg. Class B Highway	120	Schedule A
332.1	Overweight on axle ... kg. Class B Highway—liftable axle lifted	120	$200.00 + Schedule A
332.2	Overweight on axle ... kg. Class B Highway—liftable axle deployed improperly	120	$200.00 + Schedule A
333.	Overweight vehicle—violate permit ... kg.	121(1)	Schedule A
334.	Fail to have receipt in vehicle	121(3)	$75.00
335.	Fail to produce receipt	121(3)	$75.00
335.1	Overweight on axle ... kg.—reduced load period	122(1)	Schedule A
335.2	Overweight on axle ... kg.—reduced load period—liftable axle lifted	122(1)	$200.00 + Schedule A
335.3	Overweight on axle ... kg.—reduced load period—liftable axle deployed improperly	122(1)	$200.00 + Schedule A
335.4	Overweight on tire ... kg.—reduced load period	122(3)	Schedule A

Item	Column 1	Column 2 Section	Set Fine (Includes Costs)
335.5	Overweight on tire … kg.—reduced load period—liftable axle lifted	122(3)	$200.00 + Schedule A
335.6	Overweight on tire … kg.—reduced load period—liftable axle deployed improperly	122(3)	$200.00 + Schedule A
336.	Fail or refuse to stop	124(3)	$200.00
337.	Fail or refuse to drive vehicle to scale	124(3)	$200.00
338.	Fail or refuse to redistribute or remove load	124(4)(a)	$100.00
338.1	Fail or refuse to stop—commercial motor vehicle	124(5)	$310.00
338.2	Fail or refuse to drive vehicle to scale—commercial motor vehicle	124(5)	$310.00
338.3	Fail or refuse to redistribute or remove load—commercial motor vehicle	124(6)(a)	$310.00
339.	Cause vehicle to be overloaded	126	Schedule A
340.	Speeding	128	Schedule B
340.1	Speeding—liability of owner where evidence obtained through photo-radar	128	Schedule C
340.2	Speeding—community safety zone	128	Schedule D
340.3	Owner—speeding pursuant to section 207 community safety zone	128	Schedule D
340.4	Speeding—construction zone	128	Schedule E
340.5	Speeding—construction zone—worker present	128	Schedule F
341.	Careless driving	130	$260.00
341.1	Careless driving—community safety zone	130	N.S.F.
342.	Unnecessary slow driving	132	$85.00
342.1	Unnecessary slow driving—community safety zone	132	$120.00
343.	Disobey officer directing traffic	134(1)	$85.00
343.1	Disobey officer directing traffic—community safety zone	134(1)	$120.00
344.	Drive on closed highway	134(3)	$85.00
344.1	Drive on closed highway—community safety zone	134(3)	$120.00
345.	Fail to yield—uncontrolled intersection	135(2)	$85.00
345.1	Fail to yield—uncontrolled intersection—community safety zone	135(2)	$150.00
346.	Fail to yield to vehicle on right	135(3)	$85.00
346.1	Fail to yield to vehicle on right—community safety zone	135(3)	$150.00
347.	Disobey stop sign—stop wrong place	136(1)(a)	$85.00
347.1	Disobey stop sign—stop wrong place—community safety zone	136(1)(a)	$120.00
348.	Disobey stop sign—fail to stop	136(1)(a)	$85.00
348.1	Disobey stop sign—fail to stop—community safety zone	136(1)(a)	$150.00
349.	Fail to yield to traffic on through highway	136(1)(b)	$85.00
349.1	Fail to yield to traffic on through highway—community safety zone	136(1)(b)	$150.00
350.	Traffic on through highway—fail to yield	136(2)	$85.00
350.1	Traffic on through highway—fail to yield—community safety zone	136(2)	$150.00
351.	Fail to yield—yield sign	138(1)	$85.00
351.1	Fail to yield—yield sign—community safety zone	138(1)	$150.00
352.	Fail to yield from private road	139(1)	$85.00
352.1	Fail to yield from private road—community safety zone	139(1)	$150.00

Item	Column 1	Column 2 Section	Set Fine (Includes Costs)
353.	Fail to yield from driveway	139(1)	$85.00
353.1	Fail to yield from driveway—community safety zone	139(1)	$150.00
354.	Fail to yield to pedestrian	140(1)(a)	$150.00
354.1	Fail to yield to pedestrian—community safety zone	140(1)(a)	$300.00
355.	Fail to yield to pedestrian approaching	140(1)(b)	$150.00
355.1	Fail to yield to pedestrian approaching—community safety zone	140(1)(b)	$300.00
356.	Fail to yield to person in wheelchair	140(1)(a)	$150.00
356.1	Fail to yield to person in wheelchair—community safety zone	140(1)(a)	$300.00
357.	Fail to yield to person in wheelchair approaching	140(1)(b)	$150.00
357.1	Fail to yield to person in wheelchair approaching—community safety zone	140(1)(b)	$300.00
358.	Pass stopped vehicle at crossover	140(2)	$150.00
358.1	Pass stopped vehicle at crossover—community safety zone	140(2)	$300.00
359.	Pass stopped street car at crossover	140(2)	$150.00
359.1	Pass stopped street car at crossover—community safety zone	140(2)	$300.00
360.	Stopped vehicle at crossover—fail to yield to pedestrian	140(2)(a)	$150.00
360.1	Stopped vehicle at crossover—fail to yield to pedestrian—community safety zone	140(2)(a)	$300.00
361.	Stopped street car at cross over—fail to yield to pedestrian	140(2)(a)	$150.00
361.1	Stopped street car at crossover—fail to yield to pedestrian—community safety zone	140(2)(a)	$300.00
362.	Stopped vehicle at crossover—fail to yield to person in wheelchair	140(2)(a)	$150.00
362.1	Stopped vehicle at crossover—fail to yield to person in wheelchair—community safety zone	140(2)(a)	$300.00
363.	Stopped street car at crossover—fail to yield to person in wheelchair	140(2)	$150.00
363.1	Stopped street car at crossover—fail to yield to person in wheelchair—community safety zone	140(2)(a)	$300.00
364.	Stopped vehicle at crossover—fail to yield to pedestrian approaching	140(2)(b)	$150.00
364.1	Stopped vehicle at crossover—fail to yield to pedestrian approaching—community safety zone	140(2)(b)	$300.00
365.	Stopped street car at crossover fail to yield to pedestrian approaching	140(2)(b)	$150.00
365.1	Stopped street car at crossover—fail to yield to pedestrian approaching community safety zone	140(2)(b)	$300.00
366.	Stopped vehicle at crossover—fail to yield to person in wheelchair approaching	140(2)(b)	$150.00
366.1	Stopped vehicle at crossover—fail to yield to person in wheelchair approaching—community safety zone	140(2)(b)	$300.00
367.	Stopped street car at crossover—fail to yield to person in wheelchair approaching	140(2)(b)	$150.00
367.1	Stopped street car at crossover—fail to yield to person in wheelchair approaching—community safety zone	140(2)(b)	$300.00
368.	Pass front of vehicle within 30 m of crossover	140(3)	$150.00
368.1	Pass front of vehicle within 30 m of crossover—community safety zone	140(3)	$300.00

Item	Column 1	Column 2 Section	Set Fine (Includes Costs)
369.	Pass front of street car within 30 m of crossover	140(3)	$150.00
369.1	Pass front of street car within 30 m of crossover—community safety zone	140(3)	$300.00
370.	Pedestrian fail to yield at crossover	140(4)	$35.00
371.	Person in wheelchair—fail to yield at crossover	140(4)	$35.00
371.1	Cyclist—ride in crossover	140(6)	$85.00
372.	Improper right turn	141(2)	$85.00
372.1	Improper right turn—community safety zone	141(2)	$120.00
373.	Improper right turn—multi-lane highway	141(3)	$85.00
373.1	Improper right turn—multi-lane highway—community safety zone	141(3)	$120.00
374.	Left turn—fail to afford reasonable opportunity to avoid collision	141(5)	$85.00
374.1	Left turn—fail to afford reasonable opportunity to avoid collision—community safety zone	141(5)	$150.00
375.	Improper left turn	141(6)	$85.00
375.1	Improper left turn—community safety zone	141(6)	$120.00
376.	Improper left turn—multi-lane highway	141(7)	$85.00
376.1	Improper left turn—multi-lane highway—community safety zone	141(7)	$120.00
377.	Turn—not in safety	142(1)	$85.00
377.1	Turn—not in safety—community safety zone	142(1)	$150.00
378.	Change lane—not in safety	142(1)	$85.00
378.1	Change lane—not in safety—community safety zone	142(1)	$150.00
379.	Fail to signal for turn	142(1)	$85.00
379.1	Fail to signal for turn—community safety zone	142(1)	$120.00
380.	Fail to signal—lane change	142(1)	$85.00
380.1	Fail to signal—lane change community safety zone	142(1)	$120.00
381.	Start from parked position—not in safety	142(2)	$85.00
381.1	Start from parked position—not in safety—community safety zone	142(2)	$150.00
382.	Start from stopped position—not in safety	142(2)	$85.00
382.1	Start from stopped position—not in safety—community safety zone	142(2)	$150.00
383.	Start from parked position—fail to signal	142(2)	$85.00
383.1	Start from parked position—fail to signal community safety zone	142(2)	$120.00
384.	Start from stopped position—fail to signal	142(2)	$85.00
384.1	Start from stopped position—fail to signal—community safety zone	142(2)	$120.00
385.	Improper arm signal	142(4)	$85.00
385.1	Improper arm signal—community safety zone	142(4)	$120.00
386.	Improper signal device	142(6)	$85.00
386.1	Improper signal device—community safety zone	142(6)	$120.00
387.	Use turn signals improperly	142(7)	$85.00
387.1	Use turn signals improperly—community safety zone	142(7)	$120.00
388.	Fail to signal stop	142(8)	$85.00
388.1	Fail to signal stop—community safety zone	142(8)	$120.00

Item	Column 1	Column 2 Section	Set Fine (Includes Costs)
389.	Fail to signal decrease in speed	142(8)	$85.00
389.1	Fail to signal decrease in speed community safety zone	142(8)	$120.00
390.	Improper signal to stop	142(8)	$85.00
390.1	Improper signal to stop—community safety zone	142(8)	$120.00
391.	Improper signal to decrease in speed	142(8)	$85.00
391.1	Improper signal to decrease in speed community safety zone	142(8)	$120.00
392.	Brake lights—improper colour	142(8)(b)	$85.00
392.1	Brake lights—improper colour—community safety zone	142(8)(b)	$120.00
392.2	Fail to yield to bus re-entering lane from bus bay	142.1(1)	$85.00
392.3	Fail to yield to bus re-entering lane from bus bay—community safety zone	142.1(1)	$120.00
393.	U-turn on a curve—no clear view	143(a)	$85.00
393.1	U-turn on a curve—no clear view community safety zone	143(a)	$150.00
394.	U-turn—railway crossing	143(b)	$85.00
394.1	U-turn—railway crossing—community safety zone	143(b)	$150.00
395.	U-turn near crest of grade—No clear view	143(c)	$85.00
395.1	U-turn near crest of grade—no clear view—community safety zone	143(c)	$150.00
396.	U-turn—bridge—no clear view	143(d)	$85.00
396.1	U-turn—bridge—no clear view community safety zone	143(d)	$150.00
397.	U-turn—viaduct—no clear view	143(d)	$85.00
397.1	U-turn—viaduct—no clear view community safety zone	143(d)	$150.00
398.	U-turn—tunnel—no clear view	143(d)	$85.00
398.1	U-turn—tunnel—no clear view community safety zone	143(d)	$150.00
399.	Improper stop—traffic signal at intersection	144(5)	$85.00
399.1	Improper stop—traffic signal at intersection community safety zone	144(5)	$120.00
400.	Improper stop—traffic signal not at intersection	144(6)	$85.00
400.1	Improper stop—traffic signal not at intersection—community safety zone	144(6)	$120.00
401.	Fail to yield to pedestrian	144(7)	$150.00
401.1	Fail to yield to pedestrian—community safety zone	144(7)	$300.00
402.	Fail to yield to traffic	144(8)	$85.00
402.1	Fail to yield to traffic—community safety zone	144(8)	$150.00
403.	Proceed contrary to sign at intersection	144(9)	$85.00
403.1	Proceed contrary to sign at intersection—community safety zone	144(9)	$120.00
404.	Disobey lane light	144(10)	$85.00
404.1	Disobey lane light—community safety zone	144(10)	$120.00
405.	Green light—fail to proceed as directed	144(12)	$85.00
405.1	Green light—fail to proceed as directed community safety zone	144(12)	$120.00
406.	Flashing green light—fail to proceed as directed	144(13)	$85.00
406.1	Flashing green light—fail to proceed as directed community safety zone	144(13)	$120.00
407.	Green arrow—fail to proceed as directed	144(14)	$85.00
407.1	Green arrow—fail to proceed as directed community safety zone	144(14)	$120.00

TRAFFIC MANAGEMENT

Item	Column 1	Column 2 Section	Set Fine (Includes Costs)
408.	Amber light—fail to stop	144(15)	$150.00
408.1	Amber light—fail to stop community safety zone	144(15)	$300.00
409.	Amber arrow—fail to stop	144(16)	$85.00
409.1	Amber arrow—fail to stop community safety zone	144(16)	$120.00
410.	Amber arrow arrow—fail to proceed as directed	144(16)	$85.00
410.1	Amber arrow—fail to proceed as directed community safety zone	144(16)	$120.00
411.	Flashing amber light—fail to proceed with caution	144(17)	$85.00
411.1	Flashing amber light—fail to proceed with caution—community safety zone	144(17)	$120.00
412.	Red light—fail to stop	144(18)	$150.00
412.1	Red light—fail to stop community safety zone	144(18)	$300.00
413.	Red light—proceed before green	144(18)	$150.00
413.1	Red light—proceed before green community safety zone	144(18)	$300.00
413.2	Red light—vehicle owner fails to stop pursuant to section 207	144(18.1)	$150.00
414.	Turn on red light—fail to yield	144(19)	$85.00
414.1	Turn on red light—fail to yield—community safety zone	144(19)	$150.00
415.	REVOKED		
416.	Flashing red light—fail to stop	144(21)	$85.00
416.1	Flashing red light—fail to stop community safety zone	144(21)	$150.00
417.	Flashing red light—fail to yield	144(21)	$85.00
417.1	Flashing red light—fail to yield community safety zone	144(21)	$150.00
418.	Pedestrian fail to use crosswalk	144(22)	$35.00
419.	Pedestrian disobey flashing green light	144(24)	$35.00
420.	Pedestrian disobey red light	144(25)	$35.00
421.	Pedestrian disobey amber light	144(25)	$35.00
422.	Pedestrian disobey "don't walk" signal	144(27)	$35.00
422.1	Cyclist—ride in or along crosswalk	144(29)	$85.00
423.	Disobey portable amber light fail to stop	146(3)	$150.00
423.1	Disobey portable amber light—fail to stop—community safety zone	146(3)	$300.00
424.	Disobey portable red light—fail to stop	146(4)	$150.00
424.1	Disobey portable red light—fail to stop—community safety zone	146(4)	$300.00
425.	Disobey portable red light—proceed before green	146(4)	$150.00
425.1	Disobey portable red light—proceed before green community safety zone	146(4)	$300.00
426.	Disobey portable red light—stop wrong place	146(5)	$85.00
426.1	Disobey portable red light—stop wrong place—community safety zone	146(5)	$120.00
427.	Disobey portable amber light—stop wrong place	146(5)	$85.00
427.1	Disobey portable amber light—stop wrong place—community safety zone	146(5)	$120.00
428.	Remove portable lane control signal system	146(6)	$85.00
428.1	Remove portable lane control signal system community safety zone	146(6)	$150.00
429.	Deface portable lane control signal system	146(6)	$85.00
429.1	Deface portable lane control signal system community safety zone	146(6)	$120.00

Item	Column 1	Column 2 Section	Set Fine (Includes Costs)
430.	Interfere with portable lane signal system	146(6)	$85.00
430.1	Interfere with portable lane control signal system—community safety zone	146(6)	$120.00
430.2	Fail to obey traffic control stop sign	146.1(3)	$85.00
430.3	Fail to obey traffic control stop sign—community safety zone	146.1(3)	$120.00
430.4	Fail to obey traffic control slow sign	146.1(4)	$85.00
430.5	Fail to obey traffic control slow sign—community safety zone	146.1(4)	$120.00
430.6	Display traffic control sign—unauthorized person	146.1(5)	$85.00
431.	Fail to keep right when driving at less than normal speed	147(1)	$85.00
431.1	Fail to keep right when driving at less than normal speed—community safety zone	147(1)	$120.00
432.	Fail to share half roadway—meeting vehicle	148(1)	$85.00
432.1	Fail to share half roadway—meeting vehicle—community safety zone	148(1)	$120.00
433.	Fail to turn out to right when overtaken	148(2)	$85.00
433.1	Fail to turn out to right when overtaken—community safety zone	148(2)	$120.00
434.	Fail to share roadway—meeting bicycle	148(4)	$85.00
434.1	Fail to share roadway—meeting bicycle community safety zone	148(4)	$120.00
435.	Fail to turn out to left to avoid collision	148(5)	$85.00
435.1	Fail to turn out to left to avoid collision community safety zone	148(5)	$120.00
436.	Bicycle—fail to turn out to right when overtaken	148(6)	$85.00
436.1	Bicycle—fail to turn out to right when overtaken—community safety zone	148(6)	$120.00
437.	Fail to turn out to left to avoid collision with bicycle	148(6)	$85.00
437.1	Fail to turn out to left to avoid collision with bicycle—community safety zone	148(6)	$120.00
438.	Motor assisted bicycle—fail to turn out to right when overtaken	148(6)	$85.00
438.1	Motor assisted bicycle—fail to turn out to right when overtaken—community safety zone	148(6)	$120.00
439.	Fail to turn out to left to avoid collision with motor assisted bicycle	148(6)	$85.00
439.1	Fail to turn out to left to avoid collision with motor assisted bicycle—community safety zone	148(6)	$120.00
440.	Fail to stop to facilitate passing	148(7)	$85.00
440.1	Fail to stop to facilitate passing—community safety zone	148(7)	$120.00
441.	Fail to assist in passing	148(7)	$85.00
441.1	Fail to assist in passing—community safety zone	148(7)	$120.00
442.	Pass—roadway not clear—approaching traffic	148(8)(a)	$85.00
442.1	Pass—roadway not clear—approaching traffic—community safety zone	148(8)(a)	$150.00
443.	Attempt to pass—roadway not clear—approaching traffic	148(8)(a)	$85.00
443.1	Attempt to pass—roadway not clear—approaching traffic—community safety zone	148(8)(a)	$150.00
444.	Pass—roadway not clear—overtaking traffic	148(8)(b)	$85.00
444.1	Pass—roadway not clear—overtaking traffic—community safety zone	148(8)(b)	$150.00
445.	Attempt to pass—roadway not clear—overtaking traffic	148(8)(b)	$85.00

TRAFFIC MANAGEMENT

Item	Column 1	Column 2 Section	Set Fine (Includes Costs)
445.1	Attempt to pass—roadway not clear—overtaking traffic—community safety zone	148(8)(b)	$150.00
446.	Drive left of centre—approaching crest of grade	149(1)(a)	$85.00
446.1	Drive left of centre—approaching crest of grade—community safety zone	149(1)(a)	$150.00
447.	Drive left of centre—on a curve	149(1)(a)	$85.00
447.1	Drive left of centre—on a curve community safety zone	149(1)(a)	$150.00
448.	Drive left of centre within 30 m of bridge—no clear view	149(1)(a)	$85.00
448.1	Drive left of centre within 30 m of bridge—no clear view community safety zone	149(1)(a)	$150.00
449.	Drive left of centre within 30 m of viaduct—no clear view	149(1)(a)	$85.00
449.1	Drive left of centre within 30 m of viaduct—no clear view community safety zone	149(1)(a)	$150.00
450.	Drive left of centre within 30 m of tunnel—no clear view	149(1)(a)	$85.00
450.1	Drive left of centre within 30 m of tunnel—no clear view—community safety zone	149(1)(a)	$150.00
451.	Drive left of centre within 30 m of level railway crossing	149(1)(b)	$85.00
452.	Drive left of centre within 30 m of level railway crossing—community safety zone	149(1)(b)	$150.00
453.	Pass on right—not in safety	150(1)	$85.00
453.1	Pass on right—not in safety—community safety zone	150(1)	$150.00
454.	Pass—off roadway	150(2)	$85.00
454.1	Pass—off roadway—community safety zone	150(2)	$150.00
455.	Disobey official sign	151(5)	$85.00
455.1	Disobey official sign—community safety zone	151(5)	$120.00
456.	Drive wrong way—one way traffic	153	$85.00
456.1	Drive wrong way—one way traffic community safety zone	153	$150.00
457.	Fail to drive in marked lane	154(1)(a)	$85.00
457.1	Fail to drive in marked lane—community safety zone	154(1)(a)	$120.00
458.	Unsafe lane change	154(1)(a)	$85.00
458.1	Unsafe lane change—community safety zone	154(1)(a)	$150.00
459.	Use centre lane improperly	154(1)(b)	$85.00
459.1	Use centre lane improperly—community safety zone	154(1)(b)	$120.00
460.	Fail to obey lane sign	154(1)(c)	$85.00
460.1	Fail to obey lane sign—community safety zone	154(1)(c)	$120.00
460.2	Improper use of high occupancy vehicle lane	154.1(3)	$85.00
460.3	Improper use of border approach lane	154.2(2)	$85.00
460.4	Driver in border approach lane—fail to stop	154.2(4)	$150.00
460.5	Fail to provide required document—driver	154.2(4)	$85.00
460.6	Fail to provide required document—occupant	154.2(4)	$85.00
461.	Drive wrong way—divided highway	156(1)(a)	$85.00
461.1	Drive wrong way—divided highway community safety zone	156(1)(a)	$150.00

Item	Column 1	Column 2 Section	Set Fine (Includes Costs)
462.	Cross divided highway—no proper crossing provided	156(1)(b)	$85.00
462.0.1	Cross divided highway—no proper crossing provided—community safety zone	156(1)(b)	$120.00
462.1	Backing on roadway—divided highway	157(1)	$85.00
462.1.1	Backing on roadway—divided highway community safety zone	157(1)	$120.00
462.2	Backing on shoulder—divided highway	157(1)	$85.00
462.3	Backing on shoulder—divided highway community safety zone	157(1)	$120.00
463.	Follow too closely	158(1)	$85.00
463.1	Follow too closely—community safety zone	158(1)	$120.00
464.	Commercial vehicle—follow too closely	158(2)	$85.00
464.1	Commercial vehicle—follow too closely community safety zone	158(2)	$120.00
465.	Fail to stop on right for emergency vehicle	159(1)(a)	$85.00
465.1	Fail to stop on right for emergency vehicle community safety zone	159(1)(a)	$120.00
466.	Fail to stop—nearest curb—for emergency vehicle	159(1)(b)	$85.00
466.1	Fail to stop—nearest curb—for emergency vehicle community safety zone	159(1)(b)	$120.00
467.	Fail to stop—nearest edge of roadway—for emergency vehicle	159(1)(b)	$85.00
467.1	Fail to stop—nearest edge of roadway—for emergency vehicle—community safety zone	159(1)(b)	$120.00
468.	Follow fire department too closely	159(2)	$85.00
468.1	Follow fire department vehicle too closely community safety zone	159(2)	$120.00
468.2	Fail to slow down and proceed with caution for emergency vehicle	159.1(1)	$400.00
468.3	Fail to move into another lane for emergency vehicle—if safe to do	159.1(2)	$400.00
469.	Permit attachment to vehicle	160	$85.00
469.1	Permit attachment to vehicle—community safety zone	160	$120.00
470.	Permit attachment to street car	160	$85.00
470.1	Permit attachment to street car community safety zone	160	$120.00
471.	Draw more than one vehicle	161	$85.00
471.1	Draw more than one vehicle—community safety zone	161	$120.00
472.	Drive while crowded	162	$85.00
472.1	Drive while crowded—community safety zone	162	$120.00
473.	Disobey railway crossing signal—stop at wrong place	163(1)	$85.00
473.1	Disobey railway crossing signal—stop at wrong place—community safety zone	163(1)	$150.00
474.	Disobey railway crossing signal—fail to stop	163(1)	$85.00
474.1	Disobey railway crossing signal—fail to stop—community safety zone	163(1)	$150.00
475.	Disobey railway crossing signal—proceed unsafely	163(1)	$85.00
475.1	Disobey railway crossing signal—proceed unsafely—community safety zone	163(1)	$150.00
475.2	Disobey stop sign at railway crossing—stop at wrong place	163(2)	$85.00
475.3	Disobey stop sign at railway crossing—stop at wrong place—community safety zone	163(2)	$150.00

Item	Column 1	Column 2 Section	Set Fine (Includes Costs)
475.4	Disobey stop sign at railway crossing—fail to stop	163(2)	$85.00
475.5	Disobey stop sign at railway crossing—fail to stop—community safety zone	163(2)	$150.00
475.6	Disobey stop sign at railway crossing—proceed unsafely	163(2)	$85.00
475.7	Disobey stop sign at railway crossing—proceed unsafely—community safety zone	163(2)	$150.00
476.	Disobey crossing gate	164	$85.00
476.1	Disobey crossing gate—community safety zone	164	$150.00
477.	Open vehicle door improperly	165(a)	$85.00
478.	Leave vehicle door open	165(b)	$85.00
479.	Pass street car improperly	166(1)	$85.00
479.1	Pass street car improperly—community safety zone	166(1)	$150.00
480.	Approach open streetcar door too closely	166(1)	$85.00
480.1	Approach open street car door too closely—community safety zone	166(1)	$150.00
481.	Pass street car on the left side	166(2)	$85.00
481.1	Pass street car on the left side—community safety zone	166(2)	$120.00
482.	Frighten animal	167	$85.00
482.1	Frighten animal—community safety zone	167	$120.00
483.	Fail to ensure safety of person in charge of animal	167	$85.00
483.1	Fail to ensure safety of person in charge in charge of animal—community safety zone	167	$120.00
484.	Fail to use lower beam—oncoming	168(a)	$85.00
484.1	Fail to use lower beam—oncoming community safety zone	168(a)	$120.00
485.	Fail to use lower beam—following	168(b)	$85.00
485.0.1	Fail to use lower beam—following community safety zone	168(b)	$120.00
485.1	Prohibited use of alternating highbeam headlights	169(2)	$85.00
485.2	Prohibited use of alternating highbeam headlights—community safety zone	169(2)	$120.00
486.	Fail to take precaution against vehicle being set in motion	170(9)	$50.00
487.	Fail to have warning lights	170(10)(a)	$50.00
488.	Fail to use warning lights	170(11)	$50.00
489.	Interfere with traffic	170(12)	$50.00
490.	Interfere with snow removal	170(12)	$50.00
490.1	Offer tow truck services in King's Highway within 200 m of accident or apparent accident	171(1)(a)	$200.00
490.2	Offer tow truck services on King's Highway within 200 m of vehicle involved in accident	171(1)(b)	$200.00
490.3	Park tow truck on King's Highway within 200 m of accident or apparent accident—sufficient tow trucks available	171(2)(a)	$200.00
490.4	Stop tow truck on King's Highway within 200 m of accident or apparent accident—sufficient tow trucks available	171(2)(a)	$200.00
490.5	Park tow truck on King's Highway within 200 m of vehicle involved in accident—sufficient tow trucks available	171(2)(b)	$200.00

Short-Form Wordings and Set Fines from the Provincial Offences Act — APPENDIX A

Item	Column 1	Column 2 Section	Set Fine (Includes Costs)
490.6	Stop tow trucks on King's Highway within 200 m of vehicle involved in accident—sufficient tow trucks available	171(2)(b)	$200.00
491.	Race a motor vehicle	172(1)	N.S.F.
491.1	Race a motor vehicle—community safety zone	172(1)	N.S.F.
492.	Race an animal	173	$85.00
493.	Fail to stop at railway crossing—public vehicle	174(1)	$85.00
494.	Stop wrong place at railway crossing—public vehicle	174(1)(a)	$85.00
495.	Fail to look both ways at railway crossing—public vehicle	174(1)(b)	$85.00
496.	Fail to open door at railway crossing—public vehicle	174(1)(c)	$85.00
497.	Cross tracks using gear requiring change—public vehicle	174(1)(d)	$85.00
497.1	Change gears while crossing railway track—public vehicle	174(1)(e)	$85.00
497.2	Fail to stop at railway crossing—school bus	174(2)	$85.00
497.3	Stop wrong place at railway crossing—school bus	174(2)(a)	$85.00
497.4	Fail to look both ways at railway crossing—school bus	174(2)(b)	$85.00
497.5	Fail to open door at railway crossing—school bus	174(2)(c)	$85.00
497.6	Cross tracks using gear requiring change—school bus	174(2)(d)	$85.00
497.7	Change gears while crossing railway track—school bus	174(2)(e)	$85.00
498.	Bus not used to transport adults with developmental handicaps or children, painted chrome yellow	175(3)	$85.00
499.	Prohibited markings	175(4)	$85.00
499.1	Prohibited equipment—school bus stop arm	175(4)	$85.00
500.	Drive chrome yellow vehicle, not used to transport adults with developmental handicaps or children	175(5)	$85.00
501.	Drive vehicle with prohibited school bus markings	175(5)	$85.00
502.	Drive vehicle with prohibited school bus stop arm	175(5)	$85.00
503.	Fail to actuate school bus signals	175(6)	$85.00
504.	Improperly actuate school bus signals	175(8)	$85.00
505.	Improperly actuate school bus signals at intersection controlled by operating traffic control system	175(9)(a)	$85.00
506.	Improperly actuate school bus signals at location, other than an intersection, controlled by operating traffic control system—at sign or roadway marking indicating stop to be made	175(9)(b)(i)	$85.00
507.	Improperly actuate school bus signals at location, other than an intersection, controlled by operating traffic control system—in area immediately before entering cross-walk	175(9)(b)(ii)	$85.00
507.1	Improperly actuate school bus signals at location, other than an intersection, controlled by operating traffic control system—within 5 m of traffic control system	175(9)(b)(iii)	$85.00
507.2	Improperly actuate school bus signals within 60 m of location controlled by operating traffic control system	175(9)(c)	$85.00
507.3	Stop school bus opposite loading zone	175(10)(a)	$85.00
507.5	Fail to stop for school bus	175(11)	$400.00
507.6	Fail to stop for school bus	175(12)	$400.00

TRAFFIC MANAGEMENT

Item	Column 1	Column 2 Section	Set Fine (Includes Costs)
507.7	Fail to stop for school bus—owner	175(19)	$400.00
507.8	Fail to stop for school bus—owner	175(20)	$400.00
508.	Guard fail to properly display school crossing stop sign	176(2)	$85.00
509.	Fail to obey school crossing stop sign	176(3)	$150.00
509.1	Fail to obey school crossing stop sign—community safety zone	176(3)	$300.00
510.	Improper use of school crossing stop sign	176(4)	$85.00
511.	Unauthorized person display school crossing stop sign	176(5)	$85.00
512.	Solicit a ride	177(1)	$50.00
513.	Solicit business	177(2)	$50.00
514.	Attach to vehicle	178(1)	$85.00
515.	Attach to streetcar	178(1)	$85.00
516.	Ride 2 on a bicycle	178(2)	$85.00
517.	Ride another person on a motor assisted bicycle	178(3)	$85.00
518.	Person—attach to vehicle	178(4)	$35.00
519.	Person—attach to streetcar	178(4)	$35.00
520.	Pedestrian fail to walk on left side of highway	179	$35.00
521.	Pedestrian on roadway fail to keep to left edge	179	$35.00
522.	Litter highway	180	$85.00
523.	Deposit snow or ice on roadway	181	$85.00
524.	Disobey sign	182(2)	$85.00
524.1	Disobey sign—community safety zone	182(2)	$120.00
525.	Disobey sign at tunnel	183(2)	$85.00
526.	Deface notice	184	N.S.F.
527.	Remove notice	184	N.S.F.
528.	Interfere with notice	184	N.S.F.
529.	Deface obstruction	184	N.S.F.
530.	Remove obstruction	184	N.S.F.
531.	Interfere with obstruction	184	N.S.F.
532.	Fail to remove aircraft	187(1)	N.S.F.
533.	Move aircraft improperly	187(2)	N.S.F.
534.	Aircraft unlawfully take off	187(3)	N.S.F.
535.	Draw occupied trailer	188	$85.00
536.	Operate air cushioned vehicle	189	$85.00
537.	Fail to maintain daily log	190(3)	$310.00
538.	Fail to carry daily log	190(3)	$310.00
539.	Fail to surrender daily log	190(4)	$310.00
540.	Driver in possession of more than one daily log	190(5)	$310.00
540.1.	Permit person to drive commercial motor vehicle not in accordance with the regulations	190(6)	$310.00
540.2.	Fail to produce proof of exemption	191(7)	$85.00
540.3	Drive motor vehicle—toll device improperly affixed	191.2(1)	$85.00

Item	Column 1	Column 2 Section	Set Fine (Includes Costs)
540.4	Drive motor vehicle—no toll device	191.2(1)	$85.00
540.5	Drive motor vehicle—invalid toll device	191.2(1)	$85.00
540.6	Engage in activity to evade toll system	191.3(1)	$85.00
540.7	Engage in activity to obstruct toll system	191.3(1)	$85.00
540.8	Engage in activity to interfere with toll system	191.3(1)	$85.00
540.9	Use device to evade toll system	191.3(1)	$85.00
540.10	Use device to obstruct toll system	191.3(1)	$85.00
540.11	Use device to interfere with toll system	191.3(1)	$85.00
540.12	Sell device designed to interfere with toll system	191.3(4)	$85.00
540.13	Offer to sell device designed to interfere with toll system	191.3(4)	$85.00
540.14	Advertise for sale device designed to interfere with toll system	191.3(4)	$85.00
540.15	Sell device intended to interfere with toll system	191.3(4)	$85.00
540.16	Offer to sell device intended to interfere with toll system	191.3(4)	$85.00
540.17	Advertise for sale device intended to interfere with toll system	191.3(4)	$85.00
541.	Fail to report accident	199(1)	$85.00
542.	Fail to furnish required information	199(1)	$85.00
542.1	Fail to report accident—specified location	199(1.1)	$85.00
542.2	Fail to furnish required information	199(1.1)	$85.00
543.	Occupant fail to report accident	199(2)	$85.00
544.	Police officer fail to report accident	199(3)	$85.00
544.1	Insurer fail to notify Registrar as prescribed re irreparable or salvage vehicle	199.1(4)	$400.00
544.2	Specified person fail to notify Registrar as prescribed re irreparable or salvage vehicle	199.1(5)	$400.00
544.3	Misclassify vehicle as irreparable or salvage in notice to Registrar	199.1(7)	$400.00
544.4	Fail to notify permit holder as prescribed re irreparable or salvage vehicle	199.1(8)	$400.00
544.5	Fail to return permit or portion of permit for irreparable or salvage vehicle to Registrar as prescribed	199.1(16)	$400.00
544.6	Drive or draw irreparable or salvage vehicle	199.1(19)	$140.00
544.7	Permit irreparable or salvage vehicle to be driven or drawn	199.1(19)	$140.00
545.	Fail to remain	200(1)(a)	N.S.F.
546.	Fail to render assistance	200(1)(b)	N.S.F.
547.	Fail to give required information	200(1)(c)	N.S.F.
548.	Fail to report damage to property on highway	201	$85.00
549.	Fail to report damage to fence bordering highway	201	$85.00
550.	Medical practitioner—fail to report	203(1)	$85.00
551.	Optometrist—fail to report	204(1)	$85.00
552.	Failing to forward suspended licence to Registrar	211(2)	$85.00
553.	Fail to surrender suspended driver's licence	212(2)	$60.00
554.	Refuse to surrender suspended driver's licence	212(2)	$60.00
554.0.1	Fail to assist in examination of commercial vehicle	216.1(1)	$310.00
554.0.2	Fail to stop commercial vehicle for examination	216.1(2)	$310.00

Item	Column 1	Column 2 Section	Set Fine (Includes Costs)
554.0.3	Fail to surrender documents	216.1(3)	$310.00
554.0.4	Fail to furnish information	216.1(3)	$310.00
554.0.5	Fail to comply with direction of officer	216.1(7)	$310.00
554.1	Cyclist—fail to stop	218(2)	$85.00
554.2	Cyclist—fail to identify self	218(2)	$85.00
555.	Obstruct officer	225(5)	$260.00
556.	Withhold record	225(5)	$260.00
557.	Conceal record	225(5)	$260.00
558.	Destroy record	225(5)	$260.00

SCHEDULE A
HIGHWAY TRAFFIC ACT
SET FINE

Overweight	Penalty
0-2,499 kg.	$4.00 per 100 kg. or part kg.*
2,500-4,999 kg.	$5.00 per 100 kg. or part kg.
5,000-7,499 kg.	$6.00 per 100 kg. or part kg.
Over 7,500 kg.	No set fine

* Regardless of the overweight, the penalty will not be less than $100.00

SCHEDULE B
HIGHWAY TRAFFIC ACT
SPEEDING

Kilometres	Set Fines
a) 1-19 kilometres per hour over the maximum speed limit	$2.50 per kilometre
b) 20-29 kilometres per hour over the maximum speed limit	$3.75 per kilometre
c) 30-49 kilometres per hour over the maximum speed limit	$6.00 per kilometre
d) 50 kilometres per hour or more over the maximum speed limit	No out of court settlement

SCHEDULE C
HIGHWAY TRAFFIC ACT
SPEEDING—PHOTO RADAR

Kilometres

a) 1-19 kilometres per hour over the maximum speed limit

b) 20-34 kilometres per hour over the maximum speed limit

c) 35-49 kilometres per hour over the maximum speed limit

d) 50-60 kilometres per hour over the maximum speed limit

e) 61+ kilometres per hour over the maximum speed limit

Set Fines

$2.50 per kilometre

$3.75 per kilometre

$6.00 per kilometre

$8.00 per kilometre

No set fine

SCHEDULE D
HIGHWAY TRAFFIC ACT
SPEEDING—COMMUNITY SAFETY ZONE

Kilometres

a) 1-19 kilometres per hour over the maximum speed limit

b) 20-29 kilometres per hour over the maximum speed limit

c) 30-49 kilometres per hour over the maximum speed limit

Set Fines

$5.00 per kilometre

$7.50 per kilometre

No out of court settlement

SCHEDULE E
HIGHWAY TRAFFIC ACT
SPEEDING—CONSTRUCTION ZONE

Kilometres

a) 1-19 kilometres per hour over the maximum speed limit

b) 20-29 kilometres per hour over the maximum speed limit

c) 30-49 kilometres per hour over the maximum speed limit

d) 50 kilometres per hour or more over the maximum speed limit

Set Fines

$2.50 per kilometre

$3.75 per kilometre

$6.00 per kilometre

No out of court settlement

SCHEDULE F
HIGHWAY TRAFFIC ACT
SPEEDING—CONSTRUCTION ZONE—WORKER PRESENT

Kilometres

a) 1-19 kilometres per hour over the maximum speed limit

b) 20-29 kilometres per hour over the maximum speed limit

c) 30-49 kilometres per hour over the maximum speed limit

Set Fines

$5.00 per kilometre

$7.50 per kilometre

No out of court settlement

APPENDIX B

Provincial Offence Ticket and Summons

A blank Provincial Offence Ticket and a blank Provincial Offence Summons are reproduced on the following pages. Identifying numbers have been removed. Make photocopies of the ticket and the summons to practise filling them out properly.

TRAFFIC MANAGEMENT

Provincial Offence Ticket — Top Page

Provincial Offence Ticket — Top Page (Reverse)

Provincial Offence Ticket   Second Page

Provincial Offence Ticket   Second Page (Reverse)

228 TRAFFIC MANAGEMENT

Provincial Offence Ticket Third Page

Provincial Offence Ticket Third Page (Reverse)

Provincial Offence Ticket and Summons APPENDIX B 229

Provincial Offence Ticket   Fourth Page

Provincial Offence Ticket   Fourth Page (Reverse)

Enforcement Agency notes/*Notes de l'agence d'exécution*

230 TRAFFIC MANAGEMENT

Provincial Offence Ticket   Last Page

Provincial Offence Ticket   Last Page (Reverse)

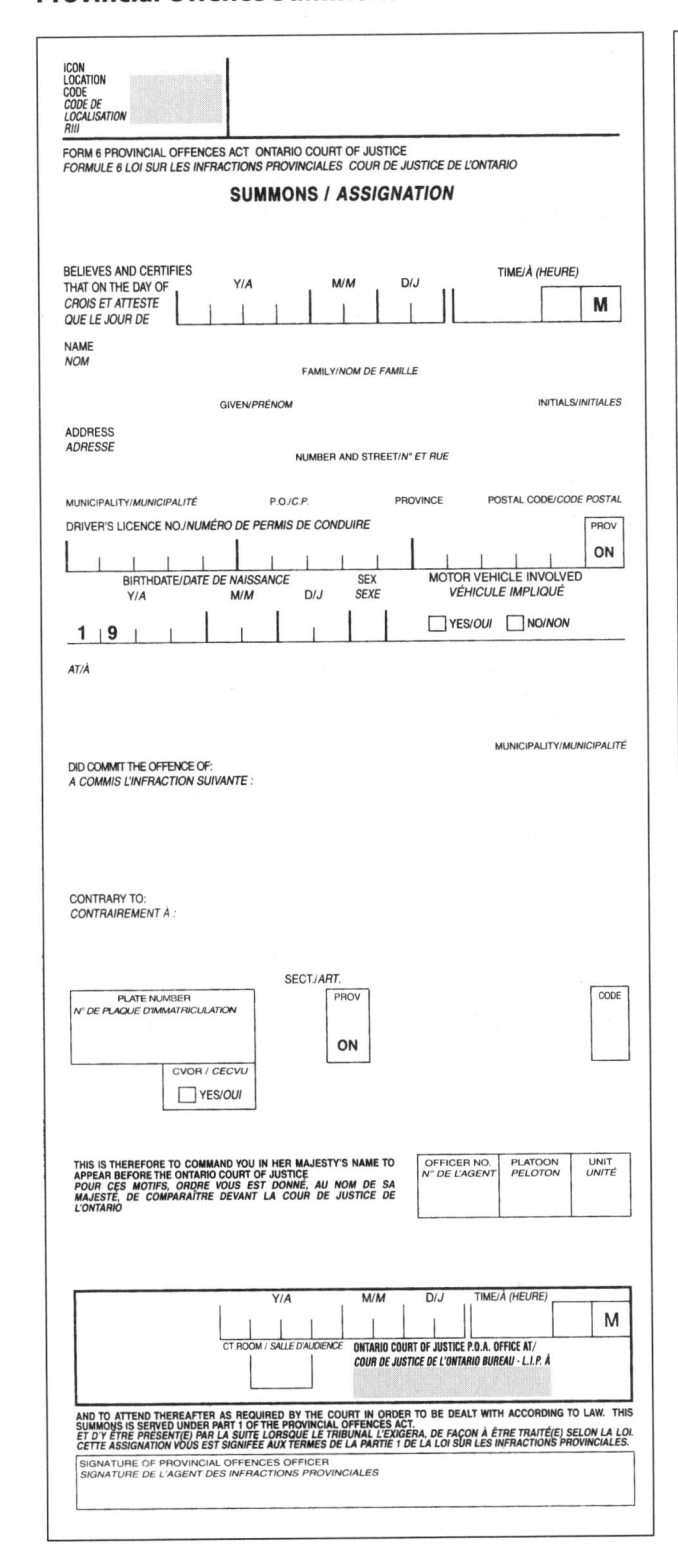

Provincial Offence Summons

FORM 6 PROVINCIAL OFFENCES ACT   ONTARIO COURT OF JUSTICE
FORMULE 6 LOI SUR LES INFRACTIONS PROVINCIALES   COUR DE JUSTICE DE L'ONTARIO

SUMMONS / ASSIGNATION

BELIEVES AND CERTIFIES THAT ON THE DAY OF / CROIS ET ATTESTE QUE LE JOUR DE — Y/A   M/M   D/J   TIME/À (HEURE) M

NAME / NOM — FAMILY/NOM DE FAMILLE — GIVEN/PRÉNOM — INITIALS/INITIALES

ADDRESS / ADRESSE — NUMBER AND STREET/Nº ET RUE

MUNICIPALITY/MUNICIPALITÉ — P.O./C.P. — PROVINCE — POSTAL CODE/CODE POSTAL

DRIVER'S LICENCE NO./NUMÉRO DE PERMIS DE CONDUIRE — PROV ON

BIRTHDATE/DATE DE NAISSANCE   Y/A   M/M   D/J   SEX/SEXE   MOTOR VEHICLE INVOLVED/VÉHICULE IMPLIQUÉ   ☐ YES/OUI   ☐ NO/NON

1 9

AT/À — MUNICIPALITY/MUNICIPALITÉ

DID COMMIT THE OFFENCE OF: / A COMMIS L'INFRACTION SUIVANTE :

CONTRARY TO: / CONTRAIREMENT À :

PLATE NUMBER / Nº DE PLAQUE D'IMMATRICULATION — SECT./ART. — PROV ON — CODE

CVOR / CECVU ☐ YES/OUI

THIS IS THEREFORE TO COMMAND YOU IN HER MAJESTY'S NAME TO APPEAR BEFORE THE ONTARIO COURT OF JUSTICE
POUR CES MOTIFS, ORDRE VOUS EST DONNÉ, AU NOM DE SA MAJESTÉ, DE COMPARAÎTRE DEVANT LA COUR DE JUSTICE DE L'ONTARIO

OFFICER NO. / Nº DE L'AGENT — PLATOON / PELOTON — UNIT / UNITÉ

Y/A   M/M   D/J   TIME/À (HEURE) M

CT. ROOM / SALLE D'AUDIENCE — ONTARIO COURT OF JUSTICE P.O.A. OFFICE AT / COUR DE JUSTICE DE L'ONTARIO BUREAU - L.I.P. À

AND TO ATTEND THEREAFTER AS REQUIRED BY THE COURT IN ORDER TO BE DEALT WITH ACCORDING TO LAW. THIS SUMMONS IS SERVED UNDER PART 1 OF THE PROVINCIAL OFFENCES ACT.
ET D'Y ÊTRE PRÉSENT(E) PAR LA SUITE LORSQUE LE TRIBUNAL L'EXIGERA, DE FAÇON À ÊTRE TRAITÉ(E) SELON LA LOI. CETTE ASSIGNATION VOUS EST SIGNIFIÉE AUX TERMES DE LA PARTIE 1 DE LA LOI SUR LES INFRACTIONS PROVINCIALES.

SIGNATURE OF PROVINCIAL OFFENCES OFFICER
SIGNATURE DE L'AGENT DES INFRACTIONS PROVINCIALES

Provincial Offence Summons   (Reverse)

NOTE TO DEFENDANT

YOU ARE REQUIRED TO APPEAR IN COURT. YOU MAY APPEAR PERSONALLY OR BY AGENT.

WHEN YOU APPEAR YOU MAY:
- (A) PLEAD GUILTY TO THE OFFENCE
  OR
- (B) SET A DATE FOR TRIAL
  OR
- (C) THE TRIAL MAY PROCEED.

IF YOU DO NOT APPEAR:
- (A) THE COURT MAY ISSUE A WARRANT FOR YOUR ARREST.
  OR
- (B) THE TRIAL MAY PROCEED IN YOUR ABSENCE.

REMARQUE AU DÉFENDEUR

VOUS ÊTES REQUIS DE COMPARAÎTRE EN COUR. VOUS POUVEZ VOUS PRÉSENTER EN PERSONNE OU PAR L'INTERMÉDIAIRE D'UN MANDATAIRE.

LORSQUE VOUS COMPARAÎTREZ VOUS POURREZ :
- *(A) PLAIDER COUPABLE RELATIVEMENT À L'INFRACTION
  OU*
- *(B) DEMANDER UNE DATE DE PROCÈS
  OU*
- *(C) LE PROCÈS POURRA SE DÉROULER*

SI VOUS NE COMPARAISSEZ PAS :
- *(A) LA COUR PEUT DÉCERNER UN MANDAT D'ARRESTATION CONTRE VOUS
  OU*
- *(B) LE PROCÈS PEUT SE DÉROULER EN VOTRE ABSENCE.*

FOR INFORMATION ON ACCESS FOR PERSONS WITH DISABILITIES, CALL
POUR PLUS DE RENSEIGNEMENTS SUR L'ACCÈS DES PERSONNES HANDICAPÉES

APPENDIX C

Suspect Apprehension Pursuits Regulation

O. REG. 546/99
IN FORCE JANUARY 1, 2000

1. For the purposes of this Regulation, a suspect apprehension pursuit occurs,

 (a) when a police officer attempts to direct the driver of a motor vehicle to stop;

 (b) the driver refuses to obey the police officer; and

 (c) the police officer pursues in a motor vehicle for the purpose of stopping the fleeing motor vehicle or identifying the fleeing motor vehicle or an individual in the fleeing motor vehicle.

2. A suspect apprehension pursuit is discontinued when police officers are no longer pursuing a fleeing motor vehicle for the purpose of stopping the fleeing motor vehicle or identifying the fleeing motor vehicle or an individual in the fleeing motor vehicle.

3. (1) A police officer may pursue, or continue to pursue, a fleeing motor vehicle that fails to stop,

 (a) if the police officer has reason to believe that a criminal offence has been committed or is about to be committed; or

(b) for the purposes of motor vehicle identification or the identification of an individual in the vehicle.

(2) A police officer shall, before initiating a suspect apprehension pursuit, determine that there are no alternatives available as set out in the written procedures of the police force established under subsection 7(1).

(3) A police officer shall, before initiating a suspect apprehension pursuit, determine whether in order to protect public safety the immediate need to apprehend an individual in the fleeing motor vehicle or the need to identify the fleeing motor vehicle or an individual in the fleeing motor vehicle outweighs the risk to public safety that may result from the pursuit.

(4) During a suspect apprehension pursuit, a police officer shall continually reassess the determination made under subsection (3) and shall discontinue the pursuit when the risk to public safety that may result from the pursuit outweighs the risk to public safety that may result if an individual in the fleeing motor vehicle is not immediately apprehended or if the fleeing motor vehicle or an individual in the fleeing motor vehicle is not identified.

(5) No suspect apprehension pursuit shall be initiated for a non-criminal offence if the identity of an individual in the fleeing motor vehicle is known.

(6) All suspect apprehension pursuits for a non-criminal offence shall be discontinued once the fleeing motor vehicle or an individual in the fleeing motor vehicle is identified.

4. (1) A police officer shall notify a dispatcher when the officer initiates a suspect apprehension pursuit.

(2) The dispatcher shall notify a communications supervisor or road supervisor, if a supervisor is available, that a suspect apprehension pursuit has been initiated.

5. A communications or road supervisor shall order police officers to discontinue a suspect apprehension pursuit if, in his or her opinion, the risk to public safety that may result from the pursuit outweighs the risk to public safety that may result if an individual in the fleeing motor vehicle is not immediately apprehended or if the fleeing motor vehicle or an individual in the fleeing motor vehicle is not identified.

6. Every police services board shall establish policies that are consistent with this Regulation about suspect apprehension pursuits.

7. (1) Every police force shall establish written procedures that set out the tactics that may be used in its jurisdiction,

(a) as an alternative to suspect apprehension pursuit; and

(b) for following or stopping a fleeing motor vehicle.

(2) Every police force shall establish written procedures that are consistent with this Regulation about suspect apprehension pursuits in its jurisdiction.

8. A police officer shall not discharge his or her firearm for the sole purpose of attempting to stop a fleeing motor vehicle.

9. A police officer in an unmarked police vehicle shall not engage in a suspect apprehension pursuit unless a marked police vehicle is not readily available and the police officer believes that it is necessary to immediately apprehend an individual in the fleeing motor vehicle or to identify the fleeing motor vehicle or an individual in the fleeing motor vehicle.

10. (1) During a suspect apprehension pursuit, a police officer shall consider the tactics for stopping a vehicle as set out in the written procedures referred to in subsection 7(1).

(2) A police officer may only intentionally cause a police motor vehicle to come into physical contact with a fleeing motor vehicle for the purposes of stopping it where the officer believes on reasonable grounds that to do so is necessary to immediately protect against loss of life or serious bodily harm.

(3) In considering the action referred to in subsection (2), a police officer shall assess the impact of the action on the safety of other members of the public and police officers.

(4) Despite subsection (2), a police officer may cause a police motor vehicle to come into physical contact with a fleeing motor vehicle for the purposes of pinning it if the fleeing motor vehicle has lost control or collided with an object and come to a stop and the driver of the motor vehicle continues to try to use it to flee.

(5) Nothing in subsection (2) precludes police officers involved in a pursuit, with assistance from other police officers in motor vehicles, from attempting to safely position the police vehicles in such a manner as to prevent the movement either forward, backward or sideways of a fleeing motor vehicle.

(6) Every police force shall ensure that its police officers receive training about the intentional contact between vehicles that is described in subsection (2). The training must address the matters described in subsections (2) and (3).

11. (1) Every police force shall establish written procedures on the management and control of suspect apprehension pursuits.

(2) The procedures must describe the responsibilities of police officers, dispatchers, communications supervisors and road supervisors.

(3) The procedures must describe the equipment that is available for implementing alternative tactics.

12. (1) If more than one jurisdiction is involved in a suspect apprehension pursuit, the supervisor in the jurisdiction in which the pursuit begins has decision-making responsibility for the pursuit.

(2) The supervisor may hand over decision-making responsibility to a supervisor in another jurisdiction involved in the pursuit.

13. A police officer does not breach the code of conduct when he or she decides not to initiate or chooses to discontinue a suspect apprehension pursuit because he or she has reason to believe that the risk to public safety that may result from the pursuit outweighs the risk to public safety that may result if an individual in the fleeing motor vehicle is not immediately apprehended or if the fleeing motor vehicle or an individual in the fleeing motor vehicle is not identified.

14. Every police force shall ensure that its police officers, dispatchers, communications supervisors and road supervisors receive training accredited by the Solicitor General about suspect apprehension pursuits.

15. A police force shall ensure that the particulars of each suspect apprehension pursuit are recorded on a form and in a manner approved by the Solicitor General.

16. This Regulation comes into force on January 1, 2000.

GLOSSARY

arrest
results when a person's physical liberty is inhibited by conveying an intention to restrict the person's liberty; the actual restraint may involve physical force, although an arrest may occur without the use of force

bill of lading
a receipt for merchandise that accompanies the merchandise when it is being transported from one place to another; it should provide detailed information about the cargo carried by a commercial vehicle

chain
a surveyor's measure, consisting of a chain or line that is 66 feet long

CVOR certificate
the Commercial Vehicle Operator's Registration Certificate, which must be held by the operator of a commercial vehicle unless he or she is excluded or exempted under the HTA; requires commercial vehicle operators to comply with safety requirements under the HTA and other legislation

equestrian
a person riding on a horse

exigent
requiring immediate aid or action

gross weight
the total weight of the motor vehicle, its trailer, and the load it is carrying; can be determined only by weigh scales

headway
the distance between one vehicle and another behind it

Judge's Rules
rules that were developed by the English courts in the early 20th century, which govern the questioning of suspects; they have generally been applied in Canada and some of the rules have been incorporated into the *Canadian Charter of Rights and Freedoms*, particularly s. 10, which requires that a suspect be cautioned and advised of a right to counsel

legal presumption
the proof of one fact by the Crown means that a second fact is presumed to be true without the Crown having to adduce evidence to prove the second fact; however, the accused may present evidence to disprove the second fact, thereby rebutting the presumption

motor vehicle
includes automobiles, motor-assisted bicycles (mopeds), and motorcycles (which includes motor scooters), unless otherwise indicated in the HTA, as well as other vehicles propelled by anything other than muscular power, but does not include snowmobiles, farm tractors, self-propelled implements of husbandry (such as reapers and combines), road-building machinery, streetcars, and traction engines

oxidizer
a substance that combines with oxygen, which may be quite volatile, flammable, or otherwise chemically active and therefore dangerous

prohibition order
made on conviction for a CC driving offence and disqualifies a person from driving a motor vehicle as defined in the CC

registered gross weight
the weight of the vehicle and the load set out in the motor vehicle permit; the owner has prepaid the government to have the legal right to haul loads of that size in that vehicle on the highway

road allowance
a continuous strip of land dedicated for the location of a public highway, usually one chain (66 feet) wide; the actual roadway may be considerably narrower, but the whole width of the road allowance constitutes the highway, within the meaning of the HTA

suspension
may be made under the authority of the HTA for either a CC offence or an HTA offence; disqualifies a driver from driving a motor vehicle as defined in the HTA on a highway as defined in the HTA

total weight
determined from either the gross weight of the motor vehicle, trailer, and load or the registered gross weight of the motor vehicle, whichever is more

towed weight
the weight of the trailer and its load

valtag
short for "validation tag," which is attached to metal number plates to show that the plate is currently valid

vehicle
includes a motor vehicle, trailer, traction engine, farm tractor, road-building machine, bicycle, and any vehicle drawn, propelled, or driven by any kind of power, including muscular power, but does not include a motorized snow vehicle or a streetcar

voir dire
a "trial within a trial" conducted by a trial judge to determine whether evidence to be tendered is admissible in the main proceeding; an officer may have to give evidence on whether the accused was given a warning and whether his or her statement was voluntary and not compelled or coerced

"will say" statements
a brief description or summary from an officer's notebook of what the witness will say in court; its primary audience is the Crown attorney and defence counsel, who will likely see the statement under evidentiary disclosure rules

INDEX

aggressive driving, 71
alcoholic influence, *see* impaired driving
arrest
    authorities, 134-35
    defined, 127
    differentiated from charge, 127, 133-34

barricades, 181
bill of lading, 176
bus, defined, 20

careless driving, 70-71
chain, defined, 21
collision investigation
    approaching the scene, 173-74
    caution statements, 185-86
    management of people, 182
    mental role playing, 173
    police attendance, reasons for, 172
    prioritizing emergencies
        dangerous goods, 175-78
        downed hydro lines, 180
        fighting drivers, 182
        injuries, 178-79
        protecting the scene, 180
        road conditions, 182
        theft protection, 182
        vehicle fires, 180
    questions to ask, 183-85
    statements required by statute, 186
    steps in investigation, 172
    unruly spectators, 186
commercial motor vehicle, defined, 19
Compulsory Automobile Insurance Act
    failure to disclose particulars of insurance, 59
    failure to have insurance, 57-59
    failure to surrender insurance card, 59

Criminal Code
    motor vehicle, defined, 145
    motor vehicle law, and, 2, 143-44
    offences under, 136, 144
        criminal negligence, 146
        dangerous operation of a motor vehicle, 147
        failure to stop, 147-48
        flight from pursuing peace officer, 147
        impaired driving, 148-62
        street racing, 95, 148
    procedure, 144, 145
    vehicle searches
        incidental to arrest, 163
        vehicle as a place, 163
criminal negligence, 146
crosswalk, defined, 24
CVOR certificate, 135

dangerous goods, 175-78
dangerous operation of a motor vehicle, 147
demerit point system, 101-4
driver's licences
    "Big Eddie" technique, 55-56
    graduated licences
        duration, 53
        G1 driver's licence, 50-51
        M1 driver's licence, 52
        M2 driver's licence, 52
        penalties, violating conditions, 53
    non-graduated licences
        air brakes, 55
        class A licence, 53
        class B licence, 54
        class C licence, 54
        class D licence, 54
        class E licence, 54
        class F licence, 54

driver's licences (continued)
    non-Ontario, plates and licence, authority for use, 57
    offences relating to, 56

equestrian, 88
exigent, 163

failure to stop, accident scene, 147
flight from pursuing peace officer, 147

gross weight, 46

headway, 90
highway, defined, 21
Highway Traffic Act
    abbreviated forms of offences under, 6
    bus, defined, 20
    commercial motor vehicle, defined, 19
    crosswalk, defined, 24
    highway, defined, 21
    index, 5, 7-8, 12
    interpretation of, 13
    intersection, defined, 24
    King's Highway, defined, 21
    motor vehicle, defined, 18, 145
    offences, *see also Criminal Code*
        aggressive driving and road rage, 71
        arrest authorities, 134-35
        arrestable offences under, 133-34
        careless driving, 70-71
        charge versus arrest, 127
        driver's licence, 56
        driving, demerit points, 101-4
        fines, 196-223
        motor vehicle stops, 124-26
        plate and permit, 44-45
        POA ticketing procedure, 127-33
        seizure authorities under, 135-36
        short-form wording, 196-223
        speeding, 69-70
        suspect apprehension pursuits, 126-27, 233-35
        victim surcharges, 100-1
    parking, defined, 26
    pedestrian crossover, defined, 24
    regulations under
        general regulation, 6-7
        table of contents, 6, 11
    roadway, defined, 21
    rules of the road
        approaching and passing streetcars, 92-93
        approaching horses, 93
        blocking intersections, 88
        crowding driver's seat, 92
        direction of traffic by police officer, 71
        divided highways, 90
        erection of and effect of signs, 72
        headlights, use of, 93
        hitchhiking, 96
        left-hand turns, 74, 78
        littering/snow deposits on highway, 97
        logs kept by drivers, commercial vehicles, 97
        maintaining a safe distance, 90
        multilane highways, 89-90
        one-way traffic, 89
        opening vehicle doors, 92
        parking, standing, or stopping, 93-94
        passing, 88-89
        passing on the right, 89
        pedestrian crossovers, 73, 76, 77
        pedestrians walk on left, 96
        racing on highways, 95
        railway crossings, public vehicles and, 95-96
        right-hand turns, 74, 77
        right of way, 72
        school crossing guards, 96
        signalling, 79, 81
        slow vehicles, 88
        speed, 68
        stop-sign-controlled intersections, 72
        stopping at railway crossings, 92
        tow trucks, control of, 94
        towing other vehicles, 92
        traffic signals, 83-88
        U-turns, 83
        yield-sign-controlled intersections, 73
        yielding to buses, 79, 82
    school bus, defined, 20
    school purposes vehicle, defined, 20
    section citation, 13
    standing, defined, 26
    stopping, defined, 24
    table of contents, 5, 10
    topics covered under, 1-2
    trailer, defined, 20
    vehicle
        defined, 18
        permits, 36-44
    vehicle equipment requirements
        child restraint systems, 100
        helmets, 99
        lighting, 97-98
        mufflers, 98

INDEX

radar warning devices, 98
seat belts, 99
wheels, commercial vehicles, 98
windshield wipers and mirrors, 98

impaired driving
    12-hour suspensions, 158-59
    90-day suspensions, 159
    ability impaired, 148
    alcoholic influences, stages of, 152
    approved screening device, 150-51
    belief versus suspicion, 150
    breathalyzer, 151
    care or control, 149
    disqualification, 160-61
    driver evaluation, 154
    drugs, impairment by, 158
    grounds for blood warrant, 155-56
    grounds for breathalyzer test, 153
    grounds for demand for blood, 155
    grounds for screening test, 153
    ignition interlock programs, 159-60
    operating, defined, 149
    over 80 milligrams, 148-49
        impaired and, 158
    reasonable grounds to believe, 149-50
    reasonable suspicion, 149
        versus reasonable grounds to believe, 153, 154
    three-hour limit, breath or blood samples, 156-58
intersection, defined, 24

Judge's Rules, 185

legal presumption, 157

motor vehicle, defined, 18
motor vehicle law
    Criminal Code, and, 2, 142-43
    Highway Traffic Act, topics covered, 1-2, 142-43
    statutes and regulations
        consolidation, use of, 4-5
        organization of, 4
        relationship between, 3
motor vehicle stops, 124-26

offences
    Criminal Code, 136, 144
        criminal negligence, 146
        dangerous operation of a motor vehicle, 147
        failure to stop, 147-48
        flight from pursuing peace officer, 147
        impaired driving, 148-62
        street racing, 95, 148

Highway Traffic Act
    aggressive driving and road rage, 71
    arrest authorities, 134-35
    arrestable offences under, 133-34
    careless driving, 70-71
    charge versus arrest, 127
    driver's licence, 56
    driving, demerit points, 101-4
    motor vehicle stops, 124-26
    plate and permit, 44-45
    POA ticketing procedure, 127-33
    seizure authorities under, 135-36
    speeding, 69-70
    suspect apprehension pursuits, 126-27, 233-35
    victim surcharges, 100-1
oxidizer, 176

parking, defined, 26
pedestrian crossover, defined, 24
prohibition order, 161
Provincial Offences Act
    part III information, 133
    part III summons, 133
    ticketing procedure, 127-33, 225-31

registered gross weight, 46
road allowance, defined, 21
road rage, 71
roadway, defined, 21
rules of the road
    approaching and passing streetcars, 92-93
    approaching horses, 93
    blocking intersections, 88
    crowding driver's seat, 92
    direction of traffic by police officer, 71
    divided highways, 90
    erection of and effect of signs, 72
    headlights, use of, 93
    hitchhiking, 96
    left-hand turns, 74, 78
    littering/snow deposits on highway, 97
    logs kept by drivers, commercial vehicles, 97
    maintaining a safe distance, 90
    multilane highways, 89-90
    one-way traffic, 89
    opening vehicle doors, 92
    parking, standing, or stopping, 93-94
    passing, 88-89
    passing on the right, 89
    pedestrian crossovers, 73, 76, 77
    pedestrians walk on left, 96

rules of the road (continued)
    racing on highways, 95
    railway crossings, public vehicles and, 95-96
    right-hand turns, 74, 77
    right of way, 72
    school crossing guards, 96
    signalling, 79, 81
    slow vehicles, 88
    speed, 68
    stop-sign-controlled intersections, 72
    stopping at railway crossings, 92
    tow trucks, control of, 94
    towing other vehicles, 92
    traffic signals, 83-88
    U-turns, 83
    yield-sign-controlled intersections, 73
    yielding to buses, 79, 82

school bus, defined, 20
school purpose vehicle, defined, 20
seizure authorities, 135-36
speeding, 68-71
standing, defined, 26
stopping, defined, 24
street racing, 95, 148
suspect apprehension pursuits, 126-27, 233-35
suspension, 161

total weight, 46
towed weight, 46
traffic signals
    amber signals, 86
    emergency vehicles, and, 86
    green signals, 83
    pedestrians, and, 86
    red signals, 86
    turns on, 86
trailer, defined, 20

valtag, 36
vehicle
    classes, *see* vehicle classes
    defined, 18
    permits, *see* vehicle permits and plates
vehicle classes
    buses, classed by passengers, 45
    buses, classed by weight, 46
    description, 47-48
    passenger capacity, and, 47
    weight, and, 46
vehicle equipment requirements
    child restraint systems, 100
    helmets, 99
    lighting, 97-98
    mufflers, 98
    radar warning devices, 98
    seat belts, 99
    wheels, commercial vehicles, 98
    windshield wipers and mirrors, 98
vehicle permits and plates
    non-restricted permits
        6-day temporary use of plates, 43
        buyer's obligations, 42-44
        seller's obligations, 40-42
    offences, 44-45
    restricted permits
        10-day permits, 37-38
        dealer and service permits, 39-40, 42
        in-transit permits, 39
    summary, permit requirements, 37
    use of, 36
victim surcharge, 100-1
voir dire, 185

"will say" statements, 185